THE ORIGIN OF THE

FIGHTER AIRCRAFT

THE ORIGIN OF THE
FIGHTER AIRCRAFT

Jon Guttman

WESTHOLME
Yardley

Frontispiece: Jean Navarre, "The Sentinel of Verdun," photographed in his Nieuport 11 in 1915. (*Service Historique L'Armée de l'Air*)

First trade paperback 2017
© 2009 Jon Guttman
Map © 2009 Westholme Publishing, LLC
Map by Tracy Dungan

Westholme Publishing, LLC
904 Edgewood Road
Yardley, Pennsylvania 19067
Visit our Web site at www.westholmepublishing.com

ISBN: 978-1-59416-297-8
Also available as an eBook.

Printed in United States of America.

CONTENTS

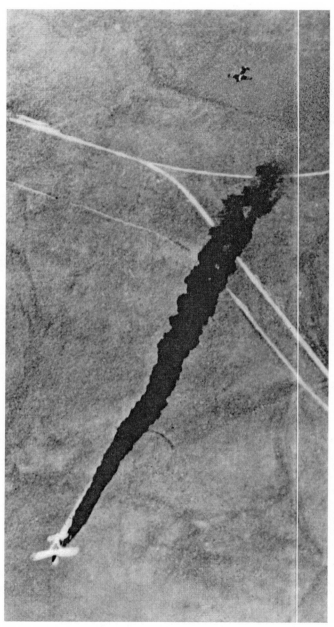

A French pusher aircraft, possibly a Voisin type, set on fire by a German aircraft, possibly a Fokker E-type. Photographs of World War I air battles are extremely rare, and while this image from the time captures the drama of the first air-to-air combat, its provenance has not been established. (*Library of Congress*)

FOREWORD

Coming fewer than 11 years after Orville and Wilbur Wright's historic takeoff at Kill Devil Hill, North Carolina, World War I has been called the first air war. Actually, warring mankind didn't wait that long—the Italians were using airplanes for reconnaissance and even bombardment as early as 1911. By World War I, however, aerial warfare's possibilities had gone from unthinkable to something serious enough for each side to want to control the sky. This gave rise to a means of achieving that goal: the fighter plane.

Although by no means the most significant development in World War I aviation, fighters soon caught the public eye to a degree their observation and bombing colleagues could not. In a war that quickly bogged down in entrenched stalemate, in which thousands of men endured wretched lives and died anonymous deaths in the mud, aerial combat often beckoned as an escape to an earlier time of heroic duels, personal fame amid relatively clean living conditions and, if one's luck ran out, a relatively clean death. And as those first pioneers developed and wielded their aerial weapons, such was indeed the case, as nations wearying of a succession of failed ground offensives found consolation in the growing victory tallies of their respective champions. The ace—the fighter pilot who had overcome five or more opponents—took his place alongside the heroes of old, as the new personification of Achilles, Horatius, Rustem, and Chevalier Bayard.

The legend those early fighter pilots created was soon overtaken by the reality that was also of their making. As both the airplane and the weapons systems it carried underwent an accelerated advancement, the transition from personal improvisations to mass-produced

viii   Foreword

fighting machines turned the sky into a battlefield in its own right. By
the end of 1916, one-on-one duels had been replaced by swirling
dogfights involving squadrons, then groups, then wings. And while a
fallen aviator might at least have the benefit of an honorable funeral,
sometimes provided by his adversaries, death in the air held its own
special horrors. While an infantryman had the option of preserving
his life from the bullets and shells in the same earth that so often made
his life miserable, only wood, canvas and an engine stood between the
airman and disaster. If he was fortunate, a bullet in the brain or the
heart would end things instantly; if he was not, a worse fate could be
spinning down out of control, bleeding to death in a lost race to an
aid station on the ground, falling from one's stricken aircraft without
a parachute—or that universal aviator nightmare, going down in
flames.

  As is the case in all human conflicts, however, the so-called "first
air war" was pursued by men who never lost sight of its purpose—to
achieve ultimate victory, as surely as their colleages on the ground
and at sea. As a result, as this book intends to show, World War I
established most of the fundamentals of aerial warfare that would be
merely brought to more efficient fruition in World War II and the
high-tech conficts of the Jet Age. Air superiority; aerial strategy and
tactics; bomber interception and escort; nocturnal aerial combat; aircraft carrier operations—all, save for electronic warfare and jet powered combat, at least took their first halting steps between 1914 and
1918.

1

SEIZING CONTROL
OF THE SKY

When Austria-Hungary declared war on Serbia on July 28, 1914, it triggered a chain reaction that escalated, country by country, alliance by alliance, into a global conflagration. The conflict caught the world in a state of technological transition that would transform—often most painfully—the conduct of warfare on land, sea, and for the first time, in the air.

Aircraft were not a complete novelty to warfare in 1914. The French had introduced observation balloons to the battlefield in 1794, and that means of intelligence gathering saw sporadic use in a number of subsequent conflicts, including the American Civil War, the Franco-Prussian War, and the Spanish-American War. In the early 1900s Alberto Santos-Dumont and Ferdinand Graf von Zeppelin perfected motorized, steerable airships that freed the gasbag from its tether. It was the achievement of powered heavier-than-air flight, however, that offered the most in terms of speed and mobility. Whatever arguments persist as to whether Orville and Wilbur Wright were first to achieve controlled heavier-than-air flight on December 17, 1903, it was Louis Blériot's precedent-setting hop across the English Channel on July 25, 1909, that served notice to the world—and in particular a nervous Great Britain—that bodies of water were no longer a protective barrier against the airplane's potential for flying over them.

The experiments began on June 9, 1910, when French Capitaine Charles Marconnay and Lieutenant Albert Féquant set a new endurance record of 160 kilometers and 2 1/2 hours in a Henry Farman pusher biplane—and used a hand-held camera to take aerial photographs of roads, railways, towns and countryside along the way. On the other side of the Atlantic, on June 30, Glenn H. Curtiss dropped dummy bombs on a battleship-shaped target at Lake Keuka, New York. On August 20, Jacob A. Fickel fired two rifle shots at a ground target and on January 7, 1911, Myron S. Crissey dropped a live bomb on a dummy target near San Francisco. On July 27, 1914— just one day before war broke out in Europe—a British Short float-plane launched a 14-inch naval torpedo.

Theory got its first opportunity to be put into practice on September 29, 1911, when the Italian army invaded the Ottoman-ruled provinces of Tripolitania, Fezzani, and Cyrenaica, bringing a small detachment of airplanes and airships with it. On October 23, Capitano Carlo Maria Piazza, in a Blériot XI monoplane, carried out the first wartime reconnaissance of the Jefara Plains outside of Tripoli. Another first swiftly followed on November 1 when Sottotenente Giulio Gavotti, holding the control stick of his Etrich Taube between his knees, dropped 17 pounds of Cipelli grenades on Turkish forces in the oases of Ain Zhara and Tajura.

The First Balkan War saw more frequent aerial bombings, including the use of specialized projectiles designed by Russian Lieutenant Vladimir Gilgar—pear-shaped aluminum cases with wooden tailfins, available in light (.25 kilogram) and heavy (1.5 kg) sizes—as well as sights he'd invented for dropping them. The Bulgarians carried out the first night bombing sortie on November 7, 1912, and during an attack on Adrianople (now Edirne) on November 30, 1912, they added a significant psychological touch by showering propaganda leaflets on the Turks.

On February 6, 1913, a Maurice Farman floatplane crewed by Greek army 1st Lieutenant Michael Moutousis and navy Ensign Aristidis Moraitinis flew over the Dardenelles, reconnoitered Turkish naval units at Nagara Point and dropped four grenades before departing. "Three of the bombs fell into the sea," the Turks reported afterward, "and the fourth hit a field near by a hospital, leaving a 15-centimeter hole in the ground." Turkish troops fired on the raider, but it

Appropriately numbered, Capitano Carlo Piazza's Blériot XI, the first airplane to fly a combat mission on October 23, 1911, shares a corner of the Hebrew Cemetery aerodrome southwest of Tripoli with an observation balloon. (*Italian Army Historical Department via Jon Guttman*)

was engine trouble that compelled the Farman to land in the Aegean Sea, to be recovered and towed by the Greek destroyer *Velos* to Mudros naval base on the isle of Lemnos. Moutousis's observer, Moraitinis, later earned a pilot's license and became a successful fighter pilot in World War I.

In March 1913, the Bulgarians tested an "automatic bomb dropping device" capable of carrying 21 bombs, which the pilot could release singly or all at once by pulling a handle. The war ended on May 30, before that invention could be used in combat, but just one day earlier another historic bombing attack had taken place off Guayamas, on the northwestern coast of Mexico.

The decade of successive power struggles collectively called the Mexican Revolution attracted a number of early fliers keen to apply their new-found skills to the battlefield—as well as adventure and "mucho dinero." Among them was 27-year-old Didier Masson, a French-born naturalized American who had illegally crossed the border with a Martin pusher to sell his services to the Constitutionalist army of Colonel Alvaro Obregón. In late May 1913, he improvised an arsenal of bombs out of 18-inch-long segments of 3-inch pipe packed with sticks of dynamite and rivets to serve as shrapnel, with fins and a push-type detonator. He also rigged a rack to his undercarriage to hold eight of the 30-pound projectiles in an upright position, a toggle device to release them, and a primitive crosshair bombsight. Thus armed, on May 29, Masson flew over the Gulf of California to attack the 1,880-ton federal gunboat *General Guerrero*. Newspaper accounts tend to be conflicting as to the nature of that first aerial strike against a warship in open waters or as to whom Masson carried with him as a bombardier, but he failed to hit the ship that day, and likewise missed during three subsequent attacks in as many days.

Another alleged aviation first in Mexico was claimed by Dean Ivan Lamb, a mercenary flying a Curtiss pusher for the Constitutionalistas, when he met and traded revolver shots with Phil Rader, a fellow American piloting a Christofferson biplane for the Federales. Again, accounts conflict as to the date—anytime from the summer of 1913 to November 1914—or even whether this aerial showdown took place at all, but even if it did, it ended in a bloodless draw.

More serious thought to seizing control of the sky from a potential enemy was well underway before World War I began. On July 23, 1910, August Euler, who held previous distinctions of earning the first German pilot's license and establishing Germany's first airplane manufacturer (Voisins under license), as well as its first airfield and flying school, applied for German Patent DRP 248.601: a fixed, forward-firing machine gun mounting for an airplane, using a "blowback shock absorber" and a special gun sight. After being awarded the patent in 1912, Euler wanted to exhibit what he called his "Airship Destroyer" at the Berlin Aeronautical Exhibition, but the War Department ordered him to withdraw it on the stated grounds that the whole concept of destroying Zeppelins, then regarded as the stately jewel in the crown of German aviation, was disgusting—but just as likely to keep it a secret.

Later in 1910, French aviation pioneer Gabriel Voisin raised eyebrows and perhaps some skeptical remarks when he displayed a sketchy mount for a 37mm naval cannon on one of his pusher biplanes. In Britain, Captain Bertram Dickson wrote a memorandum to the standing sub-committee of the Committee of Imperial Defense, advising that the use of aircraft in time of war to gather intelligence, "would lead to the inevitable result of a war in the air, for supremacy of the air, by armed aeroplanes against each other."

In the United States on June 7 and 8, 1912, U.S. Army Lieutenant Thomas DeWitt Milling piloted a Wright Model B armed with a Lewis machine gun, which his passenger, Captain Charles De Forest Chandler, demonstration-fired at ground targets. In Britain on July 24, Geoffrey de Havilland flew a "Farman Experimental" F.E.2 he had designed for the Royal Aircraft Factory, powered by a rotary engine and mounting a machine gun in the front observer's cockpit. In that same year, Vickers Ltd.'s newly created aviation branch received an order from the Royal Navy for a "fighting biplane" armed with a machine gun. After some consideration the firm opted for a two-seat pusher powered by an 80-hp Wolseley engine, with a 7.7mm Maxim gun in a ball-and-socket mounting in the nose of a two-seat nacelle. Vickers's "Experimental Fighter Biplane" or "Destroyer," was first exhibited at the Aero Show in Olympia, London, in February 1913, but as it took off for gun testing at Joyce Green, the EFB promptly nosed over. A follow-up EFB-2, with a 100-hp Gnome monosoupape rotary engine and a new nacelle with celluloid side windows, also crashed, at Bognor in October 1913. The EFB-3 reverted to the Wolseley engine and after a decent show-ing at the Olympia Aero Show in December 1913, six were ordered by the Admiralty. The EFB-4, featuring a more streamlined nacelle and only two tail booms, flew in July 1914.

Vickers finally dispensed with the "experimental" label on its FB-5, which again used a 100-hp Gnome monosoupape and mounted a .303-inch Lewis light machine gun above and in front of the observ-er's position. Dubbed the "Gunbus," this Vickers offering attracted production contracts for both the Royal Naval Air Service (RNAS) and the Royal Flying Corps (RFC) on August 14, 1914, although it would not reach the front in force for more than 11 months.

By then the war had spread across Europe and the British Expeditionary Force had landed in France, bringing with it an RFC contingent. While most of the earliest encounters between opposing aircraft ended with a harmless exchange of friendly waves by all con-cerned, it did not take long before more bellicose behavior prevailed.

On August 22, Lieutenants Louis Aubon Strange and L. Penn-Gaskell of No.5 Squadron, flying a Farman F.20, claimed to have shot at a German "Taube" or "Aviatik." Three days later, Lieutenants Hubert D. Harvey-Kelly and W.H.C. Mansfield of No.2 Squadron, flying an R.A.F.-built Blériot Experimental B.E.2a biplane, encountered a Rumpler Taube and fired on it with their sidearms until its unnerved crew landed near Le Cateau. Alighting nearby, Harvey-Kelly and Mansfield pursued the Germans into a nearby wood, but after failing to catch them, they returned to the Taube, appropriated some trophies from it, set it on fire, and took off for home.

While Harvey-Kelly and Mansfield were claiming Britain's first aerial victory after a fashion, a pilot in the Imperial Russian Air Service (IRAS) was taking more drastic measures. Born in Nizhny Novgorod (now Gorky) on February 27, 1887, Piotr Nikolayevich Nesterov had been a qualified pilot for six months when he put his Nieuport IV through a complete loop in the vertical plane over Syretsk military aerodrome, near Kiev, on September 9, 1913. His initial reward for that unprecedented achievement was 10 days in jail for "undue risk with a machine, the property of his government," until the accolades bestowed upon French aviator Adolphe Pégoud for the same feat on the 21st led to his being pardoned, promoted to Shtabs-Kapitan and awarded the Russian Aero Club Gold Medal on November 23.

Appointed commander of the XI Air Corps Detachment of the 3rd Aviation Company in February 1914, Nesterov tried to develop a training regimen for his pilots that he described in prophetic terms:

> I am perfectly convinced that it is the duty of every military aviator to be able to execute looping flights and gliding flights. These exercises must certainly be included in the training program, as they will play a great part in the aero-combat. Such a combat will resemble a fight between a hawk and a crow. The aviator who is able to give his craft the mobility and flexibility of motion of the hawk will be in a better position to seriously damage his opponent.

The principal equipment of the XI Detachment was the Morane-Saulnier G and the Nieuport IV, both French single-seat monoplanes dating to 1912. In 1913, the Russians imported the Morane-Saulnier G and licensed production was undertaken by the Duks and MOSCA factories in Moscow, Lebedev and Sliurasarenko in Petrograd, and Anatra in Odessa. Powered by an 80-hp Gnome rotary engine— though in 1916 Evgeny Morunov mounted a 100-hp Petrograd-built Gnome in one—the nimble Morane-Saulnier had been a sporty success in its heyday, but in 1914 its high wing loading limited its altitude and overall efficiency as a reconnaissance plane. That did not stop the Russian units from giving some a second seat for an observer, or Nesterov from mounting a saw bladed knife on one's tailskid to tear at balloons or airships—a weapon soon abandoned due to the paucity of lighter than air activity over the Russian front.

On September 7, 1914, Nesterov's unit was based near the town of Zholkov when a Lohner biplane of Austro-Hungarian *Fliegerkompagnie* (*Flik*) 11, based at Zurowica, flew over and dropped a bomb on the Russian aerodrome. The Austrian observer, Oberleutnant Friedrich Freiherr Rosenthal, owned several large estates in the area that had been occupied by the Russians, so there may have been some personal spite to his attack. In any case, Nesterov took it just as personally.

When Rosenthal reappeared over Zholkov the next morning, Nesterov set out to put his theories into practice, taking off and firing at the Lohner with a pistol. He failed to damage his opponent, which flew a second sortie over the airfield soon afterward, to be greeted once more with a futile fusillade from Nesterov.

When the Austrians came over for a third time that day, an outraged Nesterov jumped into the cockpit of Morane-Saulnier G No. 281 without bothering to fasten his seat belt. When one of his lieutenants came up to offer his Browning pistol, Nesterov replied, "That's all right; I shall manage without it."

This time, after climbing above the Lohner, Nesterov went into a dive and rammed it. He may have actually intended to recover from this deliberate collision, but fabric from the enemy plane's wing wrapped around his propeller shaft, momentarily binding the two planes together. The Morane-Saulnier tore free before the Lohner spun into the ground, but any hopes Nesterov may have had of regaining control were dashed when he was thrown from his plane. His body was found 30 or 40 feet from the wreckage. Oberleutnant Rosenthal and his pilot, Feldwebel Franz Malina, were also dead.

For his sacrificial victory, Nesterov was buried in Askold's Grave, a resting place for heroes in Kiev, and posthumously awarded the Order of St. George, 4th Class, on July 22, 1915. His status as an aviation pioneer was further honored by the Soviet Union on December 3, 1951, when it renamed the town of Zholiva in Lvov province Nesterov, and the Zholkovsky region as the Nesterov region.

Arguably the first deliberate attempt to seize complete control of the air was made by the Japanese during the siege of Tsingtao, which began in the immediate wake of their declaration of war against Germany on August 23, 1914. The concession port's sole airplane at that time was a Rumpler Taube flown by navy Kapitänleutnant Günther Plüschow, whose reconnaissance sorties were nevertheless enough to prod the Japanese into a concerted effort to eliminate his lone machine.

On September 5, navy Lieutenant Hideho Wada, piloting a Maurice Farman floatplane from the seaplane tender *Wakamiya Maru*, dropped 14- and 45-pound artillery shells on Fort Bismarck. The next day, two Japanese planes dropped three bombs on Plüschow's hangar, but failed to hit their target. Plüschow responded to the threat by having a second hangar erected and cobbled together a decoy plane from bamboo, tin, bicycle wheels and canvas. In several subsequent raids the Japanese bombed the fake Taube, only to experience puzzled frustration soon after at the sight of Plüschow scouting their lines or harassing them with bombs of his own, improvised from coffee cans.

With nine Japanese army and navy planes gunning for the Germans' only air asset, Plüschow was under strict orders to avoid contact, but on September 28 he attacked a Farman with his Parabellum Mauser pistol, firing 30 9mm rounds until he saw it spin down to crash. Plüschow did not report the encounter at the time, since it occurred in violation of direct orders. On October 13, Wada's and three of the army's Maurice Farmans made a concerted effort to bring down Plüschow's Taube, but he eluded them in a cloud.

A Maurice Farman M.F. 7 of the Japanese Army, as used during the 1914 siege of Tsingtao. (*Library of Congress*)

In spite of their efforts, the Japanese never did eliminate Plüshow's Taube before Tsingtao itself fell. He had been constructing a second, float-equipped biplane for the garrison, but on November 5 he was ordered to destroy it and the next day the governor ordered him to leave the doomed city with war diaries and official documents. Plüschow flew 150 miles south to Haichow, were he crash-landed in a muddy field and sold the remains of his plane to a local mandarin. From there he embarked on an eventful odyssey that included escape from Chinese internment at Nanking and imprisonment in Britain, to finally reach Germany by way of the Netherlands in July 1915.

The first use of a machine gun in aerial combat had a somewhat ironic outcome. Formed in August 1914 and assigned to the *Vème Armée* in September, French *Escadrille* V.24 flew Voisin 3LA two-seat pushers, several of which were equipped with an 8mm Hotchkiss M1909 machine gun on a front-mounted tripod for the observer. On October 5, Sergent Joseph Frantz and Sapeur Louis Quénault were flying an armed Voisin when they attacked an Aviatik B.I over Jonchery-sur-Vesle, near Reims. Quénault expended two 48-round magazines, but failed to get a decisive hit before running out of ammunition. At that point the Germans were firing at the French with rifles and Quénault produced one of his own, with which he managed to hit the enemy pilot. The Aviatik crashed, killing Sergeant Wilhelm Schlichting and Oberleutnant Fritz von Zangen of *Feldflieger Abteilung* (Field Flying Section) 18.

A Voisin 3LA was the first airplane to use a machine gun in air-to-air combat. This one optimistically mounts Le Prieur rockets on the wings as well. (Jon Guttman)

Further incidents proliferated in the wake of that precedent. On November 2, a Morane-Saulnier L two-seat parasol monoplane of *Escadrille* MS.23 was returning from a reconnaissance mission when its crew noticed a Taube following them. Taking umbrage, Sergent Eugéne Gilbert slowed to let the enemy plane catch up until it was 20 meters away, at which point his acting observer—and squadron commander—Capitaine Marie de Vergnette de Lamotte fired 30 carbine rounds into it until the Taube fluttered down to crash land in German lines.

Born in Riom on July 19, 1889, Gilbert had been a garage mechanic before a fascination with aviation led him to build a monoplane in 1909. It didn't fly, but the next year he trained on Blériots at Étampes, earning civilian pilot brevet No.240 on September 24, 1910, and went on to fly airplanes and balloons in both a military and civilian capacity. Before war broke out, Gilbert set several city-to-city speed records, including a 3,000-kilometer flight in 39 hours, 35 minutes that won him the 1914 Coupe Michelin.

On November 5, the Germans claimed their first official success. Leutnant Richard Flashar of *Feldflieger Abteilung* 33 was flying a long-range reconnaissance mission in a Rumpler B.I when he heard two cracks. Suspecting structural or mechanical failure, he looked back and saw a French parasol monoplane on his tail, with the observer taking pot-shots at him with a rifle. Flashar's evasive swerve jarred his observer, Oberleutnant Demuth, from concentrating on items of interest below and, as Flashar reported, Demuth "grabbed his *Schnelladegewehr* (rapid-fire or semi-automatic rifle) and let off a string of shots." When next Flashar glanced aft, the enemy plane was gone, but after landing the German crew learned that the parasol had crashed about thee kilometers from their airfield, within German lines. Curiously, the only casualties the French acknowledged that day were Adjutant Rondeau and Soldat Vernier of V.21, a Voisin unit supporting their IV*e Armée*, and their loss was attributed to anti-aircraft fire.

Sergent Joseph Frantz and Soldat Louis Quénault of escadrille V.24 used a Voisin 3LA to score the first official air-to-air shoot-down in aviation history on October 5, 1915. Their opponent, Aviatik B.1 B114/14, crashed near Reims, killing Sergeant Wilhelm Schilling and Oberleutnant Fritz von Zangen of Feldflieger Abteilung 18. (*Musée de l'Air et l'Espace*)

Although the Rumpler crewmen were cited within the German 1. *Armee*, they got no medals for their feat. At Christmas 1916, however, Flashar received an inscribed gold watch acknowledging the first German aerial victory from the *Inspektion der Fliegertruppe* (Inspectorate of Aviation Troops, or *Idflieg*).

Eugène Gilbert was flying a sortie with his mechanic, Soldat Auguste Bayle, serving as his observer on November 18, when they encountered an LVG B.I near Reims. Gilbert attacked and Bayle's carbine fire punctured its fuel tank. The disoriented Germans landed in French lines and their plane was later exhibited at St.-Cyr.

The New Year brought a third victory Gilbert's way when he and Lieutenant Alphonse de Puéchredon stalked a Rumpler B.I of *Feldflieger Abteilung* 23 on January 10. Approaching with the sun at his back, Gilbert closed to 20 meters when Puéchredon's first two carbine shots hit the pilot, Leutnant Franz Keller, in the neck and arm. The observer, Hauptmann Otto Karl Ferdinand Vogel von Falkenstein, pulled off a glove and raised his own rifle when Puéchredron's third shot fatally struck him. When a fourth shot holed his radiator, Keller landed between Villers-Bocage and Raineville. The French airmen landed nearby and administered first aid to Keller, who they found sitting beside his plane in great pain. Upon learning that he had been shot down by a prewar hero of his, Keller struggled to his feet to shake Gilbert's hand. The next day, in a gesture that would become commonplace throughout the war, Gilbert flew over German lines to drop a message regarding his opponents' fates, as well as a letter from Keller to his mother and sister. Both Gilbert and Puéchredon were made *Chevaliers de la Légion d'Honneur* for this action.

The next month saw another daredevil aviator add an aerial combat to his prewar laurels. Born a farmer's son in Monteferrat on June 13, 1889, Adolphe Celestin Pégoud had enlisted in the army at age 18 and campaigned in North Africa before returning to France and becoming an accomplished horseman. On October 16, 1911, Pégoud went up as a passenger in an airplane flown by Capitaine Louis Carlin, and set his ambitions on aviation. He started out as Carlin's mechanic, but obtained his own pilot's brevet on March 1. Over the next seven months Pégoud carried out a series of aerial experiments, including the first parachute jump in France on August 19. Louis Blériot, ever keen to promote his aircraft, put one of his Model XI monoplanes with strengthened wings and tailplane at Pégoud's disposal and on September 1, the daredevil scored another first by flying it inverted. He topped that feat on the 21st by putting his plane through what was initially hailed as the world's first loop—until news of Piotr Nesterov's slightly earlier achievement reached the West.

Performing his loop throughout Europe and Britain in a Blériot XI with his name emblazoned across the wings, Pégoud had achieved international fame and was planning a tour in the United States when war broke out. Initially Pégoud and his mechanic, Léon Lerendu, joined the *Camp Retranché de Paris* (CRP), a unit formed to defend the French capital. From there they were transferred to MF.25, a reconnaissance escadrille equipped with Maurice Farman 11 pusher biplanes, in which Pégoud got his first citation for a mission to Maubeuge on September 2. After moving to the Verdun sector later that month, Pégoud dropped steel darts called flechettes on German supply parks on September 29, used them to destroy an enemy balloon on the ground the next day, and dropped 2,000 flechettes on a balloon nest at Deux-aux-Bois on October 1.

Even while he performed reconnaissance and bombing missions, Pégoud took the growing presence of German aircraft in French air space as an affront to his national pride. On November 25, he made his first attack on an enemy airplane and though his observer's gun malfunctioned, he pursued his unnerved opponent until engine trouble forced him to land near Montfaucon. Pégoud was promoted to sergent for that deed, and after another mission on December 27, in which he braved bad weather, a faulty compass, and anti-aircraft fire to drop eight bombs on a balloon site, he was promoted to adjutant.

On January 23, 1915, Pégoud and Soldat Lerendu were transferred to MS.37, a new escadrille equipped with Morane-Saulnier L parasol monoplanes forming at Châteaufort. The unit moved to Sézanne on February 5, and during a reconnaissance later that same day, Pégoud and Lerendu spotted a Taube. Pégoud closed on the enemy and fire from Lerendu's rear mounted Lewis caused it to crash land south of Grandpré at 1000 hours. Continuing the mission, Pégoud encountered two Aviatiks east of Montfaucon at 1145, and several hits from Lerendu's gun sent one of them diving away. Climbing to 1,500 meters, Pégoud attacked the other Aviatik and Lerendu's fire compelled that plane to force-land as well. Although their citations were vague as to how terminal the damage to their opponents had been, the Frenchmen were credited with a triple victory, and Pégoud was awarded the *Médaille Militaire*.

Hardly one to rest on his laurels, Pégoud attacked a Taube on April 2 and drove it down in French lines, where Unteroffizier Otto von Keussler and Oberleutnant Brobnuggle of *Fl. Abt.* 40 were taken prisoner. A day before that, another Frenchman was making his presence known over the front.

Like the British B.E.2c, the Aviatik B.II had the observer up front, and this early machine gun mounting on B.1349/15 provided him with as limited an amount of safe traverse as the BE observer had. *(Jon Guttman)*

Born in Jouy-en-Morin on August 9, 1915, Jean Marie Dominique Navarre was one of twins among the 11 children of a wealthy paper manufacturer. An undisciplined child, Jean kept running away from school, but he became enthralled with mechanics and aviation, and managed to obtain his civil pilot's brevet on August 22, 1911. When war broke out, he immediately enlisted and after a short time in MF.8, he transferred to MS.12.

On April 1, 1915, Sergent Navarre attacked an Aviatik B.I near Fraisnes. His observer, Sous-Lieutenant Louis Robert, had only a carbine, but with three shots he managed to wound both Germans, Leutnant Engelhorn and Oberleutnant Wittenburg, who then landed and were taken prisoner. Both Frenchmen were awarded the *Médaille Militaire* five days later.

On April 12, Navarre and Soldat 2e Classe Gérard drove down another Aviatik. It was not confirmed, but the next day Navarre—adding the firepower of his pistol to Gérard's carbine—chased an Aviatik low over the French trenchline where poilus' rifles settled the issue, with the wounded Germans again force landing to be taken prisoner. On August 2, Navarre was made a *Chevalier de la Légion d'Honneur*.

Britain's first fighter unit fully equipped as such, No. 11 Squadron, used the two-seat Vicker F.B.5 "Gunbus" to some good effect before the Fokker E.I eclipsed it. *(Jon Guttman)*

By now the wartime skies of Europe had become decidedly unsafe, as every firearm from pistols to cannons were directed at the questing observation planes. Above the trenches, opposing aircraft traded broadsides like aerial frigates—first from rifles and carbines, then from machine guns for which crude pivots quickly evolved into sophisticated ring mountings with elevating mechanisms. At the same time, the rival air arms sought out more specialized aircraft for seizing control of the air.

Initially, there were two schools of thought regarding such fighting machines. One envisioned flying fortresses with anything from one to three gunner's positions. Stemming from the Voisin's early success, this philosophy led not only to two-seat "fighters," a term that the British generally reserved for two-seat pushers at the time, but to twin-engine gunships such as the German AEG G.II and the Gotha G.I, both of which evolved into bombers, and the French Caudron R.4 and R.11, nominal reconnaissance planes whose formidable armament made them quite effective as escorts for other reconnaissance planes or bombers. As aircraft performance improved in the course of the war, however, these heavy planes proved to be too slow and clumsy to play an active role in taking control of the sky. The only way they could shoot down enemy fighters was for the enemy fighters to come to them.

As 1915 dawned, however, Britain's first operational fighter was a two-seat pusher design, the Vickers F.B.5 "Gunbus." The first of them, Serial No. 1621, arrived in France on February 5, but did not survive the month before an unscheduled forced landing in German lines on the 28th resulted in its crew, 2nd Lts. M. R. Chidson and D. C. W. Sanders, becoming "guests of the Kaiser" and their plane falling into enemy hands virtually intact. The Germans were so impressed by their prize that their airmen were referring to any armed British pusher they encountered as a "Vickers" long after the F.B.5 had been replaced by other types.

In spite of that dubious start, more F.B.5s were sent to the front. On July 25, 1915, No. 11 Squadron, the RFC's first fully equipped fighter unit, arrived at Vert Galand aerodrome.

By then, the other air superiority concept had begun to prove itself. This was built around fast, nimble single-seat scouts such as France's Morane-Saulnier monoplanes, the German Fokker and Pfalz Eindeckers whose designs they influenced, and Britain's Bristol Scout biplane. As its name implied, the scout was originally conceived to dart over the front, its pilot taking in whatever he saw and rushing back to provide immediate intelligence on the tactical level, while the two-seaters ventured deeper into enemy lines to gather more detailed information or photographs. The inherent speed and agility of the scout naturally brought out the aggressive side in its pilot, who soon determined that the best way to shoot at an enemy was to aim his own plane toward it. To prove the scout's worth as a fighter, however, required solving one further problem: how to fire the machine gun in the same direction as the plane without shooting one's own propeller off.

2

POINT AND SHOOT

The Emergence of the Single-Seat Fighter

There were essentially two aircraft configurations on which to mount forward-firing machine guns in 1915. Pushers, with the engine and airscrew in the back, provided the pilot with an uninterrupted field of fire. The placement of the engine's weight and the propeller's torque aft of the pilot presented him with some handling idiosyncrasies, however, and the booms or, more often, latticework of struts and wires necessary to clear the propeller while supporting the tail surfaces imposed more inherent drag for a pusher to overcome than a tractor airplane. The tractor scout, on the other hand, required a means of firing through or around the propeller without riddling it or shooting it off altogether.

The first airplane builder to find a way around the problem—literally—was Giovanni Battista Caproni, and he did so before there was an air war for it to wage. As early as June 1911—three months before his country embarked on its first war using airplanes—Italian military theorist and army officer Giulio Douhet had declared, "aircraft will find their most formidable opponent in the air, in enemy aircraft, and even in these new forms of fighting the lighter than air shall be much more vulnerable than the heavier than air." In September 1913, Douhet had declared that air arms would need a single-seat airplane with a forward-firing gun "for fighting in the air." No less of a visionary than Douhet, Caproni tried to turn theory to reality early in 1914, when he unveiled a sleek, single-seat derivative of his Ca.18 observation monoplane called the Ca.20, whose 110-hp Le Rhône

The first single-seat fighter, the sole Caproni Ca.20 has survived to be exhibited since 1999 at the Museum of Flight in Seattle, Washington. (*Jon Guttman*)

rotary engine was neatly cowled behind a giant aluminum spinner with eight cooling vents. With a length of 27.43 feet and a wingspan of only 26 feet, the Ca.20 had an announced maximum speed of 103 mph. The Ca.20's most striking feature, however, was the machine gun fixed atop the tall supporting pylon that held its upper wing-bracing wires. This somewhat unsteady looking arrangement, which accounted for much of the plane's 9.5-foot height, allowed the pilot to fire his weapon forward above the propeller arc, aiming by a means of a sight mounted at eye level.

Although touted in retrospect as the world's first single-seat fighter, the Ca.20 proved to be roughly a year ahead of its time. More impressed with Caproni's Ca.1 twin-boom trimotor biplane, Douhet, then commanding the *Battaglione Aviatori*, placed higher priority on its production and development to advance his theory that strategic bombing would be the decisive factor in modern warfare. Thus Italy let slip an opportunity to field an effective indigenous fighter at the outset of its entry into the war in May 1915 and made it, like the United States, primarily dependent on France for its first-line fighters when it did join the fighting. Stored in a monastery, the historic Ca.20 managed to survive in its dry environment with little deterioration other than having its rubber tires gnawed away by rodents until 1999, when it was sold to the Museum of Flight in Seattle, Washington.

The Nieuport 10 prototype displays the sesquiplane configuration that dominated the firm's creations until well into 1917, and a flexible Hotchkiss machine gun for the forward observer that evolved into a fixed overwing mounting. (*SHAA B87.437*)

Caproni's idea of firing above the propeller came into its own on biplanes, whose strut-buttressed wings offered a more stable gun platform than a wire-braced pylon. The first plane to use that arrangement in combat, however, was not quite a biplane or exactly a monoplane. Developed by Gustave Delage from the Nieuport Type X monoplane, the Nieuport XB, or 10 as the military designated it, was powered by an 80-hp Clerget or Le Rhône 9B rotary engine, and featured a sesquiplane, or 1 1/2-wing configuration, in which a lower wing of much reduced chord, built around a single spar, was secured by V-shaped interplane struts to the two-spar upper wing. In an age of wire-braced, wooden-framed aircraft, this offered a wing cellule that was sturdier than a pylon-and-wire braced monoplane's, but less robust than a true biplane's. On the other hand, the sesquiplane offered the crew a better downward view and was more maneuverable than most biplanes.

Initially the Nieuport 10's observer sat in front of the pilot, though those positions would later be reversed. When it entered service in early 1915, both sides were seeking ways to arm their aircraft and Nieuport's first solution was to cut a central aperture in the upper wing center section, on which was mounted a flexible Hotchkiss machine gun that the observer could stand up to fire over the propeller arc. Soon, however, pilots improvised a fixed forward-firing

A prewar flier of some fame, Sergent Roland Garros established the primacy of the single-seat fighter in less than three weeks in April 1915. (*SHAA B75.279*)

mount for a lightweight, drum-fed Lewis gun above the Nieuport 10's upper wing, and often flew solo, without the observer. From there, an articulated framework was devised so that the pilot could pull the weapon down, change the magazine, and resume firing. The advantage of the upper-wing gun was obvious; the disadvantage was added drag, a limited ammunition supply, and a hazardous means of reloading, since a strong backdraft could blow the Lewis drum into a careless, butter-fingered pilot's face.

By that time, however, a crude means of firing a machine gun through, rather than above or around, the propeller had been tested in combat. This involved attaching steel wedges on the propeller to deflect any bullets that struck it. One of the earliest advocates of that idea was Eugène Gilbert, but he changed his mind when two of his friends were killed by ricocheting bullets during ground testing. The concept, however, appealed to Sergent Roland Garros, a pilot at neighboring MS.26 who had attained prewar fame as the first to fly over the Mediterranean Sea, from Saint-Raphaël to Bizerte, Tunisia, on September 23, 1913. Garros chanced to be doing exhibition flights in Germany when war broke out, but before the Germans impounded his Morane-Saulnier, he escaped to the airfield that evening, and took off. After a hazardous night flight he reached Switzerland, from which he eventually made his way back to France.

Garros discussed the deflector idea with Raymond Saulnier, who had devised a mechanical, camshaft and rod-activated system for interrupting a machine gun's fire back in April 1914, but who found it unworkable on open-bolt light machine guns such as the Hotchkiss and Lewis. As an interim measure until a better solution could be worked out, Saulnier produced a set of steel wedges that could be bolted onto the propeller blades. Garros and his mechanic, Jules Hue, improved on Saulnier's design by narrowing the width of the propeller blades at the point where the deflectors were attached.

Sergent Eugène Gilbert examines a Morane-Saulnier L modified as a single-seater. The plane is mounting a Hotchkiss machine gun and the airscrew has steel deflectors devised by Roland Garros and his mechanic, Jules Hue, at MS.23's aerodrome at St. Pol-sur-Mer. In spite of Gilbert's skepticism, Garros used this arrangement to down three enemy planes between April 1 and 18, 1915. (Jon Guttman)

After installing the modified airscrew and a forward firing Hotchkiss machine gun on a Morane-Saulnier L, Garros temporarily attached himself to the escadrille of his friend Gilbert, MS.23 at St. Pol-sur-Mer aerodrome outside Dunkirk. He then went looking for trouble. He found it during a bombing mission to Ostende on the morning of April 1, 1915, when he encountered a lone Albatros two-seater and coming head-on, opened fire on the startled Germans. Down went the Albatros, and Gefreiter August Spacholz and Leutnant Walter Grosskopf of *Feldflieger Abteilung* 40 had the dubious distinction of being the first victims of a single-seat fighter.

Over the next two weeks, Garros made himself the terror of the Western Front, attacking any German aircraft he could find. He brought down an Aviatik on April 15, and another Albatros three days later, but shortly after scoring his third confirmed victory he was forced down in enemy lines—either due to engine trouble or an infantryman's rifle bullet through his fuel line, depending on whose story one believed. The Germans were delighted to have captured France's hero of the hour and even more so to get their hands on the secret of his success.

On the same day Garros went missing, another new escadrille, MS.49, was formed at Fontaines, east-northeast of Belfort in the

Lorraine sector. Among the veteran airmen transferred to give it an experienced cadre were Eugène Gilbert, Adolphe Pégoud, and Léon Lerendu. Gilbert arrived in a Morane-Saulnier N, a unique single-seat shoulder-wing monoplane built for racing and aerobatics that Garros and he had flown before the war. Unlike the boxy looking Morane-Saulniers G and H, the N featured extra stringers that gave its fabric-covered fuselage a rounded, streamlined shape and a large cone-like propeller spinner covered its 80-hp Le Rhône engine. This was the plane for which Garros's deflectors had really been meant, and Gilbert set out to continue what his friend had started by installing them and a Hotchkiss gun on it. He also inscribed large letters on the fuselage sides proclaiming his purpose, "*Le Vengeur.*"

It was Pégoud, however, who was next to score. On April 28, he and his veteran mechanic teamed up to bring down an Aviatik between Guebwiller and Thann, credited as Lerendu's fourth and Pégoud's fifth victory. Pégoud was thus the first to achieve a status for which a French term for an outstanding aviator in general would soon be specifically applied: *as*, or "ace." He would not, however, be the first to be bestowed that title—except later, retrospectively and posthumously.

Gilbert's quest to avenge Garros began on June 6 with a combat that was recorded as indecisive, although he may in fact have killed the German observer, Leutnant Fritz Rössler of *Fl. Abt.* 34. The next day, he was credited with driving an enemy plane down in German lines near St. Amarin. On the 11th he claimed a two-seater in flames. It was never confirmed, but German records suggest that he may again have killed the observer, Leutnant Joachim von Maltzahn of *Fl. Abt.* 48, and wounded his pilot, Vizefeldwebel Rudolf Weingarten. Gilbert destroyed another Aviatik of *Fl. Abt.* 48 northeast of St. Amarin on June 17, this time killing the pilot, Vizefeldwebel Hugo Grabitz, and wounding his observer, Leutnant Karl Schwartzkopff, though their return fire pierced an engine cylinder, holed a propeller blade and slightly wounded Gilbert in the elbow.

Gilbert now had five confirmed victories, but his career as "*Le Vengeur*" ended 10 days later as he was returning from a bombing

Sergent Jean Navarre of MS.12 in the Morane-Saulnier Nm he used to bring down an LVG C.II near Jaulgonne on October 26, 1915. Its wounded crew, Unteroffizier Otto Gerold and Leutnant Paul Buchholz of Fl. Abt. 33, were taken prisoner. *(Jon Guttman)*

raid on Zeppelin sheds at Friedrichshafen, when the engine of his Morane-Saulnier L quit and he had to force land in Rheinfelden, Switzerland. After two unsuccessful attempts, he finally escaped from Swiss internment on June 1, 1916. Recurring ear problems due to a 1911 injury prevented him from returning to the front, but Gilbert served on as a test pilot, only to be killed in a crash at Villacoublay on May 17, 1918.

As a consequence of Garros's and Gilbert's brief but well-publicized runs of success, a somewhat modified version of Gilbert's Morane-Saulnier, the Model Nm (the last letter signifying "*militaire*") was put into production and saw some use in the summer of 1915. Deflectors were never a reliable means of firing a machine gun through the propeller arc, however, and the Morane-Saulniers were only allotted to French escadrilles in twos or threes. Some early aces, such as Jean Navarre, Georges Pelletier d'Oisy and Jean Chaput, scored a few victories in them before moving on to the more practical Nieuport scouts.

The British and Russians used Morane-Saulnier Ns far more than the French. No. 60 Squadron, RFC, was fully equipped with them in the summer of 1916. By that time, the deflector system and the plane on which it was mounted were completely outdated, and the unit suffered heavy casualties. No. 60 Squadron also had four specimens of the Morane-Saulnier I, with a 110-hp Le Rhône in place of the original 80-hp rotary and Alkan-Hamy interrupter gear—a Fokker-like system developed by Sergent-Méchanicien Robert Alkan of N.12 in place of the deflectors. The heavier and more powerful engine only made a tricky aeroplane even harder to control and one of 60 Squadron's pilots, Lieutenant William M. Fry, tellingly described it as the only plane he flew that gave the constant impression that it was doing its sincere best to kill him. Increasing the wing area on the Morane-Saulnier V did little to alleviate the problem. In October 1916, No. 60 Squadron exchanged the last of its Morane-Saulniers for Nieuport 16s and 17s, but they left behind an almost pathological distrust of, and prejudice against, monoplanes in the minds of the RFC's senior officers that would, like the Morane-Saulniers that inspired it, remain far longer than it should have.

While Garros and Gilbert were taking their chances with the hazardous deflectors, Adolphe Pégoud was flying a Nieuport 10 when he spotted an Aviatik of *Fl. Abt.* 48 over Bale on July 11. Diving to the attack, he fired a long burst that sent the two-seater crashing in flames near the train depot at Altkirch, killing the pilot, Unteroffizier Walter Hoffmann, and severely wounding the observer, Leutnant Heinrich Calberla. In addition to Bastille Day, Pégoud could celebrate being commissioned a sous-lieutenant on July 14, and he was officially cited for his sixth victory four days later.

The tables were turned on Pégoud as he closed on new prey over Mulhausen on August 28, when the German two-seater's alert observer scored a lucky hit on his engine at 600 meters. Even so, his conduct earned him a citation as a *Chevalier de la Légion d'Honneur*:

> Sous Lieutenant (Reserve) of Escadrille MS.49, with a spirit and bravery beyond words, also a modest and skillful pilot, who had never ceased since the start of the war to put his marvelous aptitudes to the service of his country. Accumulating daily the traits of courage and audacity, he has attacked heavily armed planes alone countless times. On 28 August 1915, during the course of an aerial duel, his plane

was riddled by bullets, and he was forced to land and immediately took every means available to save his plane in spite of
intense German fire.

On August 31, Pégoud attacked another two-seater of *Fl. Abt.* 48
over Montreux, but failed to score a telling hit. Turning away to
reload his Lewis gun, he then came on for another pass, but return
fire from the German observer, Leutnant Julius Bielitz, struck him in
the heart and his plane nosedived 2,000 meters into the ground near
Petit-Croix. Ironically the enemy pilot, Sergeant Walter Kandulski,
had been a student of Pégoud's before the war. Two hours later, the
German crew flew over the lines to drop a wreath with a band
inscribed, "His adversaries honor the flyer Pégoud, fallen in combat
for his country."

Adolphe Pégoud was buried in the cemetery at Brosse-de-Belfort
on September 3, but on September 23, 1920, his body was exhumed
and reinterred under a monument to his honor in the Montparnasse
cemetery in Paris.

At about the same time that France was producing its first aces,
Britain was finding a fighting innovator of its own. In October 1914,
the same month that Frantz and Quénault scored their groundbreaking aerial victory, No. 6 Squadron, RFC arrived in France, its pilots
including the 23-year-old scion of a distinguished military family
named Lanoe George Hawker. When his unit replaced its Henry
Farman pushers with B.E.2c tractor biplanes, Captain Hawker began
supplementing his reconnaissance patrols with more aggressive activities, such as bombing Zeppelin sheds, for which he received the
Distinguished Service Order.

In May 1915, No. 6 Squadron began to receive Farman
Experimental F.E.2b two-seat pushers, to escort the BEs. Soon afterward, Hawker wrote home about a single-seater he had just ferried in
from St. Omer on June 3: "I have a beautiful new toy, a new Bristol
Scout that goes at 80 and climbs 5 or 600 feet a minute! I'm having a

Bristol Scout C No. 1611 was the second on which Captain Lanoe G. Hawker installed his angled Lewis machine gun mounting and became the first single-seat pilot to earn the Victoria Cross. (Jon Guttman)

machine gun fitted to see how they like it." The plane to which he referred was Bristol Scout C No. 1607, a compact biplane powered by an 80-hp Gnome Lambda nine-cylinder rotary engine that embodied the fundamental scout configuration that would remain standard for the next 20 years. It was Hawker, however, who intended to make a fighter out of it. With the help of Air Mechanic Ernest J. Elton he devised a mounting for a Lewis gun that avoided the propeller arc by firing forward, downward, and outward at an angle.

In spite of the challenges of aiming such a weapon, on June 21, Hawker attacked a DFW two-seater over Poelcapelle, which was officially credited to him as "brought down out of control," or OOC. During a forced landing the next day, Hawker overturned his "toy," but managed to obtain a replacement, Bristol C No. 1611 and installed his angled Lewis gun mount on it.

On June 25, Hawker attacked three German two-seaters in as many sorties. During his second combat he forced an Albatros of *Fl. Abt. 3* to land near Passchendaele at about 1845 hours and shot another *Fl. Abt. 3* plane down in flames southeast of Zillebeke 15 minutes later, killing Oberleutnant Alfred Uberlacker and Hauptmann Hans Roser. Hawker was credited with both aircraft and subsequently received the first Victoria Cross awarded for air-to-air combat.

When Hawker was not flying his scout, he was piloting his squadron's FEs with equal ferocity. The F.E.2b was a large, ungainly looking but surprisingly capable pusher aircraft, powered by a 120-

hp Bearmore engine and armed with a Lewis gun in the forward observer's pit, which was usually supplemented by a second gun on a pole behind him that he had to stand up to fire against attacks from the rear. To augment the observer's armament Hawker brought along his own Lee-Enfield rifle. Flying F.E.2b 4227 on August 2, Hawker and Lieutenant A. Payze forced a German two-seater to land at Wulverghem. On the 11th Hawker was credited with a second "double" when he and his observer, Lieutenant Noel Clifton, sent an Aviatik nose-diving down near Houthem at 0545 hours, and similarly claimed a Fokker E.I outside Lille at 1915 that evening. Britain's pioneer single-seat fighter pilot was now its first ace, and on September 7, back in the cockpit of Bristol Scout 1611, he shot down an enemy biplane over Bixschoote for his seventh victory.

Later that month Hawker was called home for a well-earned rest—to be swiftly followed by command of a new squadron, equipped with a new fighter design. There was a serious challenge to be met, for the Germans had unleashed a new threat to Allied possession of the air that beleaguered RFC airmen were calling the Fokker Scourge.

The "Scourge" had begun with the capture of Roland Garros, the German examination of his deflectors and an order from their High Command to have it adapted or adopted to a fighting plane of their own. They quickly found an intrinsic flaw in the system, however. While French copper or brass-jacketed ammunition bounced off the deflectors, steel-jacketed German bullets tended to shatter them.

A Dutch-born aircraft designer who had been called upon to copy Garros's deflectors, Anthony Fokker, had a better idea. Since July 15, 1913, Franz Schneider of the Luft Verkehrs Gesellschaft (LVG) had held a patent for using a series of cams and rods attached to the trigger bar, to interrupt the machine gun's fire whenever the propeller was in its way. Schneider's idea, like Raymond Saulnier's parallel concept, had been theoretical up to that time, but Fokker, who had probably known of it and studied it long before getting this wartime stimulus, now put it into practice. Devising what Fokker called a *Gestängesteuerung*, or pushrod control, he and one of his employees, Heinrich Lübbe, adapted it to the 7.92 mm Parabellum LMG 08/14 machine guns installed on his A.III and M.5K scouts. Shoulder-wing monoplanes similar in appearance to the Morane-Saulnier H, the Fokker A.III and M.5K were powered by the 80-hp Oberursel U.0 rotary engine, a German-built version of the Gnome Lambda.

After testing at Döberitz on May 19–20, the German High Command was impressed enough to order five A.IIIs and M.5Ks armed with synchronized machine guns—designated M.5KMGs and bearing the serial numbers E 1/15-E 5/15—followed on August 28 by a production order for 36 E.I Eindecker (monoplane) scouts armed with the new weapon system. Production E.Is subsequently had their wings lowered on the fuselage to somewhat improve the pilot's view downward.

Although closed-bolt machine guns proved more amenable to Fokker's interrupter gear than the Hotchkiss and Lewis had to Saulnier's, even their suitability varied. The first armed scout to emerge from Fokker's Schwerin factor was A.III A16/15, armed with a Parabellum LMG 14 and issued in July to Leutnant Otto Parschau at *Fl. Abt.* 62, based at Douai aerodrome. In a letter to Fokker on the 28th, Parschau complained of the Parabellum's incessant tendency to jam after a few shots, but noted that Fokkers using the Spandau-produced Maxim LMG 08/15 were performing excellently. Parschau later got the first production E.I, 1/15, while the fifth, 5/15, went to Leutnant Kurt Wintgens.

A bespectacled 20-year-old army officer's son from Neustadt, Wintgens had previously earned the Iron Cross 2nd Class as an observer over the Eastern Front. He had then trained to be a pilot and demonstrated sufficient skill to be assigned Fokker E.I 5/15, which he flew while with *Flieger Abteilungen* 67 and 6b. It was with the latter Bavarian unit that Wintgens claimed a Morane-Saulnier L east of Lunéville on July 1, 1915, which went down too far in French lines for witnesses to confirm. For not the first or last time in the war, what failed to be officially recorded as the first German fighter victory actually turned up on the enemy's casualty list as Capitaine Paul du Peuty and Lieutenant Louis de Boutiny of MS.48, both wounded, and forced to land.

After another unconfirmed Parasol claimed on July 4, Wintgens transferred to *Fl. Abt.* 48 at Mülhausen on July 5, although he wrote to a friend that he had what amounted to a roving commission. Finally, on the 15th, Wintgens was credited with a Morane-Saulnier over Schucht— although it is curiously ironic that the French recorded no casualties between July 14 and 18!

Leutnant Kurt Wintgens may have scored the first victories in the new Fokker E.I in July 1915. He went on to earn the *Orden Pour le Mérite* and total 19 victories before he was himself shot down on September 25, 1916. (SHAA B82.505)

Wintgens went on to score two more victories by early 1916, when he came down with influenza. Returning to action with *Fl. Abt.* 6b that spring, he resumed his scoring by downing a Nieuport 12 two-seater—probably flown by Maréchal-des-Logis Léon Beauchamps and Sous-Lieutenant Debacker of N.68—on May 20, and by June 30 he had brought his total up to eight, for which he became the fourth fighter pilot to receive Germany's highest honor for officers, the blue-enameled *Orden pour le Mérite* (equally well, if less formally, known as the "Blue Max") on July 1.

Another early Eindecker recipient at *Fl. Abt.* 62 was a 24-year-old Leutnant der Reserve from Dresden named Max Immelmann, who had been flying LVG two-seaters with the unit since March 1915. Yet another pilot who got to fly the new type was Leutnant Oswald Boelcke, who had already proven his mettle in an LVG C.I when he and his observer, Oberleutnant Heinz von Wühlisch, destroyed a Morane Saulnier L over Valenciennes on July 4, killing Lieutenants Maurice Tetu and Georges comte de la Rochefoucault Beauvicourt of MS.15.

Although Immelmann and Boelcke were close friends and both came from Saxony, the only other things they held in common were an aggressive spirit and a shared belief that the Fokker E.I represented the future of aerial warfare. Immelmann was self-centered and arrogant, accused by one of his instructors as having "a truly childish temperament." Boelcke, though almost a year Immelmann's junior, seemed more mature and got along better with both fellow airmen and with the ladies. Whereas Boelcke thought nothing of taking German nurses up on "joy rides," (for which he was censured by his superiors) and courted a young French girl who lived near his base, Immelmann seemed to have only one woman in his life—his mother.

The most significant difference between the two men, however, was that while Boelcke preferred to think of himself as being as much of a loner as Immelmann, he proved to be a natural leader. Boelcke himself once wrote, "You can win the men's confidence if you associate with them naturally and do not try to play the high and mighty superior." That attitude would soon make him the mentor for a generation of German fighter pilots.

Boelcke had more overall flight experience than Immelmann, so he got the first chance to fly the section's new Eindecker, and attacked a French two-seater in June 1915. However, the monoplane's tricky flight characteristics gave him trouble, and on top of that, as he dove and loosed a long burst at his quarry, his gun jammed. A nearby German two-seater crew swore it saw the French plane go down, but nobody saw it crash and it went unconfirmed.

On August 1, flying crews of *Fl. Abt.* 62 were sleeping off the previous evening's drinking binge when they were rudely awakened by exploding bombs as B.E.2cs of No.2 Squadron raided Douai. Donning whatever flying garb was in reach, Immelmann scrambled up in Fokker E.I 3/15, soon followed by Boelcke in E.I 1/15. The BEs, too stable for their own good, made easy prey for the Fokkers and Immelmann quickly brought one down, landed next to it and took its pilot, Lieutenant William Reid, prisoner. Boelcke also lined up a target, only to suffer another gun jam.

Boelcke's frustrating spate of false starts finally ended on the evening of August 19, when he downed what he described as an "English Bristol biplane." This may in fact have been another B.E.2c of No. 2 Squadron whose crew, Captains J.G. Hearson and Barker, force landed in Allied lines with a severed fuel line.

A Fokker E.III "on the prowl" (actually 210/16, which fell into British hands after suffering engine failure on the wrong side of the lines on April 8, 1916, here photographed while being test flown at Upavon in May) epitomizes the "Fokker Scourge" that lasted roughly from the summer of 1915 to the summer of 1916. (*SHAA B83.1039*)

Now both blooded, Boelcke and Immelmann were soon wreaking enough havoc on Allied reconnaissance planes as to achieve a measure of local air superiority. "They treat my single-seater with a holy respect," Boelcke wrote. "They bolt as quick as they can."

Disobeying orders to keep within his own lines, Boelcke began to hunt in Allied territory—until an incident in which he was almost shot down by an Allied plane while attacking another came as something of an epiphany to him. Lone wolf tactics would not suffice, he realized, if fighters were to gain a meaningful control of the sky.

Boelcke formulated the idea of two Fokkers working as a team, with a wingman flying slightly above and to the side, to guard the leader's tail. In spite of the friendly rivalry that developed between them, Boelcke and Immelmann worked quite effectively together, with encouraging results. Their scores were tied at six on January 12, 1916, when both were awarded the *Orden pour le Mérite*.

By then too, the Fokker E.I had been joined by some improved progeny: the somewhat enlarged E.II, powered by a 100-hp Oberursel U.I engine, and the E.III, whose fuel capacity had been increased to raise its flight duration from 90 to 150 minutes. By the end of October there were 75 Fokkers at the front, 23 of them E.IIIs. Allotted to various other units, the Eindeckers were flown with enthused élan to produce a new generation of German fighting heroes, such as Hans Berr, Wilhelm Frankl, Walter Höhndorf, Gustav Leffers, Max Mulzer, Otto Parschau, and Kurt Student.

Two other early German aces bore firsthand witness to the difference between the agile scout and the "battle plane" at that stage of the air war. Based at Roupy, *Fl. Abt.* 23's ranks held three future *Pour le Mérite* recipients: Leutnants Ernst Freiherr von Althaus, Rudolph Berthold, and Hans-Joachim Buddecke. In September the unit received its first Fokker E.I, which the 25-year-old Buddecke, a well-traveled prewar flier who had flown monoplanes in the United States, got the privilege of flying. Berthold, in contrast, was flying an AEG G.II with twin engines, four crewmen and three flexibly mounted machine guns. On September 15, Berthold crashed AEG G.II 21/15, but was soon issued a replacement. He and Buddecke were then detached to form a tiny *Kampfstaffel* (combat squadron) to operate from Château Vaux.

On September 19, Buddecke was patrolling at 2,000 meters altitude south of Saint Quentin when he spotted "something" which turned out to be a B.E.2c of No. 8 Squadron. In the ensuing fight, Buddecke found the British observer to be his equal as a marksman, but he eventually managed to bring the BE down with the pilot, Lieutenant W.H. Nixon, dead. The wounded observer, Captain John N.S. Stott, remained in surprisingly sporting spirits as he showed his captor his bullet-riddled leather flying coat and remarked, "You are some good shot."

Berthold, flying AEG G.II 26/15, took on a British pusher on October 2, only to come back without success and two of his gunners mortally wounded. Buddecke went on to down B.E.2cs on October 23 and November 11. Soon after that he was sent to the Dardanelles with the German Military Mission to Turkey, bequeathing his Fokker to a grateful Berthold, who was by then sold on the single-seater's superiority to his far-from-invincible "flying fortress." Berthold used the Eindecker to down a Voisin on February 2, 1916, and scored his second of an eventual 44 victories over a B.E.2e three days later.

Bottom: AEG G.II 24/15 typified the "battle plane" approach to aerial combat that the Germans soon abandoned in favor of the single-seat Fokker Eindecker. *(Johan Visser)*

The now-proven "point and shoot" philosophy went beyond fighters. Anthony Fokker's interrupter gear was also used by every German airplane using a forward-firing machine gun, with the manufacturers paying Fokker for every one they installed.

That privilege did not go undisputed. In January 1916, Franz Schneider and LVG sued Fokker for patent infringement, and on June 30, 1917, the royal supreme court ruled for the plaintiffs and levied a million-mark fine on Fokker. Fokker refused to pay "even a single Pfennig," even after a second ruling by a court in Berlin in 1926, and a third, unsuccessful attempt by Schneider in 1933. Oddly, though, Fokker did submit to a ruling requiring him to pay a percentage of his patent fees to August Euler, who successfully sued him for infringement of his 1912 patent, to a total of 750,000 marks. Those conditions notwithstanding, the "Flying Dutchman's" enterprising decision to put theory into practice paid off handsomely.

On the Allied side, the Fokker Scourge became a genuine threat. In March 1916, Member of Parliament Noel Pemberton-Billing expressed what was on the minds of many RFC aircrewmen when he dismissed the B.E.2c in particular and Royal Aircraft Factory products in general as "Fokker Fodder." Meanwhile, British and French airplane and weapons designers sought means of countering the menace.

Britain's only nominal fighter at that time was the Vickers F.B.5 Gunbus, which had begun full-squadron operations at about the same time the Fokker E.I was making its combat debut. Among the first of No. 11 Squadron's pilots to directly challenge the Eindeckers was an aggressive Welsh warrior named Captain Lionel Wilmot Brabazon Rees, who with his observer, Flight Sergeant J. M. Hargreaves, was credited with "driving down" an Eindecker on July 28. On August 31, the duo destroyed an LVG C.II near Achiet le Grand, followed by an Ago C.I driven down on September 21 and an Albatros the next day. On September 30, they forced an Albatros down in British lines at Gommecourt, where the crew, Leutnant der Reserve Fritz Kölpin and Oberleutnant Ernst Leonhardi of *Fl. Abt.* 23, died of their wounds. Rees was awarded the Military Cross and Hargreaves the Distinguished Conduct Medal for their exploits. On October 31, Rees added an LVG to his tally, in concert with another observer, Flight Sergeant Raymond. With six victories at that point, Rees was destined to be the only pilot to make ace in the Vickers Gunbus, but another would earn a greater distinction.

In September, No. 11 Squadron moved from Vert Galand to Villers Bretonneux aerodrome. On the 6th of the month Lieutenant Gilbert Stuart Martin Insall and 2nd Lt. G. Manley attacked two LVGs, forcing one to dive away and the other to flee eastward.

On November 7, Insall was flying F.B.5 5074 with 1st Class Air Mechanic T. H. Donald as his observer when they forced an Aviatik to land southeast of Arras. Ignoring ground fire—including shots from the downed enemy aircrewmen, who were sent fleeing from their plane when Donald shot back—Insall swooped down to finish off the Aviatik with a small incendiary bomb. On the way home the British strafed the German trenches until return fire holed their fuel tank. Insall managed to get only 500 yards into Allied lines before having to land in a wood. There he and Donald stood by their plane while German artillery sent 150 well-directed shells their way. Working by

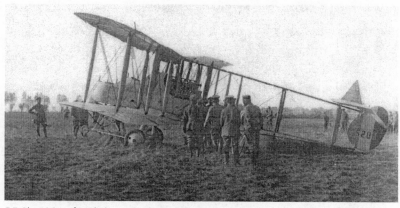

F.E.2b 5206 of B Flight, No. 20 Squadron, was brought down near Houthem on May 21, 1916, the fifth victory for Vizefeldwebel Wilhelm Frankl of Fl.Abt. 40. Captain Charles Ernest Hilton James and 2nd Lt. Henry Leslie Cautley Aked were taken prisoner. (*Greg Van Wyngarden*)

torches and other lights in the night, the two repaired their Gunbus and took off at dawn to return safely to their aerodrome.

For their dedication to recovering their plane, literally at all hazards, Insall was awarded the Victoria Cross and Donald the Distinguished Conduct Medal on December 23. Neither man was there to receive them, however—they had been brought down and taken prisoner nine days earlier, either by ground fire or by a German two-seater they had engaged, crewed by ace-to-be Hauptmann Martin Zander and Leutnant Gerche of *Fl. Abt.* 9b. After two failed attempts Insall and two companions escaped from Strohen prison camp on August 28, 1917, reaching the Dutch border nine nights later.

Awarded the Military Cross, in mid-1918 Captain Insall was put in command of a flight in No. 51 (Home Defence) Squadron, flying Sopwith Comics, night-fighting versions of the Camel, from Bekesbourne. He would remain in Royal Air Force service until July 30, 1945, dying at Bawtry on February 17, 1972.

On November 19, 1915 the second all-F.B.5 unit, No. 18 Squadron, reached France. By then, however, the Gunbus, with its maximum speed of 70 mph at 5,000 feet and a service ceiling of no more than 9,000 feet, was clearly no match for its single-seat opposition. On March 16, 1916, the RFC's commander, Major-General

Hugh Trenchard, beseeched the Deputy Director General of Military Aeronautics to, "say when you will be able to replace these machines by F.E.2bs with either 160-hp Beardmore or Rolls-Royce engines or some other type of machine." Those replacements were indeed forthcoming, but not before F.B.5 5079 of No. 11 Squadron was attacked by two Fokkers on April 23—Easter Sunday—driven down with a riddled petrol tank near Pelves. Its crew, 2nd Lts. William C. Mortimer-Phelan and William A. Scott-Brown, was taken prisoner. Their assailants were Leutnants Max Immelmann and Max Ritter von Mulzer of *Fl. Abt.* 62, and they were credited as Immelmann's 14th victory.

Notwithstanding Garros's and Gilbert's brief rampages, the French swiftly decided that the Nieuport 10 with its overwing machine gun was the most viable counterweapon of the moment. One of the earliest units to receive it in quantity was MS.3, whose airmen had already shown considerable élan even while flying Morane-Saulnier L parasols. The escadrille's first victory had been scored on July 3, 1915 when its commander, 30-year-old Capitaine Félix Antonin Gabriel Brocard, used a carbine to bring down an Albatros two-seater of *Fl. Abt.* 2 over Dreslincourt, killing the observer. Then, on July 19, Caporal Georges Marie Ludovic Jules Guynemer, a sickly 20-year-old Parisian whose patriotic insistence had gotten him into the air service as a mechanic and then as a pilot, used a Morane-Saulnier L with an improvised rear machine gun manned by his mechanic, Soldat Jean Guerder, to shoot down an Aviatik, killing Unteroffizier August Ströbel and Leutnant Werner Johannes of *Fl. Abt.* 26. *Escadrille* MS.3 began receiving Nieuports that same month and on August 28, Brocard used one to down an enemy plane north of Senlis.

The French were not alone in making aggressive use of their Nieuports. On September 12, a modified Nieuport 10 of the Belgian *2e Escadrille* sent an Aviatik crashing at Oudstuivekenskerke. The Nieuport's pilot, Sous-Lieutenant Jan Olieslagers, was a prewar champion motorcycle racer and aviator, known as the "Antwerp

Caporal Georges Guynemer and Soldat Jean Guerder pose in front of their Morane-Saulnier L after scoring their first victory on July 19, 1915. (Jon Guttman)

Devil." The kill was confirmed as Belgium's first single-seat victory, and the first of an eventual six for Olieslagers.

On September 20, MS.3 was fully re-equipped with Nieuport sesquiplanes and officially redesignated N.3. On December 5, Sergent Guynemer used a single-seat Nieuport 10 with an infantry Lewis gun, complete with stock, mounted above the wing to bring down an Aviatik over Bois de Carré. Three days later he destroyed an LVG between Roye and Nesle, killing Vizefeldwebel Kurt Diesendahl and Leutnant Hans Reitter of *Fl. Abt.* 27. On the 14th, Guynemer teamed up with a two-seater Nieuport 10, crewed by Adjutant André Bucquet and Lieutenant Louis Pandevant, to down an Eindecker over Hervilly.

The single-seat Nieuport 10's successes were encouraging, but it was not fast or nimble enough to engage a Fokker E.I on equal terms. Gustave Delage was already addressing the matter with a sesquiplane version of the Nieuport XI racing monoplane called the BB-XI, which first flew in the summer of 1915. Accepted for production that autumn under the military designation of 11, this aesthetically pleasing "offspring" of the Nieuport 10, whose smaller, lighter airframe

The Nieuport 11 preserved at the Musée de l'Air et l'Espace at Le Bourget bears the personal marking of Commandant Charles Tricornot de Rose, father of French air superiority strategy. (Jon Guttman)

allowed its 80-hp Le Rhône 9C engine to speed it along at a then-sprightly 88 mph, was popularly known as the *Bébé* ("baby").

The availability of the Nieuport 11 at a time when the Eindeckers were threatening to dominate the sky led to the next logical step: the all single-seat fighter squadron. In the late summer of 1915, Major Jean Baptiste Marie Charles, Baron de Tricornot, Marquis de Rose—one of the first French officers to embrace airplanes as the new Pegasus—was in charge of the air assets of the V*e Armée.* He ordered MS.12 to re-equip with *Bébés.* On September 23, the unit was fully restocked and redesignated N.12, the first single-seat fighter squadron in history. Always one to set the example, de Rose took to the air in his own Nieuport 11, bearing a rose on the fuselage side for easy personal identification.

Bébés soon made their way into other French units and the Royal Naval Air Service, which had already made substantial orders for Nieuport 10s, in November 1915. The RFC soon followed suit, and Nieuport 11s subsequently served in the Russian, Belgian, and Italian air services as well.

At N.3 Georges Guynemer achieved a personal milestone in Nieuport 11 N836, on the fuselage of which he applied the legend "*Le Vieux Charles*" in reference to Sergent Charles Bonnard, a popular squadron mate who had transferred to the Macedonian front. On February 3, 1916, Guynemer used it to shoot an LVG down in German lines near Roye. "I had my fifth," he wrote afterward. "I was really in luck, for less than ten minutes later another plane, sharing the same lot, spun downward with the same grace, taking fire as it fell through the clouds." German records only noted one fatality from the combat—Leutnant Heinrich Zwenger, an observer of *Fl. Abt.* 27, killed between Roye and Chaulnes—but both LVGs were confirmed. Guynemer downed another at Herbecourt on the 5th, again killing the observer, Leutnant Rudolf Lumblatt of *Fl. Abt.* 9.

Another early Nieuport fighter unit was C.65, which was originally formed at Lyon-Bron on August 2, 1915 as an *"escadrille provisoire de chasse,"* with two Nieuport 11s, three Nieuport 12 two-seaters and three Caudron G.4s. The unit's first success, an enemy plane forced to land on October 16, involved a two-seater crew. Months before being officially designated as N.65 on February 21, the escadrille chalked up its first Nieuport victory, courtesy of a hero about as far removed from Guynemer in temperament as could be imagined.

Unlike the sickly, single-minded Guynemer, Charles Eugène Jules Marie Nungesser was an athletic man of the world who had raced cars, boxed, and learned to fly while in Argentina before the war. During the conflict's early days, Nungesser had served with distinction in the *2ème Régiment des Hussards*, earning the *Médaille Militaire* before transferring into aviation in November 1914 and earning his military pilot's brevet on 17 March 1915. Assigned to VB.106, he flew 53 bombing missions in a Voisin 3, the front nacelle of which he personalized with a black skull and crossbones. In the early morning hours of July 31, Adjutant Nungesser and his mechanic went up in a new Voisin 3LA armed with a Hotchkiss machine gun—an unauthorized flight, since he was supposed to be on standby duty that night—but as fortune would have it, they caught five Albatros two-seaters staging a night raid on Nancy and sent one down to crash. For deserting his post, Nungesser was confined to his quarters for eight days. For downing the enemy plane he received the *Croix de Guerre*—and later, a transfer to train in Nieuports.

Arriving at N.65 in November 1915, Nungesser was assigned Nieuport 16 N880. This was essentially a Nieuport 11 powered by a 110-hp Le Rhône 9J that gave it somewhat higher performance, but also made it nose-heavy and gave it a higher wing loading (8.46 pounds per square foot, compared to the 11's 7.4 pounds per square foot) that made it trickier to handle than the 80-hp *Bébé*. Many pilots considered it a handful, but Nungesser was delighted with the new fighter. While ferrying it to N.65's aerodrome at Malzéville on November 26, he celebrated over Nancy by flying around the church steeples, looping over the town square and zooming as low as 30 feet down the main street. Upon landing he got a dressing-down from his commander, Capitaine Louis Gonnet-Thomas, who caustically remarked that he should be terrorizing the *Boche*, not his fellow Frenchmen.

Nungesser obeyed in his own way—he refueled his Nieuport, flew over the lines, buzzed a German aerodrome and returned to report: "It is done, *mon capitaine*!" His reward was another eight days under house arrest.

On November 28, Gonnet-Thomas let Nungesser fly a local sortie for gunnery practice on ground targets. He had barely taken off, however, when he spotted two Albatros two-seaters crossing the lines near Nomeny. Climbing to 8,000 feet and placing the sun at his back, Nungesser attacked. One of the Germans fled, but the other put up a spirited fight until Nunsesser, using his last ammunition drum at a range of 30 feet, finally drove it down in a dive.

What Nungesser saw next took much of the luster out of his second victory. "The observer, still alive, clung desperately to the mounting ring to which his machine gun was attached," he reported. "Suddenly the mounting ripped loose from the fuselage and was flung into space, taking with it the helpless crewman. He clawed frantically at the air, his body working convulsively like a man on a trapeze. I had a quick glimpse of his face before he tumbled away through the clouds. . . it was a mask of horror."

The observer whose fall Nungesser witnessed was Leutnant Wilhelm von Kalkreuth of *Brief A.M.*, whose body was found at

Sous-Lieutenant Charles Nungesser of *Escadrille* N.65 shows off his Nieuport during a visit to a Belgian Aerodrome in 1916. *(Jon Guttman)*

Nomeny. His pilot, Vizefeldwebel August Blank, crashed at Mailly. Nungesser had trouble eating and sleeping for some time after that, but he eventually got over it. Gonnet-Thomas helped—he commuted the remaining six days of his arrest and recommended him to be made a *Chevalier de la Légion d'Honneur*.

By the end of 1915, both sides had reasonably effective fighting scouts. It was in 1916, however, that those fledgling fighters would truly be put to the test.

3

THE FIRST AIR BATTLES

N either side's ground forces had made significant progress on the Western Front in 1915, in spite of Italy entering the war on the Allied side in May—and being swiftly stalemated by the Austro-Hungarian army. The next year would see a number of attempts to break the deadlock and with them, the first serious attempts to achieve control of the sky above the battlefield.

The first began on the morning of February 21, 1916, when the old fortresses around Verdun-sur-Meuse came under a 10-hour artillery bombardment, followed by an offensive involving nearly 150,000 troops. Conceived by German Chief of Staff Erich von Falkenhayn, the push was expected to overrun the weakened defenses in that sector with an attack from three sides. After some initial successes in the first few days, however, the German advance slowed when the French XX Corps arrived to bolster the shaken 30,000 defenders of the XXX Corps. Further help came on February 25 with the arrival of General Henri Philippe Pétain's IIe *Armée*. By the 29th the German momentum was faltering and 90,000 French reinforcements, as well as 23,000 tons of ammunition, were arriving via their sole railroad through Bar-le-Duc.

At that point, Falkenhayn's strategy changed from one of conventional breakthrough to a battle of attrition, in which he expected the Germans, using their superior positioning and firepower, to bleed the French army white. What it became was the longest and most agonizing battle of the war. As such, Verdun also became the crucible of the

Sometimes confused with the Fokker E.I by its enemies, the Pfalz E.I was harder to control and less popular with German pilots. Typically, E.I 479/15 was assigned to the Eastern Front, operating from Vilna aerodrome in the winter of 1915-16. (Jon Guttman)

war's first deliberate effort to achieve control above the battlefield through the massed concentration of air assets.

While the French and British had already begun equipping entire squadrons with scouts or two-seat fighters, the most specialized fighting unit the Germans had by February 1916 was the *Kampf Einsitzer Kommando*, or KEK. Created originally by Inspektor Major Friedrich Stempel, the staff officer in charge of aviation to Prince Rupprecht of Bavaria's 6. *Armee*, the KEKs consisted of two to four Fokker or Pfalz Eindeckers that were no longer attached to reconnaissance or artillery spotting *Flieger Abteilungen*. Officially tasked with *Luftwachtdienst* (aerial guard duty), the Fokkers had a freer hand to roam the front and eliminate whatever Allied planes they encountered.

At the start of the Verdun battle the staff officer in charge of the German 5. *Armee*'s air arm, Hautpmann Wilhelm Haehnelt, had 168 aircraft on hand. Of those, only 21 were Fokker and Pfalz monoplanes, which operated with KEKs based at Avillers, Jametz, and Cunel. Haehnelt's original strategy was for the fighters to patrol the front constantly to form a *Sperre*, or "blockade" against any French aircraft trying to penetrate airspace over the 5. *Armee*. This task was impossible for the Eindeckers at his disposal, making it necessary to supplement their numbers with two-seaters drawn from army battlewings, the *Kampfgeschwader der Obersten Heeresleitung*, or *Kagohls*. Even then, constant patrolling took its toll on the Eindeckers' rotary engines, which could not stand up to the same sustained activity that their more conventional water-cooled contemporaries could.

While the French army reeled under the shock of the German onslaught on February 21, its air arm had the best of that first day, suffering two men wounded and four injured, but claiming eight German aircraft, of which half were confirmed. Among the latter was a two-seater claimed but not confirmed to Adjutant Jean Navarre, recently transferred to N.67.

There was no disputing the validity of Navarre's double victory on February 26, when he shot down a two-seater and an escorting Fokker E.III of *Kampfstaffel* (or *Kasta*) 4 at Drienne-sur-Meuse, where both pilots, Leutnants Georg Heine and Alfons von Zeddelmann, died and the observer, Oberleutnant Heinrich Kempf, was taken prisoner. That brought Navarre's score up to five and for the first time the French were referring to him as an *as* or "ace," a title already applicable to Pégoud and Gilbert.

Flying relentlessly in search of new prey, Navarre soon acquired an additional sobriquet, "*la Sentinelle de Verdun*." Ever the individualist—with more than a *soupçon* of ego—he advertised his presence to the *poilus* he supported by painting the fuselage of one of his Nieuport 11s red and that of another, N576, in blue, white and red bands like the French flag. On March 2, he brought another Albatros down between Fleury and Fort Douaumont, where its wounded occupants were taken prisoner.

More future French aces opened their accounts in March. On the 8th, Adjutant Pierre Henri Edmond Dufaur de Gavardie of N.12 scored his first of an eventual six victories over Warmeriville and Lieutenant Paul Louis Malavialle of N.69 downed an LVG over Étain—his first of five. Also having his baptism of fire with N.69 was Aspirant Pierre Navarre, Jean's twin brother, driving down an enemy plane near Verdun that was only counted as a "probable." In a second combat minutes later, Navarre himself came down wounded in French lines. He was probably the first victory for Oberleutnant

An in-air photograph embodies Navarre's sobriquet "La Sentinelle de Verdun" as he patrols in Nieuport 11 N576, patriotically decked with blue-white-red bands on the fuselage and cockades on the wheel hubs. (*SHAA B92.4115*)

Hans Berr, who would ultimately score 10 with KEK Avillers, earn the *Orden Pour le Mérite* and command his unit when it expanded into *Jagdstaffel* 5, only to die in a mid-air collision with a squadron mate on April 6, 1917.

On March 11, Oswald Boelcke reported for duty at KEK Jametz. He had, in fact, been detached from *Fl. Abt.* 62 for duty over Verdun at the onset, but was grounded by what he called "some stupid intestinal trouble." Upon recovery, he got Hauptmann Haehnelt's permission to establish his own *Kommando* at Sivry, north of Verdun, for two and later three Fokkers.

Boelcke, whose score then stood at nine, recognized the inherent flaws in the *Sperre* concept—and, as he would do several times in future, devised his own solution. With Sivry lying just 11 kilometers behind the front, he established direct contact with a forward observation post that would telephone his aerodrome of any French plane's approach. Upon being alerted, Boelcke or one of his men could scramble up to intercept the intruder, thus conserving fuel and lubricant for the plane, to say nothing of time and energy for the pilot. The success of Boelcke's system at Verdun did not go unnoticed, becoming the German fighter defense model for the rest of the war.

March 12 saw N.3's recently commissioned Sous-Lieutenant Georges Guynemer score his eighth success over an LVG near Thiescourt, killing Unteroffizier Friedrich Ackermann and Leutnant Friedrich Marquardt of *Fl. Abt.* 61. On the same day, Boelcke drove a Farman of MF.63 down just outside of French lines, where its dead pilot and wounded observer were recovered, but it was subsequently destroyed by German artillery fire. Adjutant Auguste Metaire of N.49 was also driven down wounded in French lines by another rising Fokker star attached to *Kagohl* 1, Leutnant Otto Parschau.

The next day Boelcke engaged a Nieuport that had been attacking a two-seater over Fort Douaumont and drove it off—coinciding intriguingly with the fact that while attacking another LVG that day, Guynemer was hit twice in the arm and wounded in the face and scalp by fragments from his windscreen. Boelcke then spotted what he described as Voisin bombers heading toward Dun-sur-Meuse and attacked a straggler. As he closed in from the rear, he reported seeing its observer climb out onto the wing and wave at him—trying, he believed, to keep the crippled plane on an even keel. Boelcke had to disengage when another enemy plane attacked him, but later saw his victim crash in French lines. *Escadrille* BM.118 lost a Breguet-Michelin V bomber that day whose crewmen, Sergent Alphonse Vitry and Brigadier Augereau, were both wounded. It is also intriguing to note that French artist Henri Farré painted a similar (or the same?) incident, in which the Breguet's desperate observer lies prone on the wing, clear of the pusher's airscrew, shooting at the Fokker with his carbine.

March 14 saw foreign volunteers in the fore, as Sous-Lieutenant Leith Jensen, a Dane in *Escadrille* N.31, downed an enemy plane over Montfaucon, and Sergent Viktor Georgyevich Federov, an aggressive Russian Caudron G.4 pilot with C.42 who the French were calling the "Don Cossack of the Air," was credited with his second in cooperation with Soldat Pierre Lanero. Also actively serving alongside his fighters, de Rose claimed a German over Verdun, too far in enemy territory to be confirmed. But the French lost at least two Caudron G.4s that day, one being credited to Hans Berr.

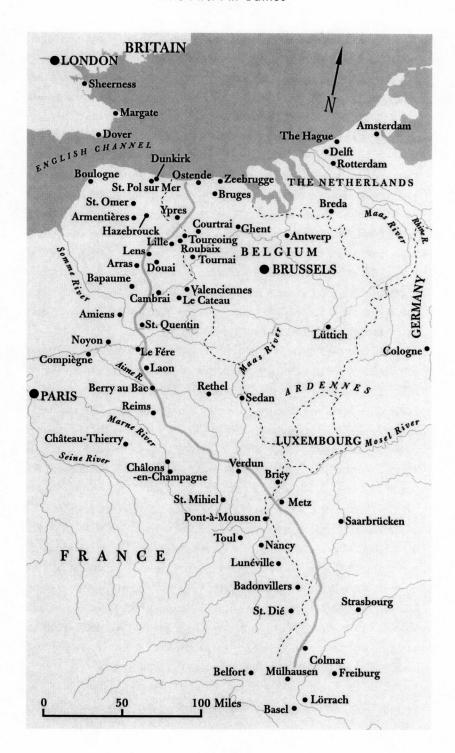

BRITAIN

●LONDON

●Sheerness

●Margate

●Dover

ENGLISH CHANNEL

Boulogne●   Dunkirk●

St. Pol sur Mer●   Ostende●   ●Zeebrugge

St. Omer●   ●Bruges

Armentières●   Ypres●

Hazebrouck   Courtrai●   ●Ghent

Lille●   ●Tourcoing   ●Antwerp

Lens●   Roubaix●   BELGIUM

Arras●   Douai●   ●Tournai   ●BRUSSELS

Bapaume●

Cambrai●   ●Valenciennes

Amiens●   ●Le Cateau

●St. Quentin   ●Lüttich

Noyon●   Le Fére●   ●Cologne

Compiègne●   Laon●

Berry au Bac●   Rethel●   ARDENNES

●PARIS   ●Sedan

Reims●

Château-Thierry●   Marne River   LUXEMBOURG   Mosel River

Seine River   Châlons   ●Verdun

-en-Champagne●   ●Briey

St. Mihiel●   ●Metz

Pont-à-Mousson●   ●Saarbrücken

Toul●   ●Nancy

F R A N C E   Lunéville●

●Badonvillers

St. Dié●   ●Strasbourg

0   50   100 Miles   Colmar●

Belfort●   Mülhausen●   ●Freiburg

●Lörrach

Basel●

Amsterdam●

The Hague●   ●Delft

●Rotterdam

THE NETHERLANDS

●Breda

Maas River   Rhine R.

GERMANY

Somme River

Aisne R.

Maas River

In spite of the accumulation of odd French successes, the Fokkers, between their *Sperre* flights and Boelcke's alert system, were managing to interfere so effectively with French reconnaissance missions that General Pétain felt compelled to issue a significant order to his chief of air operations: "De Rose, I am blind, sweep the skies for me."

He certainly did not have to tell de Rose twice. By March 15, the major had responded by concentrating his scout escadrilles around the Verdun-Bar-le-Duc sector in provisional hunting groups, or *groupes de chasse provisoires*. One consisted of N.65 and N.67 supporting the II*e Armée* from Bar-le-Duc, with N.23 serving as a reserve at Vadelaincourt. N.15 and N.69, also at Bar-le-Duc, were tasked with driving off German aircraft in the X*e Armée* sector. N.57 soon joined the effort from Lemmes. Instead of conducting barrage patrols in certain assigned sectors, all of these units were to aggressively seek out and destroy any enemy plane they saw, a shade of difference that was welcomed by the budding fighter pilots.

At 1500 hours on March 18, 23 Farmans, Breguets and Caudrons left Belfort to bomb the German Alsatian town of Mülhausen. When they arrived, they found Fokker E.III monoplane and new D.III biplane fighters waiting to intercept them, courtesy of a *Kampf Einsitzer Kommando* detached from *Fl. Abt.* 68, based at Habsheim. Led by Leutnant Otto Pfälzer, KEK Habsheim consisted of Feldwebel Karl Weingärtner, Unteroffizier Willy Glinkermann and Vizefeldwebel Ernst Udet.

Told that there were two Allied planes approaching, Udet was astonished to find himself facing 23, but dived his Fokker E.III 105/16 into the middle of the formation, fired at a Farman and saw it go down in flames. Maréchal-des-Logis Edouard Leroy of MF.29 went down with it but his observer, Capitaine Emile Victor Bacon, jumped or fell from the plane, right in front of Udet. Regaining his shaken composure, Udet attacked a Caudron and disabled one of its engines, but his gun jammed before he could finish it. It was the first of 62 victories for Germany's future second ranking ace.

All three of Udet's comrades claimed a Farman as well—one in flames—but Pfälzer's was disallowed, and indeed only three French aircraft failed to return from the raid. In contrast to the Germans' strict confirmation criteria, *Escadrilles* MF.29 and MF.123 claimed four enemy planes in the action, three of them Fokkers, but all of the fighters returned to Habsheim. The German's only loss was an AEG G.II of Royal Bavarian *Fl. Abt.* 48, also based at Habsheim, which had joined the action, only to collide with the Farman crewed by Caporal Henri Rins of MF.29 and Sergent Robert Dubar of MF.123, killing both Frenchmen along with German Offizierstellvertreter Fritz Hopfgarten, Leutnant der Reserve Walter Kurth and Vizefeldwebel Max Wallat.

The Habsheim raid served notice that airplanes could attack cities en masse—and that airplanes were equally capable of making the bombers pay for doing so. It also reinforced what everyone was coming to realize: that single-seat scouts made more effective interceptors than twin-engine, multi-place "battleplanes."

Back at Verdun, Navarre destroyed a two-seater at Vigneville that day, killing Oberleutnants Heinrich von Blanc and Robert Framich of *Kagohl* 1, while Sergent Jean Chaput of N.31 scored his second victory, an LVG in flames at Les Eparges.

Amid the activities of March 19, Boelcke attacked two Farmans bombing German positions on the Meuse and sent one crashing in pieces in the German trenches near Douaumont, killing Sergent Pierre Galiment and Lieutenant Jacques Marie Libman of MF.19. Two days later, exploding anti-aircraft shells guided Boelcke to a Voisin bomber that was engaging a German two-seater. His gunfire caused the fuel tank to explode, killing Lieutenant Jean Antonioli and Capitaine Félix Le Croart of VB.109. Oddly, the only German casualties on the 21st, Unteroffiizer Artur Reucschling and Hauptmann Ernst Erdmann of *Fl. Abt.* 65, were probably not victims of a scout, but the third victory for Caudron pilot Viktor Federov and the second for his observer, Lanero. The day before that, another Russian temporarily attached to N.23, 35-year-old Adjutant Eduard Martinovich Pulpe, had scored his third.

On March 30, Federov—again with Lanero manning the gun—was credited with his fourth victory, but on April 3, he was wounded and subsequently returned to Russia. There he would be involved in the 1917 Revolution, but in spite of his Socialist convictions he became disillusioned with the Bolsheviks and returned to France in 1918, to resume his combat career in a more appropriate milieu—the cockpit of a single-seat Spad XIII, with Spa.89.

March 31 saw a German two-seater shared among no less than three foreign volunteers in N.23—the third victory for Swiss-born Sergent Théophile Ingold, the third for Dutch Sergent Paul de Ram and the fourth for Pulpe before his return to Russia. N.23 later lost its Swiss member when Ingold was wounded in action on July 16, dying of his injuries three days later.

By April, there was as much a battle going on above Verdun as on the ground, although both armies and their attached air arms lay in bloody deadlock. Charles Nungesser burned a balloon on April 2. More remarkable than his braving a barrage of anti-aircraft fire deep in enemy lines to eliminate his target was the fact that he was there at all. While test-flying an unstable Ponnier M.1 biplane on January 29, he had lost control and crashed, breaking both legs, smashing and unhinging his jaw, piercing his palette and suffering internal injuries. Nobody had expected him to survive the night, but four days later Nungesser was hobbling around on crutches. In two weeks he left the hospital. In eight weeks he was back at N.65, reporting for duty! The next day, while Navarre was claiming his eighth victory, Nungesser scored his fourth over an LVG. He would account for three more enemy planes by the end of the month.

Two events of some significance occurred on April 9. First, a pilot ferrying Fokker E.III 210/16 to *Fl. Abt.* 5 got lost and landed twice to ask directions before straying into British territory, where he suffered engine failure and landed at Rensecure. Taking pilot and plane intact, the British tested the latter at nearby St. Omer and at Upavon, learning all about Fokker's interrupter gear. Soon the Allies would be introducing similar systems of their own, ending the myth of Eindecker invincibility. E.III 210/16 can still be seen in the London Science Museum.

Also on April 9, Capitaine Georges Thenault left C.42 to take command of a new squadron that, aside from him and his deputy, Lieutenant Albert de Laage de Meux, was to be made up entirely of

Americans who in defiance of their country's neutrality had joined the Foreign Legion to fight for France on the ground and later in the air. Officially formed on April 16, N.124, soon dubbed the *Escadrille Américaine*, commenced operations at Luxeuil-les-Bains in the relatively quiet Lorraine sector.

By April 28, Max Immelmann had pulled ahead of Boelcke with 14 victories, but his rival evened the score again that day. Having recently returned to Sivry from a visit to the Oberursel engine factory, Boelcke was patrolling toward Verdun when he saw three Caudrons under attack by another Fokker until it was forced to disengage—and subsequently credited as shot down to a crew of C.53. Boelcke attacked and drove one of the Caudrons down in French lines near Vaux, wounding Sous-Lieutenant Paul Fabre.

April 30 saw four Fokkers claimed by the French, including one by Chaput of N.31 for his third victory, and one by Lieutenant Albert Louis Deullin of N.3 for his fourth. The latter, falling south of Doaumont, was probably Rittmeister Erich Graf von Holck, attached to an artillery spotting detachment, *Flieger Abteilung (Artillerie)* 203, killed while engaging some Caudrons. His death was witnessed from afar by a Silesian-born two-seater pilot of *Kagohl* 2 who had once flown with Holck as an observer on the Russian front, now longing to fly single-seaters himself: Leutnant Manfred Freiherr von Richthofen. The next evening the man who would later make that transition possible for Richthofen, Boelcke, spotted a French plane, hastily took off from Sivry and shot the intruder down within two minutes for his 15th victory.

Late in April a new French scout, the Nieuport 17, reached the front. The Nieuport 16, with its 110-hp engine on a *Bébé* airframe, had proven nose-heavy and tricky to handle. Delage's solution was to redesign the airframe with more wing area—14.75 square meters compared to the *Bébé*'s 13.3. The plane also got a synchronized .30-caliber Vickers machine gun, using the Alkan-Hamy interrupter gear. The horseshoe-shaped cowling of earlier Nieuports was replaced by a circular one faired smoothly to the fuselage sides, further streamlined by a *cône de pénétration* attached to the engine shaft rather than to the propeller, so that it remained stationary instead of spinning.

Transparent cellon panels were installed in the upper wing center section to give the pilot a better view upward.

Officially designated the 17, but often referred to as the "15-meter" Nieuport, the new scout proved far more amenable to the 110-hp Le Rhône 9J, as well as the 120-hp 9Jb. A later version, using a fuselage rounded with stringers called the 17bis, used the 130-hp Clerget 9B or 9Z engine. The French encountered some problems with cracks in the cowling, which sometimes necessitated cutting the bottom away or outright replacement with a 16's cowl until a more flexible mounting was perfected. The *cône de pénétration* was eventually abandoned.

The first Nieuport 17s were allegedly sent to N.57. Sergent Louis Coudouret may have flown one when he sent an LVG two-seater crashing near Hermeville on May 4, his first of an eventual six victories. Sous-Lieutenant Jean Chaput transferred to N.57 from N.31 on May 7, and demonstrated his mettle anew nine days later by severely damaging an Aviatik over Esparges. Lieutenant André Bastien forced an enemy plane down in its own lines the next day and Adjutant Léon François Acher did the same on May 19, although he was badly wounded in the fight. Lieutenant Charles Dumas sent an Aviatik down to crash near Eparges on May 21.

In the months to come the Nieuport 17 became one of the war's most common fighters. In addition to the French, the British used it extensively, although they usually replaced the synchronized Vickers with a Lewis gun above the wing on their own Foster mounting. The Duks factory built Nieuports for Russian use and Nieuport-Macchi built them for the Italians. The Belgian 1e and 5e *escadrilles* were equipped with Nieuport 17s in 1917. American volunteers in N.124 and other French escadrilles flew them in combat, and later U.S. Army Air Service pilots trained in them. Even German aces such as Hermann Pfeiffer and Paul Bäumer were known to fly captured Nieuport 17s at times, as did Austrian ace of aces Godwin Brumowski.

On May 11, an air accident took the life of the mastermind behind France's fighter effort up to that point. Having turned down offers of a bomber command or a joint fighter and bomber command,

A Nieuport 16 escorts a Morane-Saulnier P on a reconnaissance mission late in 1916. Both aircraft were powered by 110-hp Le Rhône 9J rotary engines. (SHAA B88.3640)

Commandant de Rose had convinced the military authorities that the French fighter arm should have a free hand to preemptively seize control of the air over any critical area of the front, taking on defensive or escort roles as secondary options as needed. Upon his return to the Verdun sector, he was doing a demonstration flight for the Ve Armée's new quartermaster-general when his Nieuport suddenly crashed.

De Rose's death was a terrible loss to the Aéronautique Militaire, but it would continue the process that he started, expanding the fighter force within larger and larger organizations over the next two years. As it was, his provisional groups had at least stalemated the Eindecker units above Verdun, as Nieuports and Morane-Saulniers, flying in flights of six or more, used their numbers to cancel the advantages of the Fokkers' interrupter gear.

On May 18, Caporal Kiffin Rockwell, firing only four rounds at point-blank range, shot down an LVG in flames near Thann for N.124's first aerial victory. Upon hearing the news in Paris, Kiffin's brother Paul rushed over to Luxeuil with an 80-year-old bottle of bourbon whiskey. After Rockwell drank a shot, squadron mate Victor Chapman suggested that each pilot thereafter be "entitled to one slug" of the "Bottle of Death" after downing an enemy plane. The

Commandant de Rose's response to the Fokker threat at Verdun was to assemble entire escadrilles of Nieuport 11s along the front, later organized into *groupes provisoires* and, in the fall of 1916, permanent *Groupes de Combat*. (*SHAA B83.3489*)

next day, N.124 was ordered to transfer to Behonne, to support Général Robert Nivelle's II*e Armée* near Verdun. Now blooded, the *Escadrille Américaine* was fully "in the war."

May 19 was also a milestone for the French themselves, as Sous-Lieutenant Nungesser scored his eighth victory over an LVG and Navarre brought an Aviatik down near Chattancourt, where its crew was taken prisoner. The latter was the first French airman to achieve "double ace" status with 10 victories, but his triumph was dampened on that same day by the combat death of Sous-Lieutenant Georges Boillot, commander of N.65 and one of Navarre's closest friends.

On May 22, General Nivelle launched a counteroffensive to retake Fort Douaumont. The effort involved unprecedented coordination with the air service and its fighter arm. The *Groupe des Escadrilles de Chasse*, commanded since de Rose's death by Capitaine Auguste le Révérend, was tasked with attacking any German reconnaissance plane that ventured over or near the front lines. It was also to dispatch volunteers on a multiple attack against eight German kite balloons, or *Drachen*, which could observe the French preparations from their nests north of the Meuse River. For that purpose, the fighters would be equipped for the first time with a new weapon invented by naval

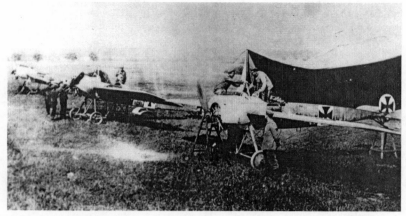

While the French assembled entire escadrilles of Nieuports at Verdun, the German Fokker E.IIIs operated with *Kampf Einsitzer Kommandos* of four or five at most. Oberleutnant Oswald Boelcke maximized their effectiveness by devising a direct early warning system for his *Kommando* at Sivry. (*SHAA B88.3477*)

Capitaine de Vaisseau Yves Le Prieur. Six to eight "rocket torpedoes" were mounted in tubes on the struts of Nieuport 11s and 16s, with aluminum sheathing over the fabric panels that might otherwise be vulnerable to their backblast. Le Prieur himself arrived at Lemmes aerodrome to oversee their installation, accompanied by Sergent Joseph Henri Guiguet, a pilot from *Escadrille* N.95 of the *Camp Retranché de Paris* who had been testing Le Prieur's rockets. Besides Guiguet, seven pilots had volunteered to participate in this dangerous but historic mission: Capitaine Louis Robert de Beauchamp and Lieutenant Georges de Boutiny of N.23; Lieutenant Jean Chaput, Lieutenant André Dubois de Gennes, and Adjutant Lucien Barault of N.57; and Sous-Lieutenant Charles Nungesser and Adjutant Henri Réservat of N.65.

The day before, while French fighters eliminated four German two-seaters—including one more by Navarre—Capitaine Philippe Féquant, escorted by two N.65 Nieuports, reconnoitered the right bank of the Meuse to pinpoint the enemy balloon nests. Five Fokkers of *Fl. Abt.* 62 attacked the trio and the German leader sent one of the escorting Nieuports crashing into French lines with its pilot, Sergent Georges Kirsch, wounded—Hauptmann Boelcke's second victory of the day and his 18th overall. Notwithstanding that, Féquant brought back the necessary intelligence and with clear skies the next morning, the eight fighters set out as planned.

Guiguet's balloon at Sivry, 30 kilometers northwest of Verdun, was arguably the most dangerous. Its location on hills that gave the Germans an unobstructed view of the valley and both sides of the Meuse made it of great strategic importance, and its heavy anti-air-craft artillery defenses were bolstered by Boelcke's fighter flight. Quickly spotting his target, Guiguet dived to what he thought a close enough range and fired all eight of his "torpedoes" as power winches swiftly pulled the balloon down to 1,000 meters altitude. One missile chanced to strike home and Guiguet's Nieuport 16 was violently thrown into a spin as the gasbag exploded into flames. Recovering, Guiguet made a beeline for Allied lines, pursued by several German fighters but returning unscathed. The *Drachen*'s observer, Oberleutnant Friedrich von Zanthier, was less fortunate, being killed in the attack.

Between Moirey and Grémilly, several of the other French "*tor-pilleurs*" were having mixed fortunes. De Beauchamp destroyed his *Drachen* east of Flabas, but de Boutiny's firing system failed. Chaput and de Gennes burned their balloons northwest and northeast of Ornes, respectively. Nungesser destroyed his target northwest of Gincrey and Réservat burned his just north of Gincrey, but Barault's rockets missed. The N.65 pilots were intercepted near Étain by German fighters, which Nungesser drove away, but as they resumed their homeward flight Réservat's Nieuport was disabled by several bullets fired from the ground. Forced to land, he was taken prisoner and his plane recovered intact along with four of the rockets—a secret weapon no longer.

A few hours after the balloon attack, the 36*e*, 54*e*, 74*e*, and 129*e* *Régiments d'Infanterie* launched their main assault. Even with their aerial "eyes" temporarily removed, however, the Germans knew something was in the offing after having undergone a heavy artillery barrage for the past several days. Consequently, instead of being "softened up," they stiffened their defenses enough to stop the French just short of Fort Douaumont.

A Caudron G.4 of C.34, flown by Caporal Gilbert Marie de Guingand, who later downed eight enemy planes with Spa.48. Many French aces got their start and sometimes scored their first victories in the slow but surprisingly agile twin-engine Caudron. (SHAA B93.979)

Although the French failed to achieve their ultimate strategic goal, the airmen had carried out their mission admirably, destroying six of their eight assigned targets. The one sour note was the loss of Réservat, but he escaped from Germany on March 19, 1917.

May 22 had also seen the French claim nine enemy airplanes, including an Aviatik over Malancourt by Sergent Weston Bert Hall, for the newly arrived N.124's second victory. On May 24, Lieutenant William Thaw surprised a Fokker E.III and brought it down north of Vaux. Capitaine Thenault was leading de Laage, Thaw, Chapman and Rockwell on the second patrol that morning when they encountered 12 enemy planes over Étain. Instead of watching for Thenault's hand signal, the overly zealous Chapman prematurely dove at the enemy, followed by Rockwell and Thaw. Chapman claimed a Fokker out of control before another wounded him in the arm. Rockwell's windscreen was hit and his face was lacerated by glass and bullet fragments, but he claimed an enemy plane before returning to Behonne, his fuel almost exhausted. Thaw also claimed a Fokker before his Lewis gun jammed and he came under fire from two Aviatiks, which put a bullet through his left elbow and his fuel tank. Gliding over the lines, Thaw pancaked near Fort Travennes, and was hospitalized with a broken arm.

Valuing their fearlessness enough to overlook their insubordination, the French promoted Caporaux Chapman and Rockwell to sergent, in addition to which Chapman received the *Croix de Guerre*, Rockwell the *Médaille Militaire* and *Croix de Guerre* with palm, and Thaw made a *Chevalier de la Légion d'Honneur*. Chapman was back in action within 24 hours, but Rockwell was ordered to a hospital for 15 days and Thaw convalesced even longer. Thenault called for a replacement from the reserve pool of American volunteers, and later that day Sergent Gervais Raoul Lufbery arrived at N.124, to be followed by Clyde Balsley and Charles Chouteau Johnson on the 29th, Lawrence Rumsey on June 4, and Dudley Hill on June 9.

On June 17, Chapman was on a lone foray when he spotted two enemy two-seaters, one of which he forced to land near Béthincourt, though it was not confirmed. At that point the two-seaters' three Fokker escorts pounced on the lone Nieuport, severing its right aileron control rod and creasing Chapman's skull. He fell into a spin, but by grabbing the ends of the control rods and controlling the stick with his knees, he managed to land safely at Froidos aerodrome. Although Rockwell believed that Boelcke had wounded Chapman, it was another German rising star, Leutnant Walter Höhndorf of KEK Vaux, who claimed a Nieuport in French lines that day for his sixth of an eventual 14 victories.

There was, however, a second French casualty that day that might just as possibly have been Höhndorf's victim. At 0600 that morning Navarre, in concert with Sous-Lieutenant Pelletier d'Oisy of N.69, had shot down a two-seater, but soon afterward Navarre came down in French lines near Samogneux, severely wounded.

At that time Navarre was the leading Allied fighter pilot with 12 victories, a record outdone by only two Germans, Boelcke and Immelmann. A succession of events would prevent his adding any further to his tally. Navarre had always been a mercurial individual whose relentless combat activity had undoubtedly taken a psychological toll that nobody, including himself, could fully understand at the time. While he was convalescing, however, his mind was pushed over the edge by news that his twin brother Pierre, recovered from his own wounds and eager to return to action, had fatally crashed during a training flight at GDE on November 15. Although he was released from the hospital to rejoin N.67 on January 31, 1917, Navarre's behavior became increasingly erratic until April 9, when a violent altercation with *gendarmes* (military police) led to his arrest and his subsequent committal for further care for what was judged to be a mental breakdown. Navarre resumed service with the air service in September 1918 and also became a pilot for the Morane-Saulnier firm, but on July 10, 1919, he was killed when his Morane-Saulnier AI monoplane crashed at Vadelaincourt aerodrome.

American volunteer Sergent Gervais Raoul Lufbery and friend pose before his monogrammed Nieuport 11 N1256 of *Escadrille* N.124, in which he scored his first four of an eventual 16 victories around Verdun in the summer of 1916. (*R. L. Cavanagh Collection*)

On June 18, Capitaine Thenault was leading Norman Prince, Rockwell and Balsley on a dawn mission to protect *reglage* (artillery spotting) aircraft when they encountered a large German formation north of Verdun. Balsley closed to 50 meters on an Aviatik, only to suffer a gun jam and find himself in a crossfire from four enemy planes. One bullet struck him in the right thigh and fragmented, sending splinters into his intestines, kidneys and lungs. After falling 12,000 feet in an inverted spin, Balsley, by using his hands to work his crippled leg, managed to level out and landed between the lines, where his plane caught on barbed wire and flipped over.

Sent to the hospital at Vadelaincourt, Clyde Balsley was out of the war. On June 23, N.124 suffered its first fatality during a fight with five German aircraft northeast of Douaumont when Chapman was shot down, credited to Leutnant Wintgens of *Fl. Abt.* 6.

Although its members flew continuously to avenge Chapman and Balsley, N.124 was unable to log its next confirmed victory for more than a month—and that was claimed by an unexpected guest. On June 22, Charles Nungesser had downed two Aviatiks over Lamorville, but crash-landed near his victims, suffering a broken nose and jaw, a dislocated knee and bullet fragments in his lip. Nungesser was soon bored with his third visit to the hospital and, since N.65 had posted him on enforced sick leave, on July 14 he flew to Behonne and attached himself to N.124's roster. Although he needed a heavy cane to hobble to and from his Nieuport 17, a week later Nungesser shot down an Aviatik and sent its Fokker escort fleeing for home.

Nungesser's success seemed to revive N.124's fortunes. On the 23rd Bert Hall was attacked by a Fokker E.III, but he turned the tables and sent it crashing between Fort Vaux and Damloup. On July 27, Lieutenant de Laage downed an Aviatik between Ornes and Bezonvaux, and on the 30th Sergent Lufbery shot down a two-seater near the Forêt d'Étain, possibly killing Oberleutnante Oskar Illing and Hermann Kraft from *Kasta 33* of *Kagohl 6*. Avowedly driven by the desire to avenge the death of his friend and prewar flying mentor, Marc Pourpe, in a flying accident on December 2, 1914, Lufbery got his second installment the next day, downing a two-seater over Fort Vaux.

On August 4, Lufbery teamed up with another future ace, Adjutant Victor Sayaret of N.57, to destroy a two-seater over Abancourt, killing Unteroffizier Peter Engel and Leutnant Otto Maiwald of *Fl. Abt.* 34. On the 8th, 'Luf' approached an Aviatik from below and behind, emptied his Lewis gun into it and sent it down in flames, killing Unteroffizier Georg Gering and Leutnant Max Sedlmair of *Kasta 36*, *Kagohl 6*.

For his impressive string of successes, Lufbery was awarded the *Médaille Militaire* and *Croix de Guerre* with palm. A globetrotting man of the world before the war, Lufbery pursued his vengeance with a cool maturity that contrasted with his more idealistic, often rash squadron mates. In addition, he exhibited remarkable endurance, flying at altitudes of 18,000 feet three or four times a day without ill effect. Further, as Pourpe's former mechanic, Lufbery personally involved himself in keeping his aircraft in peak condition. A later N.124 member, Edward Hinkle, recalled, "Anyone would rather have a secondhand Lufbery machine than a new one, anytime."

The next N.124 member to score over the Verdun front, Bert Hall, was becoming increasingly unpopular with the wealthier, more idealistic pilots comprising the bulk of the escadrille, who found his language ungentlemanly and suspected him of cheating in poker. They also applied Hall's penchant for telling tall tales to his character in general, except for Lufbery, who once told Hall, "I like a good yarn, true or not," and wryly remarked of Hall's ongoing diary, "I'll bet that'll be a prime piece of hokum when it's finished." In spite of his rough edges, however, even Hall's harshest critic, N.124 historian Paul Rockwell, admitted that he did good work for the squadron—including the destruction of an enemy photographic plane northeast of Douaumont on August 28.

N.124 concluded its operations over Verdun in fine style on September 9, when Adjutant Norman Prince teamed up with Lieutenant Victor Regnier of N.112 to down a Fokker over Fort Rozeiller. Elsewhere, Rockwell attacked a two-seater, hit its observer with his first burst and pursued it down to 4,000 feet before two intervening German fighters forced him to disengage. French ground observers subsequently confirmed the crash of his second official victory.

Transferred back to Luxeuil, the *Escadrille Américaine* had earned its laurels and, more important, had become a propaganda bonanza for the French. Although N.124's pilots often rankled at the exaggerated and even fictional exploits the press attributed to them, they approved of the imaginations they were stirring back home, inspiring other Americans to join the French air service via the Foreign Legion and fueling public sympathy that they hoped would ultimately draw their country into the war on the Allied side.

By the fall of 1915, the struggle for Verdun had fallen into complete stalemate, and would remain so until its officially declared conclusion on December 18. Even as a battle of attrition, it fell short of German hopes, with French dead listed at 543,000, but their own side faring little better with more than 434,000 fatalities. In the air, it set a rough pattern for the war as well, of German quality of aircraft and tactics being kept on the defensive by the mobilization of more Allied air assets in larger organizations. That pattern was repeated to the northwest, over the British sector.

Before examining Britain's progress in dealing with the "Fokker Scourge," it is worth noting that the air war had been following a roughly parallel course, albeit on a less grand scale, on other fronts. Russia had entered the war with a relatively small air arm operating over a vast front. Since Piotr Nesterov's sacrificial destruction of an Austro-Hungarian intruder by ramming in September 1914, other Russians had taken up arms against their foes, including a former observer of Nesterov's, Poruchik (lieutenant) Evgraf Nikolayevich Kruten. Born the son of an army colonel in Kiev on December 29, 1890, Kruten had served in the mounted artillery before entering the IRAS as an observer, but subsequently took flight training at Gatchina between January and September 1914, and went on to the XXI Corps Air Detachment on October 27. Later joining the 2nd Army Air Detachment, he was piloting a Voisin 3LA when he was credited with shooting down an enemy plane on March 6, 1915, and awarded the Order of St. Anne.

Another, more direct emulator of Nesterov was Shtabs-Rotmistr Aleksandr Aleksandrovich Kozakov, a former cavalryman who entered aviation in 1913 and in late 1914 was serving with the IV Corps Air Detachment in Poland. Flying scouting missions in Morane-Saulnier Gs, Kozakov experimented with dangling a grappling hook fitted with an explosive device full of gun cotton under his plane and on March 31, 1915, he used it to attack an Albatros. A comrade watching the encounter from the ground, Ivan V. Smirnov, later described what followed:

"A very exciting air battle developed in the clear blue sky. Then he actually did get above his opponent—so close it seemed he was on top of him—then we saw the anchor fall on its spider web's thread. It hooked on to the main wing of the enemy. The tail dropped and for a second it seemed the plane was hanging there in the air. Then the plane righted itself again, and to my dismay a wingtip connected with the tail of [Kozakov's] machine."

"The damned anchor got caught and was dangling under the bottom of the enemy plane," Kozakov reported, "so I decided to strike across the upper surface of the Albatros with the undercarriage of my plane. I pushed the elevator down and collided."

"They flew on for some minutes like this," Smirnov continued, "but then the German lost control and fell to earth like a brick, dragging [Kozakov]. Disaster seemed very near. Hardly 200 feet from the hard ground, they seemed to disentangle; a miracle! [Kozakov] tore his machine out of the deadly downward course and landed rough but safely, only breaking his propeller. His opponent was a fraction too late and dived his nose into the ground. He became our prisoner."

Shtabs-Rotmistr Aleksandr A. Kozakov and two unidentified officers stand behind members of his XIX Corps Air Detachment during operations in Stanislav, Romania, in February-March 1917. Identified pilots in the foreground are, from left: Longin Lipsky (first), Ivan V. Smirnov (third), Pavel V. Argeyev (fourth), and Ernst K. Leman (fifth). (Jon Guttman)

Kruten, Kozakov, and Smirnov were all destined to be distinguished fighter pilots. But first Russia, like its Western allies and enemies, had to come up with a fighter. This need became more apparent on October 18, 1915, when Leutnant Karl Odebrett of *Fl. Abt.* 47 used a newly acquired Fokker Eindecker to bring down a Russian pusher at Dryswiaty Lake, where its pilot was taken prisoner. Wounded on May 24, 1916, Odebrett resumed flying a Fokker with *Fl. Abt.* (A) 215 in Russia, and later served in France with *Jasta* 16 and as commander of *Jasta* 42, surviving the war with 17 victories.

At least one Russian, Ensign Aleksandr Sveshnikov of the VII Corps Air Detachment, had tried to respond to the challenge in a manner reminiscent of Gianni Caproni's Ca.20 during the summer of 1915: he mounted a Madsen machine gun on the upper pylon of a Morane-Saulnier G. Even on the pylon, however, the gun had to be set at an angle to clear the propeller arc and there was no means of aiming it. Also, the Madsen had a slow rate of fire; but by then the Morane-Saulnier G's performance, even as an unarmed scout, was hopelessly behind the times. It was the right idea applied to the wrong weapon on the wrong plane.

As with the Italians, the Russians had an excellent bomber design at their disposal, developed from the world's first multi-engine airplane, the *Bolshoi Baltitski*, designed by Igor I. Sikorsky in 1913. The follow-up four-engine bomber, the *Il'ya Murometz* or IM, was operated by the navy and proved so effective as to influence an extensive German trend toward building its own extravagantly sized *Riesenflugzeuge*, or giant airplanes. In December 1914, Tsar Nicholas II ordered the IMs to be organized into an *Eskadra Vozdushny Korabley* (Flying Ship Squadron), or EKV, based at Yablonna north of Warsaw—the world's first strategic bomber squadron.

Unlike the Italians, however, the Russians did not allow their bomber's success to negate fighter development. On the contrary, Sikorsky had produced a number of single-engine monoplane and biplane scouts for the Russian navy. In October 1914 he began work on the S.16, a biplane somewhat influenced by the Sopwith Tabloid—but employing ailerons rather than wing warping—with a wingspan of only 27 feet 6 inches and seating a crew of two within a single cockpit. Production delays, improvements by Sikorsky's design team, and problems obtaining suitable engines delayed delivery of 15 production or "serial" S.16ser aircraft until January 1916, and by the time they were delivered to the EKV to serve as trainers and scouts, a new role had been envisioned for them. Armed, the S.16ser would also escort and defend the IMs from enemy aircraft.

One of Sikorsky's design team, Lieutenant Georgy I. Lavrov, had been proposing interrupter gear for a forward firing machine gun since 1915, and that fall he devised a simple mechanism. Patented on December 1, Lavrov's gear and a Vickers machine gun were installed on the S.16ser on March 21, 1916, making it Russia's first fighter.

At that point IRAS pilots had learned of the new scout and were petitioning for its use beyond the EKV. In February 1916, Evgraf Kruten, now a Shtabs-Kapitan, wrote the headquarters of the light air service, "The commander of the fighting unit of the Flying Ships Squadron Lt. Lavrov telegraphed me that he has a Sikorsky with a machine gun for me and that I only need to notify headquarters. I request to receive a fighter plane, even one without a machine gun."

The commander to whom Kruten wrote, Grand Archduke Aleksandr Mikhailovich, was a founding father of the IRAS and quite pleased to arrange for the delivery of S.16s to the corps air squadrons attached to the Seventh and Eleventh armies. The first, powered by a Le Rhône engine, was delivered to the XXXIII Corps Air Detachment on March 17, and 10 days later Kapitan Konstantin K. Vakulovsky used it to intercept and drive off a German scout.

Three more S.16sers were delivered to the 7th Army Air Detachment at Kiev, led by Poruchik Ivan A. Orlov, and two to the 12th at Pskov under Max G. von Lerche. Sent to the front in April, the 7th settled in the Galician town of Yablonov and on April 15 it became the first Russian fighter unit to see combat when Orlov and his observer, Cornet Longin Lipsky, intercepted and drove off an Austro-Hungarian reconnaissance plane.

On April 17, Orlov discovered what would become an ongoing problem when the Lavrov interrupter gear malfunctioned and he was forced to disengage. There would be many more interceptions, but no real damage was done until April 27, when Yuri Vladimirovich Gilsher, flying without an observer in S.16ser No.201, attacked an Austro-Hungarian two-seater near Burkanov and after firing 120 rounds saw the enemy plane descend emitting a trail of black smoke.

That first victory for a Russian-built fighter was also the last. While Gilsher was returning from a second patrol that same day— which found the sky devoid of enemy planes, indicative of how shaken up the Austrians had been over their loss—his ailerons jammed and he spun down 1,200 meters. S.16 No. 201 was demolished, but thanks to its sturdy airframe, Gilsher and his observer survived.

By the middle of May, all IRAS S.16s had been withdrawn and returned to the EVK. Analysis of its short combat record concluded that the Lavrov interrupter gear was defective. Further the S.16's Russian-built versions of the Gnome rotary engine did not produce enough power for it to sustain its attacks on better-performing enemy two-seaters, since its average speed, even without the observer along, was 73 mph and its ceiling 10,000 feet.

By the summer of 1916, Russia was importing French fighters, such as the Morane-Saulnier N and I, the Spad SA and the Nieuport 10, 11, 17 and 21. The Nieuports, built under license, would be the dominant component of the IRAS's fighter force thereafter.

In spite of Giulio Douhet's prescient predictions and the bold precedent set by Gianni Caproni's Ca.20, Italy had no single-seat fighters when it declared war on Austria-Hungary on May 24, 1915. Although the frontage its air arm had to cover southwest of the Tyrolian Alps was roughly 30 kilometers compared to the Western Front's 800, it soon became clear that the *Aviazione del Regio Esercito* (Royal Army Aviation) would need something to counter Austria-Hungary's small but doughty *Fliegerkompagnien* and such formidable armed two-seaters as the Hansa-Brandenburg C.I. To do this, Italy began importing Nieuport sesquiplanes, but was soon producing its own under license thanks to Giulio Macchi, whose Società Anonima Nieuport-Macchi had been building the French planes in Varese since 1913, and who stubbornly resisted the general trend to sub-contract for bomber manufacture when war broke out.

By July 1915, two-seater Macchi-Nieuport 10s were serving at the front and on the 26th a detached flight of the *8a Squadriglia*, called the *Squadriglia Biplani Nieuport*, was established at Udine aerodrome, with six single-seat versions of the Nieuport 10. Commanding this pioneer fighter unit was Capitano Domenico Bolognesi, and among his pilots was 28-year-old Tenente Francesco Baracca, a former cavalryman who had been an aviator since 1912.

Baracca's first encounters with enemy planes, on September 9, September 13, and November 19, 1915, were frustrated by jammed guns. In February 1916, the flight, now called the 1*a Squadriglia Caccia* and operating from Santa Caterina, began getting Nieuport 11s. On April 2, Soldato Luigi Olivari shot down an enemy plane that fell too far behind the lines to be confirmed until after the war, when Austrian records revealed that it had crashed, killing Zugsführer Josef Mach and Fähnrich Victor Poiger of *Flik* 2.

On April 7, Baracca scored the first officially recognized Italian fighter victory when he attacked a Brandenburg C.I from behind and below, disabled its engine, and forced it to land in an open field near Medea. He landed nearby and discussed the fight with the pilot, Zugsfürer Adolf Ott of *Flik* 19, until troops arrived to take Ott prisoner and see to his wounded observer, Oberleutnant Franz Lenarcic, who nevertheless died in the hospital a few hours later. Ten minutes after Baracca's success, Olivari teamed up with Capitani Bolognesi and Guido Tacchini to bring down a second enemy plane whose crew, Zugsführer Ferdinand Traub and Aspirant Franz Marterer, burned their machine before surrendering to the Italians.

Future Italian ace of aces Tenente Francesco Baracca of the 1a Squadriglia Caccia poses beside the Nieuport 11 in which he scored his first victory on April 7, 1916. *(Jon Guttman)*

Baracca was awarded the *Medaglia Argento al Valore Militare* for his victory—the first of 34 for the future Italian ace of aces. On April 15, the outfit was redesignated the *70a Squadriglia*—Italy's first specialized fighter squadron.

While Italy had let slip its chance to have an indigenous land fighter, Austria-Hungary hadn't even dabbled in the concept when it invaded Serbia on July 28, and still had nothing of its own a year later. Late in 1915, it turned to the Germans, importing 13 Fokker E.Is and E.IIIs, which it designated A.IIIs—under the stipulation that the Eindeckers, still regarded by the Germans as a secret weapon, not be flown over the lines, lest they fall into Italian hands.

Among the units to which a Fokker or two were allotted was *Flik* 4, based at Haidenschaft on the Isonzo front. Their baptism of fire came on November 12, when Oberleutnant Hassan Riza Effendi Pieler attacked a Caproni Ca.1, only to be undone by a jammed gun. On November 25, however, *Flik* 4's commander, Hauptmann Mathias Bernath, downed a Maurice Farman near Lorenzo di Mossa.

More Fokkers had been distributed to *Fliks* 8 and 19 at Haidenschaft by February 1916, raising the aerodrome's total fighter strength to four. In spite of their official unit affiliations, the A.IIIs were wisely kept together on the field for the convenience of the ground crewmen, and so they could operate together should the need arise. That occasion did arise on February 18, when 10 Caproni Ca.1s of the *4a Squadriglia* departed Aviano aerodrome to bomb the city of Laibach (now Ljubljana, Slovenia). Three of the raiders turned back with mechanical troubles, but the rest carried on. In the process they overflew Haidenschaft and thus attracted the wrathful *Eindeckerflieger* coming and going.

Among the first up were Hauptmänner Bernath and 32-year-old Heinrich Kostrba ze Skalice, a member of the lower Bohemian nobility who had served as both an observer and a pilot on the Russian and Italian fronts before being assigned to *Flik* 4. At 0845 hours they attacked the rightmost Caproni in the formation northeast of Aisovizza. Bernath's gun jammed, but after firing 500 rounds, Kostrba saw the bomber go down on the Italian side of the Isonzo River. His gunfire had put a bullet through the forehead of Tenente Colonello Barbieri, mortally wounded Capitano Luigi Ballo, and grazed the skull of the pilot, Capitano Oreste Salamone. Kostrba and Bernath were jointly credited with downing the Caproni, but Salamone, though intermittently blinded by his own blood, managed to force-land at Palmonova in Italian lines. For his tenacious courage, he became the first airman to be awarded Italy's highest honor, the *Medaglia d'Oro al Valore Militare.*

After landing to replenish his ammunition, Kostrba took off again, hoping to catch the Capronis as they returned from their mission. Instead, he encountered a reconnoitering Caudron, at which he fired 200 rounds and forced it to land in Italian territory. Anti-aircraft fire discouraged him from following it down, but it was later confirmed to him. At that point he spotted the returning Capronis, one of which he dived on and fired 150 rounds. Return fire riddled Kostrba's Fokker, but he closed to 40 meters to fire the rest of his ammunition into the bomber. At that point, the Caproni was attacked by another Fokker flown by Leutnant in der Reserve Ludwig Hautzmeyer, an experienced 22-year-old veteran from Fürstenfeld, Austria, who was having his very first flight since his assignment to *Flik* 19 as its deputy commander. Other Austro-Hungarian aircraft joined in to send the Caproni down near Merna, where Capitano Tullio Visconti was found dead and Capitano Gaetano Turilli taken prisoner. The day's successes marked the first three of seven victories for Kostrba—although he would get all the rest in two-seat Brandenburg C.Is—and the first of seven for Hautzmeyer.

4

THE SOMME

While the fighting raged on in, around, and above Verdun in the summer of 1916, the British Expeditionary Force (BEF), now under General Sir Douglas Haig, had been gathering its forces for a breakthrough attempt across the Somme River. Like the *Aéronautique Militaire*, the RFC had an aggressive Tricornot de Rose of its own, in the person of Major-General Hugh Montague Trenchard.

Born in Taunton on February 3, 1873, Trenchard had not excelled academically, which prevented his joining the Royal Navy and delayed his gaining a commission in the British Army until he was 20. He went on to serve in India, in the Anglo-Boer War in South Africa—where he survived a bullet wound in the chest—and Nigeria before joining the Military Wing of the RFC in 1912. Trenchard just barely learned to fly before turning 40, which would have disqualified him, and he proved a poor pilot in any case. However, he became a first-rate administrator and swiftly came to appreciate aviation's military potential. During that time his stentorian demeanor, or the rumbling of his voice even when speaking low, earned him the nickname "Boom."

On August 25, 1915, Trenchard was promoted to brigadier and put in command of the RFC in the field. That September he directed his aircraft in support of the army at Loos, including the first tactical bombing in support of an advance, but the battle ended inconclusively and left Trenchard wishing his airmen could have done more. In the succeeding months, the Fokker Scourge so depleted the RFC's ranks that he actually had to reduce its activities in support of the ground forces—a prospect he found galling.

In December 1915 Haig replaced General Sir John French in command of the BEF and Trenchard, promoted to major-general in March, found him to be a kindred spirit who supported his ambitions of making the RFC an integral instrument of breakthrough on the Western Front. As the buildup for the Somme offensive proceeded, Trenchard assembled 107 aircraft in aerodromes behind the Fourth Army. Among them was the RFC's first single-seat fighter unit, No. 24 Squadron.

Since Britain entered the war, the rapidly expanding RFC had formed its first corps and army wings in October 1914. The former's aircraft were to scout the front lines immediately in front of a corps, whereas the army wings conducted reconnaissance and bombing missions deeper in enemy territory at the army's orders. Such fighting scouts as the British had were initially farmed out among the squadrons as the Germans had initially done with their Fokker E.Is among their *Flieger Abteilungen*. During the Battle of Verdun, however, Trenchard had taken note of the formation of specialized French *escadrilles de chasse* and German *Kampf Einsitzer Kommandos*. In late April 1916, he wanted to concentrate single-seat fighter squadrons within army wings, leaving the corps squadrons to remain heterogeneous collections of two-seaters with a few scout escorts.

Aptly, the first of the RFC's single-seat squadrons was commanded by its pioneering ace, Major Lanoe G. Hawker, VC. After being posted home for a rest late in 1915, Hawker had been sent to Hownslow on September 28 to take command of the the new unit. Like the RFC's first all-fighter unit, F.B.5-equipped No. 11 Squadron, No. 24 used a pusher, the de Havilland D.H.2.

After leaving the Royal Aircraft Factory to join Aircraft Manufacturing Co. Ltd. in June 1914, Geoffrey de Havilland had designed a two-seat pusher fighter of similar configuration to the R.A.F.'s F.E.2, the D.H.1. In the early summer of 1915, he introduced a more compact single-seat version, the D.H.2, which was sent to France for operational evaluation on July 26—and promptly fell

Captain Herman W. Von Poellnitz of No. 32 Squadron takes off in an de Havilland D.H.2. (Jon Guttman)

into German hands on August 5. In spite of the disastrous loss of the prototype, Airco put the de Havilland D.H.2 into production. The first example was delivered to No. 18 Squadron on January 9, 1916, while another went to No. 11 Squadron two days later. Back in Britain, No. 24 Squadron got its first D.H.2 on January 10, and by the time the newly promoted Major Hawker took his unit to France, its strength was up to 12.

Initially operating under direct command from RFC Headquarters at St. Omer, Hawker found much to be done before he could lead his new command into battle. The production D.H.2 carried its single Lewis gun within the front of the pilot's nacelle on a vertical shaft that gave it a considerable range of movement. Hawker judged what his men called the "wobbly mounting," which required the pilot to fly with one hand and aim with the other, to be utterly useless, and devised a clamp to fix the gun in a forward firing position. Higher authorities insisted on retaining the flexible mounting, but Hawker came up with a satisfactory compromise—a spring clip that would theoretically allow the pilot to release the gun at will. In practice, Hawker's men almost never unclipped their weapons. Hawker also devised a "double-deck" Lewis gun magazine that could hold up to 97 rounds, requiring the pilot to change drums less often in the heat of combat.

Hawker found his men intimidated by the D.H.2's reputation for falling into spins due to the rear-mounted rotary engine near its center of gravity, which caused a number of training accidents. Little was then known about how or even whether one could recover from a spin, but Hawker knew that it could be done by centralizing the controls. In February he took a plane up to 8,000 feet, then repeatedly put it into spin, both from the left and right, and then pulled out of it. After the squadron had practiced his technique, there were no further spinning-related accidents.

In the course of preparing No. 24 Squadron and its D.H.2s for battle, Major Lanoe G. Hawker VC came up with technical and tactical innovations that well earned him his German sobriquet of "the English Boelcke." (Jon Guttman)

Another problem with flying the D.H.2 was the numbing cold to be expected in an open nacelle with no engine to shield and warm the pilot. On February 9, the same day No. 24 Squadron was transferred to Bertangles, C Flight leader 2nd Lt. E.A.C. Archer was returning from a patrol when he fatally spun into the ground. Most of the men attributed the tragedy to his legs being too frozen to control his plane. In response, Hawker designed fleece-lined flying clothes, including the hip-high "fug boots" that would become a popular item among British airmen—and any German airmen lucky enough to take one prisoner—throughout the war.

From Bertangles, No. 24 Squadron was to operate with 13th Wing, 3rd Brigade, under the orders of the Third Army. Unlike France's *groupes de combat*, the RFC wings were heterogeneous collections of locally based reconnaissance, bombing and fighter squadrons. The next D.H.2 unit to arrive in France, No. 29 Squadron, was also initially to work with the 3rd Brigade, but on April 15, it moved to Abeele and was reassigned to 11th Wing, 2nd Brigade, in the relatively quiet Ypres sector in Flanders.

A third D.H.2 outfit, No. 32 Squadron, shared St. Auchel aerodrome with No. 25 Squadron's F.E.2bs from June 4 through June 7, when it settled at Treizennes to serve under 10th Wing, 1st Brigade.

Like Hawker's 24 Squadron, 32 Squadron's pilots felt in good hands under their veteran commander, Major L.W.B. Rees, who since his stint in the Vickers F.B.5 had published a booklet on how to rig the D.H.2 and did all he could to train his pilots on the new pusher scout. A fellow Welshman serving in the squadron, 18-year-old 2nd Lt. Gwilym Hugh Lewis, wrote of Rees at the time with unwitting clairvoyance: "He knows his job thoroughly and above all is a perfect gentleman. I shouldn't be surprised if he comes home with a VC; he has already got an MC."

On March 19, No. 24 Squadron had its first aerial encounter. That ended inconclusively, but on April 2, 2nd Lt. David M. Tidmarsh and Lieutenant S.J. Sibley drew first blood by shooting an Albatros down between Grandcourt and Albert, killing Unteroffizier Paul Wein and Leutnant der Reserve Karl Oskar Breibisch-Guthmann of *Fl. Abt. 32*.

On April 25, three of No. 24's men were escorting a B.E.2c of No.15 Squadron when they were attacked by a flight of Fokkers. The D.H.2s turned on the Eindeckers, driving one down and chasing off the rest. Their victim was probably Max Immelmann, then credited with 14 victories, who wrote:

> I took off at about 11 a.m. and met two English biplanes southward of Bapaume. I was about 700 meters higher and therefore came up with them and attacked one. He seemed to heel over after a few shots, but unfortunately I was mistaken. The two worked splendidly together in the course of the fight and put eleven shots in my machine. The petrol tank, the struts on the fuselage, the undercarriage and the propeller were hit. I could only save myself by a nose-dive of 1,000 meters.

The men who gave Immelmann such a nasty fight were Lieutenants N.P. Manfield and John Oliver Andrews, the latter destined to survive the war with 12 victories. At that point, as far as Hawker's men were concerned, the Fokker bogey had been laid and they attacked all German aircraft they encountered without hesitation.

On the 30th, Tidmarsh was escorting some F.E.2bs over Péronne when he engaged an approaching Eindecker. Tidmarsh claimed he never got closer than 500 yards and did not have the opportunity to fire before the Fokker dove away, but he saw its wings come off and it crashed into some houses near Bapaume. The Germans' subsequent report on the death of Leutnant Otto Schmedes of KEK Bertincourt, attached to *Fl. Abt.* 32, stated that his flying wires had been severed by bullets, but they may have snapped under the strain of his dive—a characteristic weakness in mono-planes at that time. In any case, Tidmarsh was credited with the Fokker

Lieutenant John O. Andrews beside a D.H.2 of No. 24 Squadron. As leader of A Flight, "Jock" Andrews took on Fokker E.IIIs and Albatros D.IIs with equal distinction. (*Jon Guttman*)

and would down one more two-seater on May 20 before going off on leave to Britain. He would return to the front in March 1917, flying a new Bristol F.2A two-seat fighter in No. 48 Squadron.

On May 23, General Henry Rawlinson reported that thanks to the aggressively flown D.H.2s, the reconnaissance planes were able to photograph the entire German trench system along the frontage occupied by his Fourth Army. "I cannot speak too highly of the work of these young pilots," he said, "most of whom have recently come from England, and the de Havilland machine has unquestionably proved itself superior to the Fokker in speed, manoeuvrability, climb-ing, and general fighting efficiency."

Such efficiency could not be attributed to the next British scout unit to arrive in France on May 28. By the time it settled at Vert Galant under 13 Wing, 3rd Brigade command on June 10, No. 60 Squadron, under 29-year-old Major Francis Fitzgerald Waldron, consisted of two flights of nine Morane-Saulnier Type N monoplanes each and one with four Type BB two-seater biplanes.

While the all-fighter squadrons prepared for the "Big Push" at the Somme, the odd scout pilots operating within corps squadrons developed the sort of individual flair that would make them great fighter pilots in the future. Among the early members of this intra-squadron elite was Charles Gordon Bell. Born in London on May 31, 1889, he learned to fly at Brooklands in 1910, earning Pilot's Certificate No.100 on July 4, 1911 and allegedly flew 63 different types of airplanes by the time war broke out. Joining the RFC late in 1914, he flew B.E.2s in No. 10 Squadron until the unit obtained some Bristol Scouts. Already known for his monocle, his stammer, and his quick wit, Bell became an aggressive scout pilot. On September 15, 1915, he forced an LVG to land. On October 13, he sent an Albatros down out of control and forced another LVG to land. Bell downed another Albatros OOC on November 16, and destroyed an LVG at Henin-Liétard on November 30. Posted home with ill health in December, Bell later trained pilots at Gosport, his students including the future ace James McCudden. Major Bell subsequently returned to the front as commander of No. 41 Squadron, only to be tragically killed during a test flight on July 29, 1918.

After No. 11 Squadron replaced its F.B.5s with F.E.2bs, it also acquired an escort of Bristol Scouts. Among the pilots assigned to fly them was Lieutenant Albert Ball, a 19-year-old collegiate from Nottingham, England, who after serving in the 2/7th Battalion Sherwood Foresters, had joined the RFC and entered service with No. 13 Squadron in February 1916. On May 7, he was transferred to No. 11 Squadron and assigned Bristol Scout 5312. This plane had been fitted with interrupter gear designed in January by Vickers employees Harold Savage and George Henry Challenger for their firm's machine gun. Just nine days later, Ball used the new weapon system to drive an Albatros C.III of *Kasta* 17, *Kagohl 3* down "out of control" for his first credited victory, although its wounded pilot managed to force-land in German lines. The Vickers-Challenger gear was used for a time, but its long, flexible connecting rod proved too fragile to be reliable, and it was soon replaced by other systems.

When Nieuport 11s and 16s with overwing Lewis guns were added to the scout flight, Ball truly came into his own, being credited with an LVG OOC and another forced to land on May 29. He forced a Fokker to land on June 1, and burned a balloon on June 23, to become the third British pilot credited with five victories. The RFC tended to eschew the distinction of "ace," but Ball began to acquire a notoriety that would inevitably make its way to the public eye.

In contrast to the British—but not the French—the Germans had been making the most of their Fokker pilots' success, publicizing their exploits and awarding the *Orden Pour le Mérite* to each man who scored his eighth victory—a standard that would later be raised as the state of the deadly art advanced. By the end of June 1916, Oswald Boelcke was the most success-

Lieutenant Albert Ball holds the red-painted spinner he mounted on the propeller of his Nieuport 17 while serving in No. 60 Squadron RFC. *(IWM Q107324)*

ful fighter pilot in the world, with 19 victories to his credit, closely followed by Immelmann with 15 or 16. Wintgens's and Höhndorf's scores stood at seven, Ernst von Althaus and Wilhelm Frankl had six each, and Max Mulzer and Rudolf Berthold had five. In a special category was Hans-Joachim Buddecke, who after downing three British aircraft around St. Quentin with *Fl. Abt. 23* between September and November 1915, had transferred to *Fl. Abt. 6*, based at Smyrna. From there he scored another four confirmed and seven unconfirmed victories over Gallipoli and the Dardanelles, earning the sobriquet of *El Shahin*, or "shooting hawk," from his Turkish allies.

Oberleutnant Immelmann, however, would not be around to interfere with British air operations over the Somme or further rival Boelcke's tally. On June 18, he had left Douai aerodrome in Fokker E.III 246/16, leading three other fighters from *Fl. Abt. 62* to intercept seven F.E.2bs of No. 25 Squadron. Joined by Leutnant Mulzer, he singled out F.E.2b 4909, crewed by 17-year-old Lieutenant John R. B. Savage and Air Mechanic 2nd Class T. N. U. Robinson. Flying above them in F.E.2b 6346, 2nd Lt. G. R. McCubbin from Cape Town, South Africa, observed Savage's plight and dived to his aid, pursued by two other Fokkers.

"Savage's machine suddenly got out of control, as the Fokker had been firing at it, and Savage's machine went down," McCubbin recalled in 1935. "By this time I was very close to the Fokker and he apparently realised we were on his tail, and he immediately started to do what I expect was the beginning of an 'Immelmann' turn. As he started the turn we opened fire and the Fokker immediately got out of control and went down to earth."

Crashing near Sallaumines from 2,000 feet, Immelmann, "The Eagle of Lille," was dead. The F.E.2b came down near Lens, where Savage died of his wounds and Robinson was taken prisoner, but instead of being credited to Immelmann, they were claimed by and credited to his wingman, Mulzer.

McCubbin's extraordinary aerial success earned him the DSO while his observer, Corporal J. H. Waller, got the Distinguished Service Medal and a promotion to sergeant. The Germans later claimed Immelmann's synchronization had malfunctioned, causing him to shoot his own propeller off, but Waller retrospectively asserted, "it is quite on the cards that our bullets not only got him, but his prop as well, and that would be the reason for them trying to make this statement."

Max Immelmann's name lives on in a maneuver he was credited with developing to regain altitude, involving a half loop with a half roll at the top. Oswald Boelcke's name would soon be associated with things of a more collective nature.

News of his friendly rival's death had shocked Boelcke, who flew north to visit his comrades at Douai for a couple of days. Upon returning to Sivry, he learned that an equally shaken German high command was ordering him off combat operations, rather than risk losing its surviving hero. Rankled by the prospect, Boelcke flew as often as he could before the withdrawal date, and in spite of bad weather claimed a Nieuport in German lines for his 19th victory on the evening of June 27. Curiously, the French records lack claims or losses for that entire day.

After that, Boelcke was dispatched on an inspection tour to Vienna, Budapest, Belgrade and ultimately Constantinople—with the primary intention of keeping him out of combat. Before his departure, Boelcke had several meetings with the chief of the air service, Oberstleutnant Hermann von der Lieth-Thomsen, and his staff, during which he put down on paper his ideas for the German fighter force's future. More significantly, he left behind a list of basic rules for aerial combat:

> Always try to secure an advantageous position before attacking. Climb before and during the approach in order to surprise the enemy from above, and dive on him swiftly from the rear when the moment to attack is at hand.

> Try to place yourself between the sun and the enemy. This puts the glare of the sun in the enemy's eyes and makes it difficult to see you and impossible for him to shoot with any accuracy.

> Do not fire the machine guns until the enemy is within range and you have him squarely within your sights.

> Attack when the enemy least expects it or when he is preoccupied with other duties such as observation, photography or bombing.

> Never turn your back and try to run away from an enemy fighter. If you are surprised by an attack on your tail, turn and face the enemy with your guns.

> Keep an eye on the enemy and do not let him deceive you with tricks. If your opponent appears damaged follow him down until he crashes to be sure he is not faking.

> Foolish acts of bravery only bring death. The *Jasta* must fight as a unit with close teamwork between all pilots. The signal of its leaders must be obeyed.

Known as the Dicta Boelcke, an earlier version of those instructions (the reference to *Jasta*, or *Jagdstaffel*, being added later in the year) were issued to all German fighter units. They have been expanded upon in the decades that have followed, but with one exception those fundamentals have remained applicable in every war that has involved air-to-air combat since. The exception is rule number six, for even by the autumn of 1916, the sky had become too full of fighting aircraft for it to be safe to follow an opponent down, sacrificing altitude and leaving oneself vulnerable to attack by one of the victim's squadron mates.

While Boelcke and his colleagues were laying the groundwork for an efficient German fighter force, Anthony Fokker and his chief engineer, Martin Kreutzer, had been noting and taking steps to keep up with the wave of improved Allied fighting planes appearing over the front to challenge his once-seemingly invincible E.III. Although all but one of his new offerings were biplanes, they were structurally similar to the Eindeckers they would have to replace—and all would be disappointments.

The Fokker E.IV was a stretched E.III with a humplike fairing around the pilot's cockpit that partially enclosed the machine gun, similar to the one that earned the Sopwith Camel its name. It was built to accommodate a 160-hp twin-row, 14-cylinder Oberursel U.III engine—a copy of the Gnome Double Lambda—that required a framework in front of the cowling to steady it. When the prototype arrived for testing at Essen in September 1915, Fokker had installed three 08/15 machine guns firing up at a 15-degree angle. That arrangement was soon abandoned because the triple interrupter gear mechanism was judged too complex to be practical.

As it was, when issued to Oberleutnant Parschau for front-line evaluation in October 1915, the E.IV was the first airplane to use twin machine guns in combat, and 49 eventually saw service. That more were not among the grand total of 416 Eindeckers built was due to the fact that, while the E.IV could attain 105 mph, one of its pilots called it "practically a flying engine." Still using the old wing warping technique rather than ailerons, the plane was tricky to fly and yet less

Hauptmann Oswald Boelcke and his aircrew standing in front of a Fokker E.IV. The war's first twin-gun fighter, it nevertheless proved to be a disappointment. (Jon Guttman)

maneuverable than its predecessors. On top of that, air-cooling the aft row of cylinders proved to be a recurring problem in the U.III engine, even with holes punched across the face of its cowling.

In the spring of 1916, Fokker introduced a series of two-bay biplane scouts, starting with the D.II, which used the 100-hp Oberursel Ur.I rotary engine, and of which 177 would be built. Hot on its heels came the D.I, a similar airframe adapted to the 100-hp Mercedes D.I engine. While the D.II handled reasonably well, the D.I, with its heavier liquid-cooled engine, was less successful, though it too got a modest production contract and saw service using the 120-hp Mercedes D.II engine.

While he was test-flying the D.I on June 7, 1916, Martin Kreutzer's rudder jammed, causing the plane to crash. He died of his injuries the next day. His successor as chief engineer, Reinhold Platz, was a welding specialist who would serve a major—if oft-exaggerated—role in helping Anthony Fokker move on to structurally more advanced designs. For the time being, however, Kreutzer's legacy continued, in the form of three more biplanes based on his basic formula that would drive Fokker from notoriety to obscurity until the late summer of 1917.

Paralleling the career of the Fokker Eindeckers were the less illustrious Pfalz E.I, E.II, E.III and E.IV. Although based on the Morane-

Saulnier H, which Pfalz had been building under license when war broke out, the Pfalz machines were inferior in performance and often dangerously more difficult to handle than the Fokkers. Nowhere was that more apparent than on the Pfalz E.IV, which was powered by the twin-row Oberursel U.III engine—and even more of a handful to control than its less-than-brilliant contemporary, the Fokker E.IV. On April 25, 1916 the commander of KEK Vaux, Leutnant Rudolf Berthold, whose score then stood at five, crashed in Pfalz E.IV 803/15—suffering the first of several injuries that he refused to allow to keep him from the front for more than the barest minimum of time. Incidents like that established a reputation that would prejudice German airmen against subsequent Pfalz designs for the rest of the war.

On the night before the Somme offensive began, Major Hawker issued a directive to his pilots far more simple and to the point than Boelcke's: "Tactical Orders OC 24 Squadron. Attack everything."

A massive eight-day artillery bombardment had preceded the British assault. On July 1, it lifted and the British infantry began walking toward the enemy lines—where well-entrenched German troops emerged from their dugouts, took up their defensive positions and proceeded to mow down 60,000 men in that first day. And that was only the beginning.

In the air, the sheer number of British reconnaissance, artillery spotter, and bombing aircraft assured them a measure of aerial supremacy, but the German fighters struck regularly under conditions of their choosing in an often effective effort to disrupt RFC air operations. Among the units seeking to counter that were the D.H.2s of Nos. 24 and 32 squadrons, joined by No. 60 Squadron's Morane-Saulnier N "Bullet" monoplanes.

It was 32 Squadron's Major Rees, however, who set the most noteworthy example for his men on July 1. At 0555 that morning he and Canadian-born Lieutenant J. C. Simpson took off and diverged on separate missions—Simpson to patrol the area around La Bassée,

Loos, and Souchez, while Rees skirted the line to await the return of a bombing flight and its D.H.2 escorts. In the course of his sortie Simpson encountered 10 Roland and Albatros two-seaters of *Kagohl 3*'s *Kasta* 14 on a bombing mission of their own and promptly attacked. Just as promptly, a fusillade from three of the German observers struck Simpson in his head and sent his plane crashing into the Loos Canal.

Moments later Rees spotted the formation, which he at first believed to be British. As he approached it, however, one plane dived at him shooting. Firing 30 rounds in response Rees reported he "saw the top of the fuselage splinter between the pilot and observer," and the enemy plane dived away to the east.

At that point Rees, his blood up, attacked a lone Roland. Three others rushed to its aid, but fired at a hopelessly long range while Rees closed on his quarry, emptied his Lewis drum into it and subsequently reported, "After about 30 rounds a big cloud of blue haze came out of the nacelle in front of the pilot."

As that plane fled over the lines, Rees attacked five more Germans. Gwilym Lewis, who thought Rees "the bravest man in the world," described what he learned about the melée that followed:

> The Huns were in a tight bunch when he came along—after he had finished they were all scattered in twos and ones all over the sky, not knowing which way to go. He sent the first one down out of control; the second one probably had a bullet through his engine. He turned to attack the third, whose observer was sitting with his head back and his gun aiming vertically upwards fairly blazing off bullets. I supposed he must have forgotten to take his hand off the trigger before he 'pipped out.' Just as the Major was going to get this machine as a trophy another fellow came and shot him in the leg from below. He was still going on but he discovered he couldn't steer his machine, so he came home.

Rees disengaged with a paralyzed leg, but shortly after doing so he regained some use of it and turned to pursue the enemy leader, which after dropping a bomb fled toward German lines. Expending a full

drum and even drawing his pistol—only to drop it into the nacelle—
Rees finally gave up as the two-seater was too far away and too high
to catch. As it was, he had scattered the German bombing formation
and the observer he had hit in the third plane—mortally, it turned
out—was *Kasta* 14's commander, Leutnant Erich Zimmermann,
whose wounded pilot, Leutnant der Reserve Ernst Wendler, crash-
landed near La Bassée.

"He landed in the usual manner—taxied in," Lewis wrote. "They
got the steps for him to get out of his machine. He got out and sat on
the grass, and calmly told the fellows to bring him a tender to take
him to hospital. I am afraid he had got a very bad wound, though he
is lucky not to have had an artery in his leg shot, as I understand he
would never have got back if he had.

"Of course, everyone knows the Major is mad," Lewis added. "I
don't think he was ever more happy in his life than attacking those
Huns. He said he would have brought them all down one after the
other if he could have used his leg."

Rees was credited with a Roland "out of control" and one "forced
to land," raising his total to eight, and was awarded the Victoria Cross.
His fighting days were over, though—he spent the rest of the war commanding the Air Fighting School at Ayr. Continuing his aviation
career after the war, Rees retired from the Royal Air Force as a Group
Captain in 1931, and died in the Bahamas on September 28, 1955.

Another future ace who scored all but one of his seven victories in
pushers got his first on July 1, although in this case his mount was not
a D.H.2 scout, but an F.E.2d two-seater. Born in Pakenham, Ontario
on April 19, 1888, Harold Evans Hartney had been mobilized in
October 1914, but had been married before he shipped out to
England in May 1915 and transferred to the RFC in October.
Reporting to 20 Squadron at Clamarais on June 16, he flew his first
sortie over the lines on the 30th.

The next day Hartney was in a five-plane formation over
Armentières when 20 Fokker E.IIIs descended on the FEs. The
British claimed five of their assailants in the running fight that
ensued, two of which were credited to Hartney and his observer, Air
Mechanic 2nd Class A. Stanley. Separated from his formation,

Hartney fought his way home through what Stanley believed totaled 11 "scraps" with enemy fighters attacking from fore and aft. Ultimately, with one of Stanley's guns jammed and the other out of ammunition, Hartney made it to the lines and made a pancake landing in a stretch of ploughed ground behind the Australian trenches. He wrote in his memoir *Up and At 'Em!*

> Then we began to inspect our plane, it was in horrible shape, riddled with bullets and how it held together is a mystery. The fabric in places was torn clear from the leading edge to the trailing....That motor should have been put in a museum....Seven bullets were actually sticking in the water jackets and in the plumbing. The cowling was almost a sieve. And there's the gospel truth, though my word on it has often been doubted—four of the aluminum pistons, a secret Rolls-Royce innovation, had actually fused and were holding up four of the exhaust valves. There was no water whatever in the engine and practically no oil. For those last few minutes it had been doing its bit for old England metal to metal—at melting temperatures.

Practically unnoticed on that same day was the combat debut of a scout that would be as influential as the Nieuport *Bébé*, for an equally temporary timespan. While the RFC had focused on acquiring pushers to counter the Fokker Scourge, the Royal Naval Air Service was getting something rather more progressive from Thomas O.M. Sopwith and his chief engineer, Herbert Smith. Their line began with the prewar Sopwith Tabloid racer, a boxy looking but compact single-bay biplane of wood and canvas. Although the Tabloid and a floatplane derivative, the Baby, saw service as scouts in the war's first few years, the first true fighting machine designed by Sopwith and Smith was a two-seat reconnaissance-fighter and bomber. Named for its W-shaped cabane strut arrangement, the "1-1/2 Strutter" was passed by the Sopwith experimental department on December 12, 1915. In addition to a Lewis gun on an ingeniously simple, flexible ring mounting for the observer designed by RNAS Warrant Officer Frederick W. Scarff, this plane had the first forward firing synchronized machine gun to be standard on a British warplane, using Vickers-Challenger interrupter gear. A few weeks after its test flight, however, that system was replaced by an improved one developed by Scarff and Lt. Cmdr. Viktor V. Dybovsky, an equally inventive aircraft designer from the Russian Navy who was visiting England at the time. Still later, the 1-1/2 Strutter got interrupter gear devised by a Flight Sergeant Ross, which allowed the pilot the option of hand-firing the machine gun if the synchronizing mechanism malfunctioned.

Soon after the 1-1/2 Strutter entered production, its was joined by a smaller, single-seat derivative, powered by an 80-hp Le Rhône engine and armed with a single Vickers employing Scarff-Dybovsky gear. Officially called the Scout and cleared for testing on February 9, 1916, it made an immediate impression on the Admiralty and everyone who flew it. Its maximum speed was 110 mph at 6,500 feet, it could climb to 10,000 feet in 12 minutes and it combined ease of handling, sprightly maneuverability and good cockpit visibility in one of the most aesthetically pleasing airplanes of the war.

The RNAS ordered the Scout in April, by which time Sopwith's Australian-born foreman of works, Henry Alexis Kauper, had developed another synchronizing mechanism that would soon replace the Scarff-Dybovsky system. When the RFC's General Trenchard read a copy of the Admiralty's report on the plane's performance, he penciled in the margin, "Let's get a squadron of these." Another RFC officer, Colonel Sefton Brancker, was said to have remarked upon spotting a Scout alongside its two-place forebear, "Good God! Your 1-1/2 Strutter has had a pup." In spite of official efforts to discourage it, the delightful new fighter soon became universally known by that name.

By the time the first Pups arrived at No.1 Wing RNAS at Dunkerque in July 1916, the prototype of another variant was joining them for front-line evaluation. Completed on May 30, 1916, Sopwith Triplane N500 combined the Pup's fuselage with a 130-hp Clerget engine and three sets of narrow-chord, high aspect ratio wings that gave the pilot a better view from the cockpit, a faster climb rate and superior maneuverability, even than the Pup's. Flying the new Triplane on July 1 was Flight Lieutenant Roderic Stanley Dallas of No. 1 Wing's "A" Squadron, an Australian who already had three vic-

Top: Still flyable and still a delight to fly, a Sopwith Pup in early Royal Naval Air Service markings shows off its well-proportoined lines at Lake Guntersville, Alabama in 2001. (*Jon Guttman*) Bottom: Sopwith Triplane N500 suffers a noseover. Flying this prototype on July 1, Flight Lieutenant Roderic Stanley Dallas of No. 1 Wing's A Squadron downed a German two-seater, followed by an enemy fighter on September 30. The Germans did not take serious notice of the Triplane until the spring of 1917, but then they would take very serious notice indeed. (*Brian Kehew via Rod Filan*)

tories in Nieuports. To those he added a fourth in N500, when he drove a German two-seater down out of control southwest of St. Marie Capelle. The Admiralty was again duly impressed and ordered the Sopwith Triplane into production. Meanwhile, N500 was still on hand with "A" Squadron, renamed No. 1 Squadron RNAS, on

September 30, when Dallas used it to shoot down an enemy fighter. It would take several more months before the Germans took serious notice of the Triplane, but when they did, it would be serious indeed.

Oddly, the first confirmed Sopwith Pup victory would not be scored until much later. On September 24, Australian-born Flight Sub-Lieutenant Stanley James Goble used the prototype to drive down an LVG out of control over Ghistelles—his third of an eventual 10 victories. On the 25th, Flight Sub-Lieutenant Edward Rochfort Grange attacked a Sablatnig SF.2 floatplane of *Seeflugstaffel* 1, which broke up over the sea six miles off Ostend, killing Leutnante zur See Soltenborn and Rothig. In spite of the occasional encounters off the coast, it became clear to Goble, Grange, and the rest of the Sopwith pilots at Dunkerque that they would not accomplish much in northern Flanders. Events over the Somme were to change all that.

German aerial activity had generally been moderate on July 1, at least in comparison with the days to follow. Eindecker pilots claimed six victories on July 2, two of them in their lines and three adding to the tallies of Mulzer, Parschau and von Althaus. Their only fatality, Leutnant Werner Neuhaus of *Flieger Abteilung* (A) 203, collided with a French Nieuport 17 flown by Sergent Marcel Garet of N.23—and in an ironic twist, his Fokker E.III crashed in French lines while Garet's body fell on the German side. Albert Ball of No. 11 Squadron also scored on the 2nd, claiming a Roland and an Aviatik.

While the D.H.2s and Nieuports were more than holding their own over the Somme, No. 60 Squadron's Morane-Saulnier Bullets were proving to be a source of more trouble than triumph. On July 3 the CO, Major "Ferdy" Waldron, led A Flight against several two-seaters escorted by three Fokkers. The only sure outcome of the ensuing scrap was the loss of Waldron, last seen gliding down, but later confirmed as killed by Unteroffizier Hans Howe, a Fokker pilot attached to *Fl. Abt.* 5b. Aside from that, Franz Walz, a two-seater pilot of *Kasta* 2, *Kagohl* 1, claimed his third victory, a B.E.2c of No. 16 Squadron south of Péronne whose pilot, 2nd Lt. S.H. Ellis, was wounded and taken prisoner, while Parschau burned a French balloon over La Neuville.

On July 8, Mulzer—temporarily detached from *Fl. Abt.* 32 for service in KEK B—shot down a B.E.2c of No. 4 Squadron west of Bapaume, the observer, Corporal L.R.G. Johnstone, being taken prisoner but the Australian pilot, Lieutenant Eric C. Jouett, dying the next day. With his score now eight, Mulzer became the fifth German—and the first Bavarian—fighter pilot to be awarded the *Orden Pour le Mérite.*

In spite of the growing numbers and quality of their Allied opposition, July 9 was one of the *Eindeckerflieger's* best days. Leutnant Gustav Leffers of *Abwehrkommando Nord* shot down an F.E.2b of No. 11 Squadron that had just bombed a target southwest of Bapaume. The pilot, 2nd Lt. David H. Macintyre, was taken prisoner with hand and leg wounds, but the observer, 2nd Lt. Hayden Floyd, died of his injuries three days later.

Elsewhere, Parschau demonstrated that balloon busting did more than just provide a spectacle for pyromaniacs. The French gasbag he destroyed north of Grévillers, killing Adjutant M. Mallet of the 55*e Compagnie d'Aérostiers*, had been directing artillery on the German trenches for some time. As he returned over the lines, Parschau was greeted by cheers from the soldiers and, since this was his eighth victory, he got two more tangible rewards: the *Orden Pour le Mérite* and command of *Abwehrkommando-Nord*. Walz of *Kasta* 2 scored his fourth victory on the 9th, while Leutnant Hans-Karl Müller of KEK Avillers got another balloon. Two other British planes were claimed by the Germans that day, although one Fokker E.III was brought down near Mariakerke aerodrome by Roderic Dallas, back in a Nieuport, for his fifth victory.

July 15 saw Walz and his observer shoot down a Caudron G.4 of *Escadrille* C.106 west of the Somme for the German pilot's fifth victory. It also saw the combat debut of a future American ace who was officially not supposed to be there. A cowboy from Sterling, Colorado, Frederick Libby was riding herd in Canada when war broke out and in 1915 he decided to join the army there. After some time in the trenches he transferred to the RFC as an observer in No. 23 Squadron, he noted this first impression of the F.E.2b:

> The pilot was in front of the motor in the middle of the ship
> and the observer in front of the pilot. When you stood, all of
> you from the knees up was exposed to the world. There was
> no belt and nothing to hold on to except the gun and sides of
> the nacelle. Fastened to the bottom and toward the front of
> the nacelle was a hollow steel rod with a specially mounted
> swivel mount for anchoring the machine gun, which could
> be swung from side to side or to the front as the occasion
> demanded, giving it a wonderful field of fire.
>
> Between the observer and the pilot was another gun, which
> was for the purpose of fighting a rear-gun action over the top
> wing to protect your tail. The mounting consisted of a hol-
> low steel rod, into which a solid steel rod was fitted to work
> up and down with the machine gun on top. To operate this
> you simply pull the gun up as high as possible, where it locks
> into the fitting, then you step out of the nacelle and stand
> with a foot on each side. From this position you have nothing
> to worry about except being blown out of the ship or being
> tossed out if the pilot makes a wrong move. This gun, I know,
> I am not going to like much.

Nevertheless, Libby showed himself to be an outstanding marksman. One of the squadron's sergeants had impressed on him the
importance of good teamwork with his pilot:

> The observer is the most essential part of the team. You do
> all the shooting, all the photography, all the bomb dropping,
> if bombs are used. And you're entirely responsible for your
> pilot's life. True, the pilot flies the ship. He gets you there
> and back, and a good pilot will put you in a position to shoot
> and will not get panicky, tossing the ship around, throwing
> you out of position to shoot or defend yourself.

Libby's first assigned pilot was Lieutenant E.D. Hicks, whose
advice against getting separated from their flight over enemy territory
reflected the tactics that were already evolving, "A lone ship they all

jump on, so we try to keep formation at any cost if possible. Fighting your way home in a single ship, the odds are all in favour of your enemy. The wind is almost always against you because it blows from the west off the sea—this they know and they can wait."

On July 15—Libby's 25th birthday—Hicks took him up for his first combat sortie and in a sudden, sharp encounter the fledgling gunner shared in the destruction of an Ago C.I in flames over Bapaume with another FE crew. Soon afterward Libby was assigned to Lieutenant Stephen William Price and both men were transferred to No. 11 Squadron, where Price was given command of B Flight. On August 22, the duo was credited with three Rolands south of Bapaume—two of which were shared with squadron mates 2nd Lt. Lionel B. F. Morris and Lieutenant Tom Rees. An Aviatik on the 25th and a two-seater on September 14 made Libby the first American ace of World War I, although the first American *pilot* to attain that status, Raoul Lufbery, would have to wait until October.

The first American ace— albeit not as a pilot— Coloradan Frederick Libby enlisted in Canada and became an F.E.2b observer in No. 23 Squadron, downing an Ago in his first combat flight on July 15, 1916. He later scored nine victories with No. 11 Squadron, trained as a pilot, and went on to add two to his tally flying Sopwith 11/2 Strutters with No. 43 Squadron and two more in deHavilland D.H.4 bombers with No. 25 Squadron. Fred Libby died in Los Angeles, California on January 6, 1970, aged 79. (*Sally Ann Marsh*)

If July 9 was among the Fokker pilots' best days over the Somme, July 21 was among the the worst. It was a day of activity all over the sector, with Höhndorf claiming a Nieuport over Bapaume for his 10th victory; Wintgens downing a B.E.2c of No. 12 Squadron, and a Morane-Saulnier N of No. 60 Squadron. A Voisin became von Althaus's eighth victim, qualifying him for the Blue Max. The British, however, claimed six German planes destroyed and three "driven down." Three of them were *Jagdflieger*, the highest fatalities in that category the Germans had suffered in a single day thus far.

At 0800 that morning, D.H.2s from 24 Squadron's A Flight led by Captain "Jock" Andrews took on five Roland C.IIs escorted by five Fokkers over Roisel. In the ensuing melee, Andrews shot down an Eindecker near Allaines, which Lieutenant S.E. Pither also fired at as it descended. Andrews reported seeing the Fokker smash its undercarriage in a forced landing and he subsequently fired on and scattered a group of Germans approaching the wreck.

Andrews's first confirmed victory was very likely Otto Parschau, then commanding the newly redesignated KEK B from Bertincourt, who was struck in the chest and head, and died of his wounds soon after. In addition to that Blue Max ace, Leutnant Werner Schramm of *Fl. Abt.* 32 crashed at Combles after being struck in the chest by shrapnel, and Vizefeldwebel Wolfgang Heinemann of *Fl. Abt.* 3 was killed by an F.E.2b team from No. 23 Squadron.

While the RFC's new fighters were taking the Fokker Eindecker's measure over the Somme, a potentially momentous event on the Eastern Front was going virtually unnoticed in the West. On June 4, 1916, 1,770 Russian guns opened up along a 200-mile front between the Pripet Marshes and the Romanian border—a mere six-hour prelude to a sharp assault that heralded a brilliantly conceived offensive by General Aleksei A. Brusilov. Over the next three months Brusilov's Southwestern Army Group drove an average of 20 miles into Austro-Hungarian lines, inflicted 250,00 casualties and took 450,000 prisoners, as well as 500 guns.

Brusilov's breakthrough created a crisis for the Central Powers that might have changed the course of the war if the Western Allies had paid more attention, and if it had only been achieved earlier, before the rot within Russian society was already too advanced to avoid the revolution that would soon tear it asunder. As it was, Germany and Austria-Hungary were forced to transfer 23 divisions from France, Italy, and northern Russia, while the Ottoman Empire contributed its XV Corps and two divisions to contain the potential Russian follow-up that never materialized. It adversely affected the

German effort at Verdun and compelled the Austro-Hungarian army to cancel an offensive along the Trentino River.

As with Britain's less successful Somme offensive, Brusilov's had been attended by a buildup in supporting air activity, including plenty from the IRAS's budding fighter force. Heading that effort was Aleksandr Kozakov, who had been transferred to the XIX Corps Air Detachment on September 2, 1915, and made its commander a month later. After chasing enemy planes in his Morane-Saulnier armed with a shotgun, he obtained a Nieuport 10 late that year and had his mechanics mount a Maxim machine gun on it, firing up at a 24-degree angle to clear the propeller. He first tried it out in combat on February 5, 1916, and although it was hard to aim, he managed to destroy an Albatros C.III with it on June 27. On July 29, he used it amid one of the largest air battles to occur over the Eastern Front, when 11 Russian aircraft engaged 11 German bombers over Dvinsk, and shot down another Albatros for his third victory.

Other Russian aces were opening their accounts—and another would close his—at that time. On June 8, Poruchik Ivan Orlov of the 7th Army Air Detachment shot down a Lloyd C.II of *Flik* 9 over Pelikovze, and on the 25th he and Poruchik Vassily Ivanovich Yanchenko shared in destroying an Aviatik B.III of *Flik* 27. On July 1, Eduard Pulpe, recently returned from France and commissioned a Podporuchik (sub-lieutenant) in the 10th Fighter Detachment, scored his fifth victory in the Lutz-Kovel area. On August 2, however, he was mortally wounded while engaging an Albatros C.III of *Kagohl* 2. The German pilot credited with downing his Nieuport 11, Leutnant Erwin Böhme, would later figure prominently in Oswald Boelcke's saga on the Western Front.

Throughout the Brusilov offensive, Kozakov had encouraged a spirit of fighting élan within his XIX Corps Detachment, including the adoption of a nickname, the "Death or Glory Squadron." The unit used a white skull and crossbones on a black rudder, although those colors were reversed on Kozakov's plane. In July, in emulation of the provisional *Groupe des Escadrilles de Chasse* that the French had formed at Verdun, Kozakov's unit was combined with two others, the II and IV Corps Air Detachments, into the 1st Combat Air

Group, with him in overall command. On September 6, Kozakov, now flying a Nieuport 11, shot down a German two-seater and on December 21, he downed a Brandenburg C.I of *Flik* 10 for his fifth victory. He would ultimately become Russia's leading ace with 17 to 20 victories, but the Revolution, his participation on the White side in the ensuing Russian Civil War, and the execution of the tsar were all undoubtedly contributing factors to the abrupt takeoff, stall, and crash of a Sopwith Snipe, apparently deliberate, that ended Kozakov's life on August 1, 1919.

Also making its combat debut in July was the 2nd Combat Air Group under Evgraf Kruten, who had been writing articles and books on air tactics throughout the spring of 1916. Flying a Nieuport 11 whose fuselage side was decorated with the head of a Russian knight, Kruten put his theories into practice by shooting down an Albatros C.III on August 11, followed by a Rumpler on the 14th.

In early March 1917, Kruten was visiting Paris when he heard about the revolution which—apparently expecting it to lead to much-needed military reforms—he called "the saving thunderstorm that liberated Russia from the tsarist regime." France was shipping some escadrilles east to assist Russia's air efforts, but while talking with Russians temporarily assigned to French units on the Western Front, Kruten declared, "there is nothing about flying that we could learn from foreigners, and nobody dared approach us in our ability to fly." After returning to Russia on March 24, Kruten published a book expounding on his opinion of Allied aid: *Invasion of Foreigners.* Taking command of the newly formed 2nd Combat Air Group in April, Kruten flew at the head of his squadrons in a Nieuport 21 and 17, and brought his tally up to seven on June 6. As he was returning from a sortie on June 19, however, his Nieuport 17 suddenly fell into a spin and crashed on his own airfield at Plotych. He died of his injuries minutes later.

5

DICTA BOELCKE

By the end of July it was clear to both sides that a variety of Allied scouts and two-seat fighters had canceled the Fokker Eindecker's sole advantage, its interrupter gear—in fact, the Nieuport 16 and 17, and the Sopwith 1-1/2 Strutter and Pup had similar weaponry of their own. "The start of the Somme battle unfortunately coincided with the low point in the technical development of our aircraft," wrote *Idflieg* commander Major Wilhelm Siegert, with outspoken candor. "The unquestioned supremacy we had enjoyed in early 1916 by virtue of our Fokker monoplane fighters shifted over to the enemy's Nieuport, Vickers, and Sopwith aircraft in March and April. Our monthly aircraft output did not even allow a squadron to be equipped with a common type. For example, *Fl. Abt.* 23 had a complement of five different aircraft types."

The Nieuport *Bébé* and its progeny had already caught German attention over Verdun, and they were no less formidable over the Somme. If Jean Navarre had used them to outstanding effect as the "Sentinel of Verdun," Britain's Albert Ball more than matched his notoriety over the Somme.

Although both were loners, the two heroes harbored differing temperaments. While Navarre was rebellious and somewhat unstable, Ball was a quiet, religious sort who spent his time between missions tending a vegetable garden, or in his hut reading or playing the violin. While Navarre often flew with a woman's silk stocking as a flying helmet, Ball preferred to fly bareheaded because he liked to feel the wind in his hair.

Although he professed to hate killing, Ball nevertheless felt duty bound to fight and clearly overcame his qualms once engaged in the thrill of the hunt. Unlike the French, who generally preferred the synchronized Vickers machine gun introduced on their Nieuport 17s, Ball favored the Lewis gun on the overwing Foster mount that was standard on RFC Nieuport 17s. He became exceptionally skilled at pulling the gun down to pepper the undersides of German two-seaters, which became his principal prey.

After acquiring Nieuport A201, Ball drove a Roland C.II down to land southeast of St. Leger on August 16. On the 22nd, he was escorting a bombing mission when he spotted seven Rolands heading westward at 5,000 feet altitude. Peeling off, he attacked the Germans from the rear, breaking up their wedge-shaped formation and then, coming as close as 15 yards, he emptied two Lewis drums into one until it crashed west of Bapaume. At that point Ball saw another five Rolands from *Kasta* 1 flying southwest at 7,000 feet. Climbing underneath the rearmost plane, Ball aimed his Lewis straight up, fired two drums into its belly from as close as 10 yards and saw it go down trailing smoke. The remaining Rolands attacked Ball, but after changing magazines once more he fired into the nearest one and sent it crashing into a village between Vaux and Maurepas. The observer of his last victim, Leutnant Hans Becker, died of his wounds; the wounded pilot, Unteroffizier Wilhelm Cymera, would later become a fighter ace himself.

Out of bullets, Ball dived away from the remaining Rolands, having scored the first triple victory, or "hat trick" by a British fighter pilot. Even then, he was not finished—after landing at No. 8 Squadron's aerodrome to replenish his ammunition, he took off again and attacked three more Rolands, breaking up their formation but failing to shoot any down before dwindling fuel compelled him to disengage. Along the way home he attacked two more German formations whose return fire struck his plane 11 times. Nevertheless, upon landing he emerged from his damaged Nieuport unharmed.

On August 23, Ball and Nieuport A201 were transferred from No. 11 to 60 Squadron. The unit had suffered badly during the Somme fighting, as General Trenchard reported to Haig on August 3:

A Roland C.II and a Fokker E.III. By late 1916, the streamlined Roland "Walfisch" two-seater was a more dangerous opponent to the British than was the single-seat Fokker.

I have had to withdraw one of the fighting squadrons from work temporarily and have sent it to St. André-au-Bois. This squadron, since the battle began, had lost a Squadron Commander, two Flight Commanders, and one pilot—all killed or missing, and yesterday it lost two more machines with two pilots and observers by anti-aircraft fire. Besides this, they have had several officers wounded. They have a very difficult machine to fly and I think a rest away from work is absolutely necessary.

When No. 60 Squadron, now led by Major Robert Raymond Smith-Barry, resumed operations with 13th Wing, 3rd Brigade from Izel-le-Hameau, it still had a flight of Morane-Saulnier Ns, Is and Vs, but two other flights equipped with Nieuport 16s and 17s. Those last Moranes would soon be replaced as well, and Trenchard would be loath to equip his squadrons with a monoplane fighter again.

Ball liked the "new crowd" at 60 Squadron, and quickly plunged back into action, downing a Roland on August 25, three more on the 28th, and two on the 31st. He continued to score in multiples in September—two on the 15th, three on the 21st, one on the 23rd and 25th, three on the 28th and three on the 30th, raising his total to 31. At that point, his exploits came to public attention and in October Ball, who had been promoted to captain on September 13, was recalled to England. There he would serve as both a flight instructor and a recruiting tool for the RFC. Although the 20-year-old Ball met and fell in love with 18-year-old Flora Young during that time, he was not happy with training duties and petitioned for a return to the front. He would eventually get his wish—with a new squadron and a new airplane.

While Ball wrought havoc on the Germans as a lone wolf, most RFC fighter units, such as 24 and 32 Squadrons, were collectively establishing an ascendancy over the front. The inability of the Fokkers to keep British reconnaissance, artillery spotting, and bombing planes from violating their airspace and the incessant misery they brought down on the heads of the German troops holding the line did not go unnoticed. A frequent oath heard among them was, "God punish England, our artillery and our airmen."

If the *Fliegertruppe* was to regain its fraying claim to the sky over the Western Front, it would need its own new generation of fighters. Fortunately for the Germans, the first of that generation, albeit what turned out to be a transitional stopgap, had already entered combat at the end of June.

Although Anthony Fokker had not exactly been resting on his laurels, the D.II and D.I biplanes that he unveiled in May 1916 offered little significant improvement over their monoplane predecessors. His next three efforts were essentially up-powered or refined versions of Martin Kreutzer's last design. The Fokker D.III was an enlarged D.II using the twin-row Oberursel U.III. Of the first seven to reach the front on September 1, 1916, two went to *Jagdstaffel* 2 whose commander, Hauptmann Oswald Boelcke, used them to score the unit's first seven victories in two weeks. Those successes, however, were more a reflection of his expertise than on the virtues of the D.III, which was too slow, still used obsolescent wing warping, and whose engine suffered from the same overheating of the after cylinders that had bedeviled the E.IV.

Hard on the D.III's heels in October 1916 came the D.IV, using a 160-hp Mercedes D.III engine. Only 44 were built and they served out the war as fighter trainers. So did the 216 examples of the D.V, which boasted a 100-hp Oberursel U.I engine behind a circular cowling and spinner, as well as a slightly swept-back upper wing. Patently outdated when it entered production in December 1916, the

Fokker D.III 350/16 was one of several biplane designs with which Anthony Fokker vainly tried to stem the growing onslaught of improved Allied fighters in 1916. (Jon Guttman)

D.V was nevertheless built until July 1917, at which point the development of the Fokker triplane gave it a revived relevance, as the ideal trainer to re-acquaint Dr.I pilots with rotary engine operation.

Fokker's belated efforts to supercede his Eindeckers provided nothing but a numerical supplement to the biplane fighter that truly served as the transition to Germany's next generation: the Halberstadt D.II.

Originally formed as the Deutsche Bristol Werke Flugzeug GmbH to build Bristol aircraft under license on April 9, 1912, the Halberstädter Flugzeugwerke GmbH produced its first original design, the B.I biplane, in 1914. A product of technical director Karl Thies and Swiss-born Hans Burkhard before the latter left the firm to join Gotha, the B.I was powered by an 80-hp Oberursel Ur.I rotary engine, but its successor, the B.II, used a 100-hp inline, water-cooled Mercedes D.I. Although both were used as trainers, their unusually sensitive controls were undoubtedly on Thies's mind in early 1916, when he read letters from Boelcke, Immelmann, Wintgens, Parschau, and other aces expressing an urgent need for a successor to the Fokker Eindeckers. Thies designed a more compact, sturdy single-seat version of the B.II, with ailerons on the wings, a 100-hp Mercedes D.I engine and a single machine gun. Static testing of the new Halberstadt D.I on February 26, 1916, revealed a safety factor of 5.78, which contrasted markedly with the fragility shown by the

Fokker biplanes. Only two D.Is were built, however, because *Idflieg* wanted something better and Thies provided it. The improved Halberstadt D.II featured forward staggered wings, a raised turtledeck above the fuselage, and a 120-hp Mercedes D.II engine. This earned an initial contract for 12 planes in March, and the new fighter was officially flight tested and accepted for mass production in May.

The first Halberstadt D.II was probably intended for Immelmann, but he was dead by the time it arrived at Douai on June 22. Boelcke visited the aerodrome later that month and wrote:

> One evening I flew the new Halberstadt biplane—that was the first appearance of this machine at the front. Because it had a slight resemblance to the British BE, I was able to completely surprise an Englander. Undetected I got within 50 meters and 'shot his jacket full.' But since I was too fast and did not have the machine in hand like my Fokker I had to dive under the Englander. He turned around at once and began to descend. I went after him; the belt jammed and I had to turn away. By the time I had located the problem, the enemy was gone.

Boelcke was withdrawn from combat a few days later, but by June 29, there were eight Halberstadt D.IIs at the front. Two were delivered to *Fl. Abt. 32* by Leutnants Leffers and Franz Diemer, who flew them with the unit's fighter detachment, *Abwehrkommando Nord*. Leffers was probably flying a Halberstadt when he shot down an F.E.2b of No. 11 Squadron over Miraumont on July 9, although Allied witnesses misidentified his plane as a Fokker.

While its maximum speed of 90 mph was no better than that of the Nieuports and D.H.2s it faced, the Halberstadt D.II impressed Germans and Allies alike with its maneuverability and its ability to hold together in a dive better than the Fokker monoplanes and biplanes. A total of 85 were built and the Halberstadt D.II became the backbone of new, specialized German fighter squadrons, or *Jagdstaffeln*, that began to form in August 1916.

Built around the nuclei of KEKs and other Fokker formations, the *Jagdstaffeln*, abbreviated as *Jasta*, increased their fighter complement from the original two to five to anywhere from 10 to 14. The first such unit, *Jasta* 1, was built around KEK B on August 23, led by Hauptmann Martin Zander and equipped with Fokker D.Is and D.IIs.

One day after official formation, *Jasta* 1 chalked up its first success on the 24th, when Offizierstellvertreter Leopold Rudolf Reimann was credited a Sopwith 1-1/2 Strutter east of Metz-en-Couture. The RFC unit he engaged, No. 70 Squadron, actually lost two planes in that action. In one, Captain Robert G. Hopwood and Gunner Charles R. Pearce were killed. The other, crewed by 2nd Lt. Awdry Morris Vaucour and Lieutenant Alan John Bott, was hit by an anti-aircraft shell fragment that set its fuselage fabric on fire. Crawling inside the fuselage, Bott beat out the flames with his gloved hands and tore away the smoldering fabric, then re-emerged from his cockpit to find a German fighter descending on him, gun blazing. Although his engine quit, Vaucour managed to force-land in Allied lines south of Carnoy. Both crewmen were unhurt and Bott received the MC for his quick thinking.

Both Reimann and the surviving crew he attacked in *Jasta* 1's first combat went on to acedom. Vaucour and Bott were credited with two Eindeckers on September 2, followed by a third on September 15, for which Vaucour would receive the MC. "Bunny" Vaucour went on to command No. 45 Squadron in Italy, where he scored four more victories and earned the Distinguished Flying Cross and a bar to his MC before being tragically shot down and killed on July 16, 1918—by an Italian who had misidentified his Sopwith Camel for an enemy plane. Bott subsequently learned to fly and was posted to No. 111 Squadron in Palestine, where he downed enemy two-seaters on April 14 and 15, 1918, but was himself brought down and taken prisoner on the 22nd. Writing of his experiences postwar under the pen-name of Contact, Bott went on to a successful career as a journalist, drama critic, and publisher before his death in 1952.

The second *Jagdstaffel*, which was formed on August 27, came to be a devastatingly more significant addition to the German air service than its predecessor, for its commander was Oswald Boelcke. From Turkey, Boelcke had traveled through Macedonia and Bulgaria, and then off to Kovel in the Ukraine to visit his brother Wilhelm, commanding *Kasta* 10 of *Kagohl* 2. While there, on August 11 Oswald received a most welcome order from Oberstleutnant Leith-Thomsen: "Return to Western Front as quickly as possible to organize and lead *Jagdstaffel* 2 on the Somme Front."

In the course of his travels Boelcke had met a number of young airmen who barraged him with questions on the secret of his success. Amid all the embarrassing hero-worship, the ace made some acquaintances whose combat records or demonstrated spirit impressed him enough to request them for his new unit. This began before he left Kovel with five men from *Kagohl* 2, at least two of whom came with his brother's recommendation. One was Leutnant der Reserve Erwin Böhme, a seasoned, reliable 37-year-old member of *Kasta* 10. The other, from neighboring *Kasta* 8, was a 24-year-old former cavalryman from Silesia who, though not a natural pilot, had shown his mettle over the Eastern and Western fronts, and was keen to make the transition from two-seaters to scouts: Leutnant Manfred Freiherr von Richthofen.

Hauptmann Boelcke established his new unit at Bertincourt, 20 kilometers east of Cambrai. Hauptmann Zander from nearby *Jasta* 1 helped him out by transferring over some mechanics and one of his pilots, 21-year-old Otto Höhne. On September 1, Richthofen reported for duty, along with *Offstv.* Max Müller, a 28-year-old Bavarian with an impressive record in two-seaters and Eindeckers. Also arriving that day was another bit of talent that Boelcke managed to poach from *Jasta* 1—*Offstv.* Reimann, who brought with him a newly delivered fighter that would prove to be another critical factor in *Jasta* 2's success: the Albatros D.I.

Built in the summer of 1916, the Albatros D.I was based on a racing plane developed just before the war by Robert Thelen, supervisor of the Albatros design committee. Although its single-bay, twin-spar wing structure was standard for the time, the D.I featured a streamlined plywood fuselage with a neatly cowled 160-hp Mercedes D.III engine and a spinner over the propeller. Taking advantage of the more powerful engine, Thelen built the new fighter to carry not one, but two synchronized machine guns.

Albatros D.I. 391/16 fell into British hands when the B.E. 2c it was attacking managed to put a lucky bullet through its radiator. Forced to land near Pommier, France, its pilot was taken prisoner and his plane subjected to considerable study. (*National Archives*)

Although the Albatros was not as maneuverable as most of its Allied opponents, German airmen soon decided that they could live with that, considering its superior speed and firepower. Early D.I fliers complained that the upper wing and the trestle-type center-section struts blocked their upward vision, to which Thelen responded by lowering the upper wing and supporting it with outward-splayed N-shaped cabane struts, designating the modified result the D.II. He also subsequently replaced the drag-producing "ear" type radiators on the fuselage sides of the D.I and early D.IIs with a Teeves und Braun radiator installed flush within the center section of the upper wing.

Nimble and viceless though the Halberstadt D.II had been, the Albatros fighters made an even-more dramatic impression. Böhme wrote, "Their climb rate and maneuverability are astonishing; it is as if they were living, feeling beings that understand what their master wishes. With them, one can dare and achieve anything."

As he assembled his hand-picked band of aerial huntsmen, Boelcke indoctrinated them in his tactical dicta, which, significantly, he had been improving upon since June. Simplified for swift memorization, it now went roughly as follows:

Seek advantage before attacking. If possible, keep the sun at your back.

Having begun an attack, always follow through.

Only fire at short range, and only when your opponent is positively in your sights.

Never lose sight of your opponent, and do not be fooled by his tricks.

In every attack it is important to approach your opponent from behind.

If your opponent attacks from above, do not try to evade but fly to meet him.

When over enemy territory, never forget your path home.

For the Staffel—attack on principle in flights of four or six. When single combat ensues, take care that many do not go for one opponent.

It might be noted that this revised list had eliminated reference to following a stricken foe down in item 4, in anticipation of the likelihood of more enemies in the air. On a related note, Boelcke had added instructions for massed attacks and mutual support in item 8. Instead of individuals making piecemeal contributions to overall air superiority, the *Jasta* was now to operate as a team, like soldiers on the ground, mobilized to achieve a collective goal: the annihilation, if possible, of entire enemy formations.

Using one of the first two available Fokker D.IIIs, Boelcke opened his new unit's account on September 2 by bringing down a D.H.2 whose pilot, Captain Robert E. Wilson of No. 32 Squadron, was taken prisoner. Introduced to his famous adversary the next day, Wilson remarked, "If I had to be shot down, I'm pleased that it should have been by so good a man." Boelcke returned the compliment by inviting Wilson for coffee and a tour of Bertincourt aerodrome before he was sent to a POW camp.

Boelcke went on to score another six victories in the Fokkers between September 9 and 15, while training his men for the major actions to come. Five Albatros D.Is and one D.II arrived on the 16th, and while flying a patrol in one of the D.Is later that same afternoon,

Hauptmann Oswald Boelcke, commander of Jasta 2, examines a D.H.2 he brought down intact on September 14, 1916, while Leutnant der Reserve Otto Höhne sits in the nacelle. The British pilot, 2nd Lt. J.V. Bowring of No. 24 Squadron, was wounded and taken prisoner. (*Greg Van Wyngarden*)

Leutnant Höhne brought down an F.E.2b of No. 11 Squadron at Manancourt. The crew, 2nd Lt. A.L. Pinkerton and Lieutenant J.W. Sanders, were taken prisoner.

That solo milestone was merely incidental to what occurred on September 17, when *Jasta* 2's amalgam of leader, men, machines, and tactical doctrine dramatically came together in full, deadly fruition. Leutnant Böhme started the day off at 0745 hours, when he brought down a Sopwith 1-1/2 Strutter of No. 70 Squadron whose pilot, 2nd Lt. Oswald Nixon, was killed and the wounded observer, 2nd Lt. R. Wood, taken prisoner. At 1100, Boelcke led five of his men toward Allied lines and spotted four bomb-laden B.E.2ds of No. 12 Squadron heading for Marcoing railway station under an escort of six F.E.2bs of No. 11 Squadron. Boelcke went to intercept, but the British were already bombing the station when his flight arrived over them. Targeting the higher formation of FEs, Boelcke held back in order to help anyone who got into trouble, while the other five Albatros scouts dived on the pushers.

Acting in perfect accordance with all that had been drilled into their heads in the past several weeks, the Germans broke up the FE formation, then went after lone targets—at that point joined by their commander. Picking out the flight leader, Boelcke quickly forced it down at Equancourt where the crew, Captain D.B. Gray and Lieutenant L.B. Helder, managed to set their F.E.2b afire before being captured. At about the same time, 1135, Leutnant Hans Reimann—no relation to his *Staffel*-mate Rudolf Reimann—forced F.E.2b 4844 down south of Trescault, where 2nd Lt. T.P.L. Molloy and Sergeant G.J. Morton became "guests of the Kaiser."

A third F.E.2b, 7018, was attacked by Richthofen, who reported afterward:

> I singled out the last machine and fired several times at closest range [10 meters]. Suddenly the enemy propeller stood stock still. The machine went down gliding and followed until I had killed the observer who had not stopped shooting until the last moment.
>
> Now my opponent went downwards in sharp curves. At approximately 1,200 meters a second German machine came along and attacked my victim down to the ground and then landed next to the English plane.

Also landing to inspect his first of an eventual 80 victims, Richthofen found the observer, 21-year-old 2nd Lt. Tom Rees, was indeed dead. The pilot, 19-year-old 2nd Lt. Lionel B.F. Morris, died before the ambulance could get him to Cambrai hospital.

As the British tried to make their way westward they encountered what would become another soon-to-be-frequent part of running the gauntlet home: being jumped by a second *Staffel* drawn to the scene of action. This was *Jasta* 4, formed on August 25 from KEK Vaux under the command of Oberleutnant Hans-Joachim Buddecke, now based at Roupy and equipped with Halberstadt D.IIs. In consequence a fourth F.E.2b, 6994, of 11 Squadron became Leutnant Wilhelm Frankl's 12th victory, Sergeant J.E. Glover being killed and the pilot, 2nd Lt. H. Thompson, dying of his wounds soon after.

That night, a German army tradition was broken and a new air force tradition established when enlisted men were permitted to join the officers in *Jasta* 2's *Kasino* to celebrate. Amid the festivities,

Members of Jasta 2 pose before Leutnant Manfred von Richthofen's Albatros D.II 391/16. From left: Boelcke's successor as Staffelführer, Oberleutnant Stefan Kirmaier, Leutnant Hans Imelmann, Richthofen, and Leutnant Hans Wortmann. (*Greg Van Wyngarden*)

Boelcke pinned the Iron Cross First Class on Böhme. Richthofen, who had already received that decoration, wrote a letter that evening to a jeweler in Berlin, ordering a plain silver cup, two inches high and one inch wide, on which was to be inscribed: "1.Vickers 2. 17.9.16."

On the other side of the lines, at No. 11 Squadron's aerodrome at Izel-le-Hameau, Fred Libby, who had shared two of his then-six victories with Richthofen's first victims, lamented, "This morning Boelcke and his crew went into action on our C Flight... I knew it was too good to last, for the last few times we have been over, Price and I have had no action. Now with Mr. Boelcke in his new and faster machines, we will really catch hell."

At the same time that the Albatros D.II's introduction in concert with the Dicta Boelcke was heralding a new reversal of fortune over the Somme front, the French were introducing a more advanced fighter of their own. The first Spad VIIs represented a synergistic combination of engine and airframe that would dominate the *chasse* arm for the rest of the war.

The Spad VII's serendipitous evolution began with the dissolution of the *Societé provisoire des aéroplanes Deperdussin* and its resurrection in August 1914 as the *Societé anonyme pour l'Aviation et ses dérivés*, still retaining the original company acronym. In its new incarnation, Spad also retained Deperdussin's talented designer, Louis Béchereau.

Among Béchereau's first wartime designs was the Spad SA.1, on which he had tried quite literally to find a way around the problem of firing a machine gun past the propeller arc, by placing a gunner in a pulpit held by means of struts in front of the propeller and its 80-hp Le Rhône 9C rotary engine. Introduced late in 1915, the SA.1 was succeeded by the SA.2 with a 110-hp Le Rhône 9J engine and the SA.4 which reverted to the 80-hp Le Rhône 9C due to cooling problems, and which featured ailerons only on the upper wing, rather than on both like its predecessors. All of them proved to be more terrifying to their front gunners, who stood little chance of survival in the event of a noseover upon landing, than to the enemy. The last of the Spad SA types were out of French service by May 1916, although as many as 67 were in Russian service until as late as June 1917.

Spad's two-seat fighter was a failure, but removal of the gunner's pulpit revealed a sound basic airframe. On June 4, 1915, Béchereau applied for a patent for the plane's single-bay wing cellule, which featured intermediate struts of narrow chord, to which the bracing wires were attached at the midpoint. That arrangement added strength and, by reducing vibration in the wires, reduced drag as well.

Béchereau's next fighter, the Spad SG, was essentially a single-seat SA.4 that replaced the gunner's pulpit with a remotely controlled Hotchkiss machine gun in a sizeable nacelle mounted in front of the propeller. Evaluated in April 1916, it too was swiftly rejected, but in the meantime Béchereau had altered the airframe to use the newly developed 140-hp Hispano-Suiza 8A engine. This eight-cylinder water-cooled marvel, featuring an aluminum block, had been developed in 1915 by Swiss engineer Marc Birkigt in 1915, and promised an outstanding power-to-weight ratio. It also proved readily adaptable to the new interrupter gear, a version of which Birkigt

An early Spad VII flown by Capitaine Jean Derode, the commander of N. 102 *"Eclipse de Soleil,"* at Villeselve in 1917. Note the yellow and reddish-orange colors of the unit insignia decorating the cowling and vertical stabilizer. Derode scored seven victories— four with N. 102—before being killed in action while commanding Spa. 99, on June 4, 1918.

had fabricated and incorporated into his design to fire a single .30-caliber Vickers machine gun.

Originally designated the Spad SH, the prototype had a large conical spinner in front of a circular radiator and underwent flight testing in March 1916. The spinner was soon abandoned but its rounded radiator shell was retained. A further development, using a 150-hp Hispano-Suiza 8Aa engine that was designated the Spad 5, underwent flight evaluation in July, reportedly reaching a speed of 170 kilometers per hour and climbing to 3,000 meters in nine minutes. Already impressed with its fundamental design, the *Aéronautique Militaire* had already placed an order for 268 aircraft on May 10. The final production variant was officially designated the Spad 7.C1 (the 'C1' indicating that it was a single-seat *chasseur*), although it was more commonly known as the Spad VII.

Lieutenant Armand Pinsard, commander of N.26, is alleged to have been allocated Spad VII S122 as early as August 23. Pinsard's principal claim to fame until then had been the result of his having been forced down in German territory on February 8, 1915, spending almost 14 months as a prisoner of war, then escaping with

Capitaine Victor Menard on March 26, 1916, and crossing the lines to safety on April 10. Pinsard scored his first victory of a total of 27 on November 1, 1916, and would subsequently serve as commander of N.78 and Spa.23, surviving the war as an *Officier de la Légion d'Honneur*, along with the *Croix de Guerre* with 19 palms and the British Military Cross.

Sergent Paul Sauvage of N.65 had three previous victories to his credit when he received Spad VII S112 on September 2. He scored his fourth on the 23rd, and his fifth on October 2, followed by a sixth on November 2. A Rumpler fell to his guns on December 10, and on the 27th he downed an Albatros over Moronvillers. Called *"le benjamin des As"* because of his youth, Sauvage was killed by an exploding anti-aircraft shell 20 miles east of Maissonette on January 7, 1917—one month short of his 20th birthday. Adjutant Maxime Lenoir of N.23 received Spad VII S116, but before he could add to his 11 victories he was shot down and killed on October 23.

Apart from those piecemeal issuances, the allocation of Spad VII S115 to N.3 on September 2 had the greatest impact on the new fighter's future, for it was assigned to the escadrille's leading ace, Sous-Lieutenant Georges Guynemer. Two days after receiving it, he shot down an Aviatik C.II over Heyencourt, killing Leutnants Hans Steiner and Otto Fresenius of *Kasta 37*, for his 15th victory.

On September 23, Guynemer downed two Fokkers, plus a third that went unconfirmed, within five minutes, but as he returned over the lines at an altitude of 3,000 meters, his new plane was hit by a 75mm shell fired by nervous French anti-aircraft gunners. With the water reservoir shattered and fabric torn away from his left upper wing, Guynemer spun down, but he managed to regain control at about 180 meters and crash-landed in a shell hole, emerging with a cut knee and a slight concussion. "Only the fuselage was left, but it was intact," he wrote his father. "The Spad is solid, with another [plane], I would now be thinner than this piece of paper."

Completely sold on the new fighter, Guynemer recovered from his painful injuries well enough to return to action in a replacement Spad, S132, on September 25. Another endorsement for the fighter came that same day when Lieutenant Alfred Heurteaux, a squadron

As he recrossed the lines after scoring two victories on September 23, 1916, Sous-Lieutenant Georges Guynemer's Spad VII S115 was struck by a 75mm shell fired by nervous French anti-aircraft gunners. Crash-landing in a shell hole, Guynemer was sold on the new fighter as he wrote his father, "The Spad is solid, with another [plane], I would now be thinner than this piece of paper." (SHAA B88.475)

mate of Guynemer's who had received Spad S113, claimed a "Fokker" over Villers Carbonnel, whose dead pilot turned out to be Kurt Wintgens, then serving in *Jasta* 1 and who had brought his own tally up to 19 just the day before. Although wounded often enough to be nicknamed "The Bullet Catcher," Heurteaux survived the war as a *Chevalier de la Légion d'Honneur* with 21 victories.

Other N.3 members would add significantly to their scores in Spads once they learned to play its strengths. While not as maneuverable as the Nieuport 17, the Spad VII handled well enough to hold its own in a dogfight. More important, it could dive at very high speeds for the time without fear of its wing structure succumbing to the strain.

Although not the tactical theoretician that Boelcke was, Guynemer became highly influential as both an advocate and a critic of the Spad, persuading Béchereau and his design team to keep improving what he regarded as a fundamentally sound design. Aside from having one synchronized machine gun when the Germans were introducing twin weapons, principal complaints that Guynemer and his colleagues had for the the Spad VII concerned its unreliable cooling system and the need for more power. Spad experimented with a variety of radiator arrangements before finally devising a workable one that involved a row of slats that could be adjusted to accommodate the temperatures in different seasons and altitudes. The question of performance was answered when Marc Birkigt increased the compression ratio of his Hispano-Suiza motor from 4.7 to 5.3, and the resulting output from 150 to 180 horsepower. The first Spad VII to be powered by the new 8Ab engine, S254, was presented to Guynemer in mid-December 1916. Not only did he score 19 victories in that plane, but he never changed the engine—a tribute to both its reliability and to the *méchaniciens* who maintained it, often joined in their labors by former mechanic Guynemer himself. Fortunately for posterity, the doubly historic S254 survived combat and decades of retirement, to eventually be restored and displayed at the *Musée de l'Air et l'Espace* at Le Bourget.

About 3,500 Spad VIIs were built in total, and at one time or other were flown by aces of France, Britain, Russia, Italy, and the United States, as well as André Bosson and Jacques Roques, two Swiss aces flying for the French, and the 10-victory Belgian ace Edmond Thieffry. Even after the twin-gun Spad XIII superseded it as France's main fighter, the 180-hp Spad VII remained in first-line service, still able to hold its own, until the end of the war. French fighter pilots were still training in them as late as 1928.

While the first *Jagdstaffeln* were challenging the RFC's dominance over the Somme front, a remarkable joint air raid against a German industrial target put fighters to the test in two capacities: both intercepting bombers and escorting them. It originated at Luxeuil-les-Bains, where French *Groupe de Bombardement* 4, commanded by Capitaine Maurice Happe, had been joined in June by 3 Wing, RNAS, equipped with Sopwith 1-1/2 Strutters, in the form of both single-seat bombers and two-seat fighters to escort them, as well as Breguet-Michelin V pushers purchased from the French.

The first to use the 180-hp Hispano-Suiza 8Ab engine that kept it viable throughout the war, Spad VII S254 was used by Lieutenant Georges Guynemer to score 19 of his victories without an engine change and is currently preserved at the Musée de l'Air et l'Espace at Le Bourget. (*Jon Guttman*)

By August 1916, four *groupes de bombardement* were striking at targets such as Ludwigshafen, Mannheim, Pechebronn, and Dillingen in the heavily industrialized Saar valley and even the Rhine. As aerial opposition increased, Happe developed a V-shaped formation to concentrate defensive fire against intercepting Fokker and Pfalz Eindeckers.

Then on September 14, N.124 was ordered back to Luxeuil from Behonne. By then *l'Escadrille Américaine* had fought 146 combats and was credited with 13 victories, for the loss of one pilot killed and three wounded. One reason for N.124's return to its old aerodrome was to provide escort to the French bombers in the operation to come.

On the 19th the Americans began exchanging their worn-out *Bébés* for Nieuport 17s. During that time also, while on a three-day leave in Paris, they had acquired a new mascot in the form of a four-month-old lion cub that they named Whiskey. Operations from Luxeuil resumed on a tragic note, when Sergent Kiffin Rockwell was killed while attacking an Albatros two-seater over Rodern on September 23. On October 10, however, Adjutant Norman Prince shot down a Fokker over Altkirch, probably killing Unteroffizier Julius Heck of KEK 5.

On October 12, Happe combined his
French and British assets for a raid on the
Mauser arms factory at Oberndorf-am-
Neckar, which lay 175 kilometers from
Luxeuil. GB.4 was then comprised of F.29,
F.123 and B.M.120. F.123's Farman 40
and 42 bombers were supplemented by 12
new Sopwiths, but only one of the latter
would escort them to the target. B.M.120's
Breguets were to be escorted by four
Nieuport 17s from N.124, with Lieutenant
de Laage leading Adjutant Lufbery,
Adjutant Prince and Sergent Didier
Masson. The bombers would be aloft for
five hours, more than double the
Nieuports' duration, so the latter were to fly
ahead and land at an advance airfield at
Corcieux to refuel before proceeding to—
and later returning from—the target.

Leutnant der Reserve Otto
Kissenberth of KEK Ensisheim,
photographed here with a
Pfalz E.I, was flying Fokker
D.II 540/16 when he was
credited with three victories
during the Oberndorf raid on
October 12, 1916. (Jon
Guttman)

Also participating in the strike would be two flights each of single-
seat Sopwith bombers from Blue and Red squadrons of 3 Wing,
escorted by seven Sopwith two-seaters. In addition to the total of 62
aircraft slated to bomb Oberndorf, 18 Caudron G.4s of C.61 were to
mount a diversionary raid on Lörrach to the south, though only four
actually carried out the mission.

Dense cloud cover over the Black Forest delayed the raid until just
after noon, but at 1315 the first of six Farmans from F.29 and six of
F.123 took off, followed at 1345 by seven Breguet IVs of B.M.120
and one Breguet V seconded to that unit from the British. Two
Farmans apiece from F.29 and F.123 dropped out with mechanical
problems and a fifth F.123 plane, struck by anti-aircraft fire, force-
landed in Allied territory in the Vosges Mountains.

At 1340, the first of 26 Sopwiths and Breguets from 3 Wing began
taking off. One of the Sopwith two-seaters was flown by the wing's
commander, Richard Bell-Davies, who had received the Victoria
Cross for rescuing a downed comrade in Bulgaria on November 19,

1915. Four Sopwiths had to turn back with engine trouble and a fifth crashed at Faucogney 25 minutes after takeoff.

Astride the raiders' route lay Colmar-Nord aerodrome, from which Bavarian *Flieger Abteilung* 9 operated six Ago C.I two-seat, twin-boom pusher biplanes, with a small fighter component, KEK Ensisheim, based south of that aerodrome. Farther south, at Habsheim, were *Fl. Abt.* 48 and the former KEK Habsheim, now redesignated *Jasta* 15. At 1504 hours the operations room at Colmar received a telephone call that five enemy planes were flying east from Gebweiler. Suspecting its own aerodrome to be the target, *Fl.Abt.*9b scrambled up all of its planes, including three Fokker D.IIs from KEK Ensisheim, flown by Leutnant Otto Kissenberth and Vizefeldwebels Ludwig Hanstein and Ludwig Hilz. While they climbed to intercept the raiders, a confusing succession of follow-up reports reached Colmar-Nord: seven enemy planes coming from Hilsenfirst to the east; 12 from Gebweiler to Ensisheim; five from Ensisheim to Neuf Breisach; 10 from Buchenkopf to the southeast; 15 from Thann to the northeast.

Happe's four F.29 Farmans, at the vanguard of the aerial procession, slipped past the defenses, dropped their bombs on Oberndorf unopposed and returned to Luxeuil safely, with one of his crews claiming a Fokker. As F.123's three Farmans flew over the forest between Neuf Breisach and Colmar, however, they were attacked from behind by Kissenberth and Hilz. Kissenberth shot the leading Farman down into the woods near Bidensolen, where its exploding bombs sent a funeral pyre 100 meters into the air for crewmen Adjutant Henri Baron and Sergent André Guerineau. Kissenberth next attacked Sous-Lieutenant Armand Georges and Sergent Ernest Jouan, whose Farman fell over on one wing and crashed near the Breisach-Freiburg railroad.

Out of ammunition and almost out of fuel, Kissenberth landed at *Flugpark* Neuf Breisach and phoned in his first combat report. It is possible that his retirement was mistaken for the downing of "an altogether small two-seater biplane of a type absolutely new," credited to Brigadier Jean Pierre de Gaillard de la Valdène and Caporal Pichon in F.123's Sopwith escort. Gaillard's description also suggests, however, that his opponent may have been a Fokker D.II of *Jasta* 15 whose pilot, Vizefeldwebel Ernst Udet, had installed a dummy rear gunner of sheet metal on the fuselage decking to discourage enemy planes from getting on his tail. In any event, neither German pilot was actually shot down, as B.M.120 would soon discover.

Red Squadron of 3 Wing bombed Oberndorf, but its nine Sopwiths then came under attack by German fighters, including Kissenberth and Hilz, who had taken off again after replenishing their fuel and ammunition. Kissenberth engaged a two-seater Sopwith that put up a spirited fight until its ammunition ran out. The Sopwith's engine was damaged but its Canadian pilot, Flight Sub-Lieutenant Raymond Collishaw, managed to limp back to Luxeuil. Kissenberth landed at Freiburg, where he was joined by two other aircraft— Hanstein's Fokker and one of the Sopwith bombers! Hanstein had wounded the Sopwith's Canadian pilot, Flight Sub-Lieutenant Charles H.S. Butterworth, in the neck and drove him down in tight circles until he landed at the parade field outside Freiburg.

Red Squadron's other eight Sopwiths returned safely, but the worst ordeal of the mission lay in store for B.M.120. Things began on a fairly encouraging note. While waiting to rendezvous with B.M.120's eight Breguets, N.124's pilots engaged four Fokker E.IIIs north of Colmar, one being credited to Prince. With N.124 guarding their flanks, the bombers flew on, but as they emerged from the Vosges to the southwest, *Jasta* 15 scrambled up several fighters to intercept them. Among the Germans was Ernst Udet, who wrote of the action after the war:

> Because it flew directly under me, it was easy work. I dropped down past the Nieuports, placed myself in a safe position behind the leading machine and, with 350 shots, forced it to land. It landed intact, and in order to prevent the occupants from destroying it, I landed beside it. Because my tires were punctured by shots, I turned over, but without serious consequences. It was a comical picture; the vanquished landed upright and the victor landed upside-down. Both Frenchmen clambered down and we shook hands all around.

Udet's victim was a Breguet IV whose nacelle was marked with a black and white checkered square and the ironic legend, 'Le Voilá le Foudroyant' (Behold the thunderer). After making a dead-stick landing at Rüstenhart with all their bombs still on the racks, Caporal Lucien Barlet and Soldat Luneau were elated to be alive, even if they would spend the next two years as POWs.

Three of *Fl. Abt.* 9b's Ago C.Is tried to intercept the bombers over Freiburg, but F.29 and F.123 had already passed over that city by the time they arrived. Leutnant Walther Kiliani then directed his pilot, Leutnant Hans Hartl, to turn west, where the Agos ran right into B.M.120. Kiliani and Hartl joined a *Jasta* 15 pilot, Leutnant Otto Pfälzer, in forcing down a Breguet near Bremgarten. Upon landing nearby, Kiliani tried to cut some tricoloured fabric for a souvenir, but was warned off by crewmen Sergent Nöel Bouet and Caporal Delcroix, who had already set their plane on fire. Shortly afterward, the Breguet's bombs went off.

Amid the confusion of the running fight, Ago crew Leutnants Georg Pfleiderer and Alois Simson found themselves under attack by an Aviatik from *Fl. Abt.* 48, which fortunately caused no damage before its crew realized its error and peeled off. Hilz singled out a Breguet and shot it down in flames over Umkirch, killing Caporal Robert de Montais and Soldat André Haas. Ago crew Vizefeldwebel Ertl and Leutnant Biedermann engaged another Breguet in a running fight along the Elzacher valley until Biedermann's ammunition ran out. The crew was probably Caporaux Tanner and Viaris de Lesogne, who reportedly were "violently attacked by a twin-fuselage enemy" near Emmendingen. They survived and Happe credited them with bringing down an Aviatik.

N.124 had hardly been idle. After firing 50 rounds at an Aviatik, Masson turned on a Fokker, only to see his engine sputter and die— his fuel tank had been punctured. As Masson tried to glide home, his intended victim got on his tail, shooting up his upper wing and fuselage, his windscreen and instrument panel. The German came on too fast, however, and zoomed under the Nieuport. Masson banked and emptied his machine gun into the Fokker, which spun earthward until he lost sight of it one mile west of Neuf Briesach. Resuming his glide, Masson cleared the Rhine under fire from the German infantry, so low that his wheels barely cleared the French barbed wire before he landed in a shell hole. Masson got clear of his plane just before German artillery demolished it.

Only four Breguets reached the target area to release their bombs. During the return flight Lufbery was credited with shooting down a Roland C.II over Schlettstadt. De Laage fired at a Fokker that was attacking a Breguet at the rear of the formation, but did not feel sure enough of the outcome to request confirmation.

The engine of the Breguet flown by *Maréchal-des-Logis* Léon Mottay and Caporal Marchand quit and they crash landed at the Haslach-Offenburg railway near Steinbach. Marchand was killed and the injured Mottay was taken prisoner. They were probably credited to Leutnant Kurt Haber of *Jasta* 15.

Elsewhere, Davies led Blue Squadron's Breguets through flak and drove off some German aircraft that made some desultory attacks on his tight formation. "We cleared the Black Forest and presently a small town appeared ahead," he reported. "It did not look like Oberndorf, but the bombers seemed quite sure it was. They got into a single line and went down to bomb."

As the returning British column crossed the Rhine Valley at about sunset, Davies saw a Breguet go down. Although he saw no enemy planes, the Germans reported that Pfleiderer and Simson, returning to Colmar, encountered a homeward-bound Breguet and fired into its nacelle. At that point they were joined by Kissenberth, who loosed a burst into the motor. The British gunner shot away one of Kissenberth's interplane struts, but his wing held up and he attacked again, spewing lead into the Breguet's cowling while Simson hit its gunner from below. The Breguet V came down near Oberenzen, and Pfleiderer and Simson landed to take the pilot, Flight Sub-Lieutenant Rockey, and his badly wounded bombardier, Gunlayer Sturdee, prisoners. Back at Colmar-Nord, Kissenberth was also credited with the bomber—his third for the day. Another British Breguet V was brought down over Buggingen by flak with Gunlayer Vitty mortally wounded and its pilot, Flight Sub-Lieutenant Newman, taken prisoner.

As damaged planes and wounded crews straggled back toward Luxeuil, the only F.123 Farman to bomb Oberndorf crash-landed in the Vosges, injuring its pilot, Caporal Henri Tondu. The three remaining Breguets of B.M.120, unable to find their way in the darkness, landed in some flat country to the northwest. One of 3 Wing's Breguets crashed at Buc and a Sopwith was similarly wrecked at Corbenay, but the British reported no crew casualties.

By the time the *Escadrille Américaine*'s Nieuports returned to Corcieux, darkness had fallen and oil fires were lit on the field to guide them in. Lufbery's plane bounced to a safe landing. Prince, following him at a lower altitude, caught his landing gear on a utility cable and crashed. Thrown from the cockpit with two broken legs and internal injuries, Prince was rushed to the hospital at Gerardmer, but a blood clot developed in his brain and he died on the 15th.

The Oberndorf raid was a sprawling air battle by 1916 standards and is all the more remarkable for the noteworthy participants from both sides. Jean Pierre de Gaillard de la Valdène's claims were his second or third, to which he would add two more as a fighter pilot in Spa.95. Ray Collishaw would eventually account for 60 enemy planes flying Sopwith Pups, Triplanes and Camels.

On the German side, Ludwig Hanstein went on to serve in *Jasta* 16 and command *Jasta* 35b until he was killed in action, shortly after scoring his 16th victory, on March 21, 1918. Kurt Haber's fifth victory was also his last, before transferring to *Jasta* 3 and being killed over Péronne on December 20, 1916, by Charles Nungesser. Ernst Udet's somewhat embarrassing victory was the second of an eventual 62. The day's star performer, Otto Kissenberth, went on to serve in *Jasta* 16 and command *Jasta* 23b, surviving the war with 19 victories.

As for the volunteers of N.124, Oberndorf added more triumph and tragedy to their legend. Masson, miraculously unscathed, was awarded a *Croix de Guerre* with palm that acknowledged the outstanding circumstances attending his only confirmed victory: "Accomplished his mission to the finish, despite fuel exhaustion which befell him over German lines and forced him to return by volplaning." Lufbery's victory had been his fifth, making him the first

American pilot to make ace and earning him another palm for his
Croix de Guerre.

What, however, had the raiders accomplished for the loss of 15
planes and 21 airmen? The Allies initially claimed to have dropped
four tons of bombs on the Mauser plant and shot down six enemy aircraft. The Germans reported that 60 bombs fell on or around
Oberndorf, killing three people and injuring seven, but that no significant damage was done and work at the Mauser plant had not been
interrupted. "No German machine was lost," their report concluded,
"and no aeronaut was killed or wounded in the action." That was a
slight exaggeration, for Unteroffizier August Büchner of *Fl. Abt.* 6b
was severely wounded that day. Later intelligence reports confirmed
Davies's suspicions—his six Breguets had bombed Donaueschingen,
rather than Oberndorf.

Analyzing lessons learned from the raid, the French concluded:

(1.) The bad quality of the aeroplanes or engines on the
series F.XLII (130 hp Renault engine).

(2) The difficulty for the Sopwith aeroplanes to get a proper
formation in the clouds.

Finally, other long distance raids can be foreseen without
very great losses when the Squadrons F.29, F.123 and
B.M.120 are transformed into Sopwith Squadrons which
will raid in conjunction with the English Aviation.

Until sufficient Sopwiths could be made available, the French
resorted to bombing at night, while the British did so by day. That
strategy—which would be revived by the British and Americans in
World War II—enjoyed more success, but not for long. Generals Haig
and Trenchard believed long-distance bombing only diverted aircraft
from more productive front-line tasks, so 3 Wing was disbanded,
reorganized, re-equipped with Sopwith Pups and redesignated No. 3
Squadron, RNAS.

Oberndorf also demonstrated the importance of fighters, both as
interceptors, which the Germans had used with such devastating
effect, and as escorts like N.124's Nieuports or 3 Wing's Sopwith

A Caudron R.4. Capitaine Didier Lecour-Grandmaison and his aircrews of C.46 made aggressive use of this twin-engine reconnaissance plane, reviving the multi-seat fighter concept. (*SHAA B83.5643*)

two-seaters. This aspect—which would be critical to the success or failure of bombing campaigns in the next world conflict—led to a continuing evolution of the escort. That, in turn created an emphasis on endurance and the need for a doctrine to protect bombers or long-range reconnaissance planes. These requirements differed from those of the front-line scout, whose pilot only had to concern himself with achieving air superiority relatively close to home.

October 1916 saw the debut of an additional candidate for the role, when the first Caudron R.4 arrived at *Escadrille* C.47 and another five were delivered to S.A.L. (*Section Artillerie Lourde*, or heavy artillery section) 210. The brothers Gaston and René Caudron had been prominent aircraft producers before the war, primarily influenced by Gaston's infatuation with the Wright Brothers, which inspired him to produce airplanes such as the single-engine G.3 and France's first twin-engine airplane, the G.4, with latticework-supported tail surfaces in spite of the fact that their tractor propellers made such an arrangement unnecessary. Notwithstanding their quaintly passé configuration, both planes performed and handled surprisingly well. The G.3 was soon relegated to the training role, but the G.4 was used as a reconnaissance plane and bomber well into 1917, and was aggressively—and sometimes successfully—used in air-to-air combat by future aces such as Jean Chaput, René Dorme, André Martenot de Cordoux, René Fonck and Viktor Federov. As it became clear that the G.4's fundamental design produced too much drag and precluded an effective defense against attacks from the rear for it to have a future, Gaston Caudron produced a variant with a conventional fuselage, the G.6. Hard to control and prone to fall into spins, the G.6 was never as popular as the G.4.

Meanwhile, René Caudron had been working on a twin-engine bomber design of his own, with a pilot situated between two observer-gunners, each manning twin .30-caliber Lewis guns on swivel mountings. After testing it, the *Service Fabrication Aéronautique* placed a production order on the R.4 on November 21, 1915. The prototype proved to be underpowered, but the SFA thought that would be less of a problem if it was used in the reconnaissance role, without a bomb load. Tragedy struck on December 10, when Gaston Caudron fatally crashed while test flying the prototype. An investigation traced the cause to wing spar failure near the central portion. Henri Potez aided in rectifying that flaw and the redesigned R.4, powered by either 130-hp Renault 12Db or 150-hp Hispano-Suiza 8A engines, got its delayed approval for production.

Although its speed seldom exceeded 80 mph, the Caudron R.4's 3-hour endurance made it quite successful in the long-range reconnaissance role. Its robust airframe stood up well under attack and its gunners became quite proficient at fending off or shooting down their assailants. When C.46 was fully re-equipped with R.4s its commander, Capitaine Didier Lecour-Grandmaison, encouraged his crews to engage any enemy planes they encountered as if they were flying three-seat fighters. By March 1917, the escadrille, redesignated R.46, was credited with 19 victories—more than a good many single-seat units— and several of its pilots and gunners, including Lecour-Grandmaison, had attained ace status. That astonishing record would lead to the development of further twin-engine reconnaissance planes, such as the Letord 1, 3 and 5, and the Caudron R.11. And it would plant the germ of an idea for using such "flying fortresses" as bomber escorts in the heads of French air service officers.

While the debate over long-range escort fighters had just begun, the French air service saw no reason to question the effectiveness of Tricornot de Rose's gathering of Nieuport units into a provisional *Groupe des Escadrilles de Chasse* to cancel out the Fokkers' technological edge over Verdun, or of the similar success enjoyed by Capitaine Félix Antonin Gabriel Brocard's collection of N.3, N.26, N.37, N.62, N.65, N.67, N.73, and N.103 into the provisional *Groupement de Combat de la Somme* in support of the British offensive. On October 4, the French high command took the next logical step by creating three permanent *Groupes de Combat*, which would allow four to five *escadrilles de chasse* to be deployed wherever along the front they might be needed in the future. Officially formed on November 1, these first of many such groups were: GC.11, consisting of N.12, N.31, N.48, and N.57 under the overall leadership of Chef d'Escadron Auguste le Révérend; GC.12 under Chef de Bataillon Brocard, comprising N.3, N.26, N.73, and N.103; and GC.13, commanded by Capitaine Philippe Féquant, made up of N.65, N.67, N.112, and N.124.

From that point on, two factors would make GC.12 one of the most renowned flying formations of World War I. In the months that followed, the group would adopt a common identifying insignia, each being a variation on N.3's stork in different attitudes of flight, whose habit of nesting in the chimney tops of Alsace-Lorraine symbolized France's determination to liberate that region from German occupation. The other factor was that the group would shoot down more enemy planes, and concentrate more heroes and top-scoring aces within its rolls, than any comparable fighter organization in the *Aéronautique Militaire*.

Notoriety of another sort had accumulated around N.124, whose fighting record, dramatic deeds, and colorful characters had made it both a persuasive propaganda tool for winning American sympathy for the French cause and an embarrassment to President Woodrow Wilson's administration, which was then still striving to keep the United States out of the war. One upshot of this was a plea from the U.S. Secretary of State, yielding to German diplomatic protests regarding the presence of an *"Escadrille Américaine"* in the French ranks, for them to cease referring to it by that sobriquet. On November16, the French acquiesced, ordering N.124 to use the more generic *Escadrille des Volontaires*. The Americans found that name too dull, but their organizer, Dr. Edmund Gros, came up with a more emotive one, referring to the young French marquis who in 1777 had volunteered to fight in General George Washington's Continental Army, and went on to influence his country's decision to recognize and assist the newborn United States in its War for Independence. On December 6, N.124 was officially renamed *l'Escadrille Lafayette*. Under that metaphoric title, the fighter squadron became an even more influential propaganda tool for the French and Allied causes—and as such, carved itself a permanent niche among the many legends of the first air war.

While the French fighter force was undergoing its change in organization, October 1916 also saw the German army air service undergo a change in name, from *Fliegertruppe* to *Luftstreitkräfte*. Further changes in organization were in store for it as well, but as far as the *Jagdflieger* were concerned the most significant change that month lay in a general resurgence of their air power, made possible by the Albatros D.II, combined with the wide adoption of Boelcke's tactical dicta. *Jasta* 2 had become the vanguard of this resurrection of aerial supremacy, but its success did not go unchallenged—least of all by the D.H.2 pilots of No. 24 Squadron.

Although Major Hawker's command responsibilities had reduced his own opportunities to score a single confirmed victory since his unit commenced operations, a number of aces had emerged from 24's ranks, including Lieutenant Patrick Anthony Langan-Byrne, a 21-year-old Irishman from Clopherhead, County Leith, who had transferred to the RFC from the Royal Artillery. The 10 victories he scored in little more than a month and a half were impressive, but closer scrutiny reveals a rather lax British standard for crediting such

D.H.2 5925 sits disarmed for training duties at Brooklands, still displaying remnants of its A Flight wheel and interplane strut markings. Assigned to No. 24 Squadron from February 1916 to May 1917, this remarkable veteran was used by several aces, including Lieutenant Patrick A. Langan-Byrne on October 16 1916, 2nd Lt. Eric C. Pashley on November 3, 2nd Lt. Kelvin Crawford on November 22, 1916 and April 2, 1917, and Lieutenant Robert H. M. S. Saundby on November 23, 1916. (*Greg Van Wyngarden*)

successes that resulted in tallies that did not match actual enemy losses—and in consequence could deceive the British as to how well its men and machines were doing. His first victory was recorded as "forced to land" on August 31, and his second, on September 2, was "OOC" or "out of control," which could mean a dead or disabled pilot, shot-away control wires or, just as likely, an enemy escaping by feigning such a plight, only to pull out near the ground and fly safely home.

Langan-Byrne's next two were a scout "destroyed in flames" on September 15 and a Fokker D.II "destroyed" on the 16th, although the Germans reported no casualties on either day. Langan-Byrne's next five victories—an LVG on the 21st, two enemy planes on the 22nd, a Rumpler C.I on the 23rd, and an LVG on the 28th, were all described as "forced to land." Although they made encouraging moral victories, the British would soon cease counting "forced to land" as confirmed victories when they realized that it made little or no real impact on enemy strength—as Langan-Byrne himself would soon find out.

Jasta 2 had already had its first run-ins with No. 24 Squadron. The first telling clash occurred over Thiepval on September 9, in which Lieutenant Manfield, who with "Jock" Andrews had given Max Immelmann such a difficult time back in April, was shot down and killed by Hauptmann Boelcke. In a clash on September 14, 24 Squadron's Lieutenant Arthur Gerald Knight and Sergeant Stanley Cockerell were jointly credited with a Fokker D.II in flames, but the Germans suffered no casualties, whereas 2nd Lt. J.V. Bowring was brought down wounded and taken prisoner—victory No. 24 for Boelcke.

Moderate activity at the start of October flared up on the 10th, with D.H.2s being claimed by three of Boelcke's comrades. Leutnant Böhme claimed one east of Longueval at 0950 that morning whose pilot, 2nd Lt. Maximillian J.J.G. Mare-Mortembault of No. 32 Squadron, reported being chased along the Bapaume-Albert road before coming down in British lines, but survived unhurt. Offizierstellvertreter Max Müller scored his first victory near Vraucourt at 1100, 2nd Lt. N. Middlebrook of No. 24 Squadron being taken prisoner. Hauptmann Zander of *Jasta* 1 also downed a D.H.2 at Beugny at 1730 hours for his fifth victory, but his D.H.2 also force landed in British lines near Meaulte, Sergeant Cockerell emerging wounded but alive. Boelcke himself was involved in a fight with F.E.2bs of No. 11 Squadron, during which 2nd Lt. R. P. Harvey and Lieutenant Fred Libby were credited with an Albatros OOC. *Jasta* 2 lost no men, however, while Boelcke sent another two 11 Squadron crewmen to their deaths in flames. Leutnant Richthofen also claimed a "Vikkers" over Roeux at 1800 hours, but that F.E.2b of No. 25 Squadron, whose pilot was killed and the observer wounded and taken prisoner, was disputed and ultimately credited to a two-seater crew of *Fl. Abt.* 22.

On October 16, Langan-Byrne, who by then had been awarded the Distinguished Service Order and had been put in command of B Flight, forced an Albatros D. I to land for his 10th official victory. *Jasta* 2 had a more fruitful day, however, as Boelcke and Rudolph Reimann destroyed BEs in the early afternoon and Richthofen scored his fifth victory, a B.E.12 of No. 19 Squadron, at 1700 hours.

The latter, a single-seat scout version of the B.E.2c, proved no better able to dogfight an Albatros than its notorious two-seat progenitor, and was soon relegated to the bombing role before being withdrawn from the Western Front altogether.

Soon after that fight, Boelcke reported, "We ran into a squadron of six Vickers single-seaters south of Bapaume at 1745 hours. We went into some fine turns. The English leader, with streamers on his machine, came just right for me. I settled him with my first attack—apparently the pilot was killed, for the machine spun down."

Boelcke's 34th victim was Langan-Byrne, the nacelle of whose D.H.2, A2542, was later photographed intact, but who was killed and buried in a grave that has since disappeared into the artillery-ploughed miasma lying between the two armies. Sometime thereafter Major Hawker sadly noted, "I haven't recovered from the blow of losing him, he was such a nice lad as well as the best officer I have ever met."

No. 11 Squadron was also having more encounters with *Jasta* 2. Captain Price and Lieutenant Libby claimed another Albatros OOC on the 17th, but again the only documented losses were British—an F.E.2b of No. 23 Squadron and two from 11 Squadron, one of the latter being Boelcke's 35th victory.

Price and Libby shared one more Albatros on the 20th before both men were posted back to England for some well-deserved leave. Fred Libby would return to the front as a pilot with a captain's commission in 1917, scoring two victories in Sopwith 1-1/2 Strutters as leader of No. 43 Squadron's B Flight, and another two in de Havilland D.H.4s leading B Flight in No. 25 Squadron on August 8 and 12, bringing his total to 14. He died in Los Angeles, California, on January 9, 1970, but not before writing a memoir in 1961 that was finally published in 2000, as *Horses Don't Fly*.

As the Germans and French had at Verdun, the British kept up their increasingly futile effort to achieve a decisive breakthrough at the Somme for months. Meanwhile, the aerial attrition wrought on the

RFC by Boelcke and his disciples had compelled it to appeal to the RNAS for reinforcements. This led to the formation of No. 8 Squadron, RNAS, consisting of one flight of two-seat Sopwith 1-1/2 Strutters drawn from 5 Naval Wing, a flight of Nieuports from 4 Wing and one of Sopwith Pups from 1 Wing. All the airmen were volunteers—and, given the relatively idle time they'd been having in Flanders throughout the past few months, they were enthusiastic ones, including Stan Goble and "Roch" Grange. Organized at St. Pol-sur-Mer in October, "Naval 8" was dispatched south to relieve No. 32 Squadron at Vert Galand. There, it came under the command of 22nd Wing, 5th Brigade, and commenced operations on November 3.

First blood was drawn on November 10, when Flight Sub-Lieutenant Stanley V. Trapp forced a German scout to land and Flight Sub-Lieutenant Daniel Murray Bayne Galbraith sent another down OOC ("out of control") a few hours later. Born in Carleton Place, Ontario, on April 27, 1895, Murray Galbraith learned to fly in the United States before joining the RNAS in 1915. He had already scored two victories in Nieuports and one in a Pup prior to his arrival at the Somme. On November 16, Goble and Galbraith each claimed an LVG OOC, the latter's victory making him the war's first Canadian ace. After destroying another LVG on the 23rd, Galbraith was awarded the DSC and Bar and French *Croix de Guerre*. Shipped home to rest on December 1, he later served as an instructor and flew anti-submarine patrols from Italy's Adriatic coast. After the war Galbraith joined the new Royal Canadian Air Force, but was killed in an auto accident on March 29, 1921.

November 23 also saw Flight Lieutenant Robert Alexander Little, a 21-year-old Naval 8 man from Melbourne, Australia, destroy an artillery spotter from *Fl. Abt.* (A) 221 in flames northeast of La Bassée, killing Vizefeldwebel Friedrich Schwalm and Oberleutnant Johann Köln. It was the first of 47 victories he would score in Pups, Triplanes and Camels to become Australia's ace of aces.

In December Naval 8 was fully equipped with Pups and the unit would continue making a name for itself over the sector until relieved by another Pup unit, Naval 3, in February 1917. The sprightly per-

Oberleutnant Stefan Kirmaier stands before his Albatros D.II, which was identified by a black fuselage band and black, white, and red leader's streamers that were wound around the interplane struts while on the ground. After scoring his 11th victory, Kirmaier was killed on November 22 by Lieutenant J.O. Andrews and 2nd Lt. Kelvin Crawford of No. 24 Squadron. Richthofen avenged him the following day. (*Greg Van Wyngarden*)

formance of its scouts got Sopwith noticed by the RFC, which would be making more use of that firm's products in the months to come.

On October 26, Boelcke's score reached 40, making him the highest-scoring fighter pilot in the world. On the 28th, however, he met No. 24 Squadron again, for what proved to be one time too many.

Boelcke was leading a flight in response to a call for air support during an infantry attack when they encountered two C Flight D.H.2s, flown by Lieutenant Gerald Knight, an English-born Canadian whose score then stood at six, and 2nd Lt. Alfred Edwin McKay, credited with a Roland OOC on July 20. In the swirling melee that followed, Boelcke and Böhme were converging on Knight when McKay, being pursued by Richthofen, flashed in front of them. As both Germans abruptly pulled up, Böhme's undercarriage struck

Boelcke's left upper wing. Böhme regained control after falling 200 meters, but Boelcke's Albatros D.II 386/16 went into an ever-steepening glide that ended in a fatal crash.

Oberleutnant Stefan Kirmaier took over command of *Jasta* 2. Although all of Germany was shaken by his loss, Boelcke's men would develop and expand upon his tactical principles...and take grim revenge on the RFC.

On November 22, Jock Andrews shared his seventh victory with 2nd Lt. Kelvin Crawford, described in the RFC communiqué as "a hostile machine, which crashed on our side of the lines near Les Boeufs." Their victim, killed by a single bullet in the back of the head, turned out to be Kirmaier, who had scored his 11th victory just two days before and who was last seen by his four accompanying pilots going after a "Vikkers" two-seater.

Coming less than a month after Boelcke's death, Kirmaier's was a demoralizing loss for *Jasta* 2. The special duty officer, Oberleutnant Karl Bodenschatz, assumed administrative leadership until Oberleutnant Franz Walz arrived as the new CO on the 29th. At that point, the man that *Jasta* 2 pilots looked up to was Leutnant Manfred von Richthofen, who had scored his ninth and tenth victories the same day as Kirmaier's last. It was a tacit but demanding role—but the next day Richthofen more than fulfilled his young comrades' expectations.

At 1300 hours on November 23, Jock Andrews led four A Flight D.H.2s, flown by Captain Robert H. M. S. Saundby, 2nd Lt. John H. Crutch and, as a last-minute replacement, Major Hawker. At 1330 Crutch's engine began knocking and he landed at No. 9 Squadron's field near Morlancourt, where he found "plugs damaged and tappet rods out of adjustment" in two cylinders.

Continuing on, A Flight encountered two "HA" (hostile aircraft) northeast of Bapaume at 1350 and drove them east until Andrews looked up and noticed "two strong patrols of HA scouts above me." Andrews judged it prudent to disengage, but reported, "A DH Scout, [flown by] Maj Hawker, dived past me and continued to pursue." Figuring Hawker had not noticed the enemy fighters and loath to abandon their commander, Andrews and Saundby followed him and, as Andrews noted, "were at once attacked by the HA, one of which dived on Maj Hawker's tail."

In what he described as a "violent fight," Saundby was jumped by two Albatros D.IIs, which forced him to spiral "two or three times." Andrews drove off Hawker's assailant after firing 25 rounds at close range, only to be attacked by a fourth Albatros that crippled his engine. As he tried to glide away, "obliged to try to regain our lines," Andrews's DH was further shot about until Saundby intervened, firing a double drum of Lewis rounds into the pursuing Albatros at 20 yards' range until it "wobbled" and then power-dived away. Although *Jasta* 2 recorded no corresponding casualty, the Albatros was credited as Saundby's third victory.

Before crossing the lines to make a dead-stick landing at Guillemont at 1410, Andrews claimed to have last seen his commander "at about 3,000 feet near Bapaume, fighting with an HA, apparently quite under control but going down." The only other witness to Hawker's last fight was Manfred von Richthofen. He wrote, "I attacked, together with two other planes, a Vickers one-seater at 3,000 metres altitude. After a long turning fight of three to five minutes, I had forced down my adversary to 500 metres. He now tried to escape, flying to the Front. I pursued and brought him down after 900 shots."

That terse combat report was considerably elaborated upon after Richthofen learned the identity of his 11th victim. "The gallant fellow was full of pluck," he wrote, "and when we had got down to about 3,000 feet he merrily waved at me as if he would say 'Well—how do you do?'" For a time it seemed as if the D.H.2's agility counteracted the Albatros's brisker speed and climb. Both adversaries, however, realized that the prevailing westerly winds and the possibility of more Germans intervening would inevitably compel the British pilot to choose between force landing in enemy territory or making a break for home. "Of course he tried the latter," Richthofen wrote, but as an equal matter of course he was not about to let this worthy foe get away. Still, as Hawker zig-zagged away at 300 feet altitude, Richthofen added, "the jamming of my gun nearly robbed me of my success." The 900 rounds he fired confirmed his claim that this had been his most difficult combat to date.

German Grenadiers found and buried the man Richthofen justly called the "English Boelcke" 250 yards east of the Luisenhof Farm on the Flers road. Like Kirmaier the day before, he had died from a single bullet in the back of the head.

Lanoe Hawker's death, as much a blow to the RFC as Boelcke's and Kirmaier's had been to the *Luftstreitskräfte*, had climaxed the "battle of the titans" between No. 24 Squadron and *Jasta* 2, although it was by no means the end of it. Renamed *Jasta* Boelcke, or *Jasta* B in honor of its late founder, *Jasta* 2 continued to have encounters with all three D.H.2 squadrons well into 1917.

Soon after scoring his seventh victory on November 6, Lieutenant "Jerry" Knight was promoted to captain and transferred from No. 24 to 29 Squadron, where he was made a flight commander and scored his eighth success on December 16. He was slated for 10 days' leave after completing one more patrol on the 20th. Knight did not return—and all four of the D.H.2s he led came back to Le Hameau aerodrome badly shot about. His fate was reported by his killer, Manfred von Richthofen:

> About 1130 I attacked together with four planes and at 3,000 metres altitude, enemy one-seater above [Monchy-au-Bois]. After some curve fighting I managed to press adversary down to 1,500 meters, where I attacked him at closest range (plane length). I saw immediately that I had hit enemy; first he went down in curves, then he crashed to the ground. I pursued him until 100 meters above the ground.

One week later, on December 27, Captain Harold J. Payn was leading six D.H.2s of 29 Squadron's C Flight on a patrol from Arras to Monchy, where the Canadian Corps was engaging in a major raid, when it got into a fight with some Albatros D.IIs. Seeing a German on Lieutenant Alexander Jennings's tail, Flight Sergeant James Thomas Byford McCudden rushed to his aid.

"I now fired at the nearest Hun who was after Jennings," McCudden later wrote, "and this Hun at once came for me nose-on, and we both fired simultaneously, but after firing about twenty shots my gun got a bad double feed, which I could not rectify at the time as I was now in the middle of five D.I Albatroses, so I half-rolled. When coming out I kept the machine past vertical for a few hundred feet and had started to level out again when, 'cack, cack, cack' came from just behind me, and on looking round I saw my old friend with the black and white streamers again. I immediately half-rolled again, but still the Hun stayed there, and so whilst half-rolling I kept on making headway for our lines, for the fight had started east of Adinfer Wood, with which we were so familiar on our previous little joy-jaunts.

"I continued to do half-rolls and got over the trenches at about 2,000 feet, with the Hun still in pursuit, and the rascal drove me down to 800 feet a mile west of the lines, when he turned off east, and was shelled by our A.A. guns. I soon rectified the jamb and turned to chase the Hun, crossing the trenches at 2,000 feet, but by this time the Hun was much higher, and very soon joined his patrol, who were waiting for him at about 5,000 feet over Ransart."

McCudden's squadron mates were surprised to see him return, and his dive must have seemed just as terminal to enemy witnesses, because his D.H.2 was probably the "Vickers two-seater" credited to Richthofen at that time and place. "At 1615" the Baron reported, "five planes of our *Staffel* attacked enemy squadron south of Arras. The enemy approached our lines, but was thrown back. After some fighting I managed to attack a very courageously flown Vickers two-seater. After 300 shots, enemy plane began dropping, uncontrolled. I pursued the plane up to 1,000 metres above the ground. Enemy plane crashed to ground on enemy side, one kilometer behind trenches near Ficheux."

Jimmy McCudden went on to get an officer's commission in January 1917. "Those shows I liked, so long as I came out of them," he remarked, "but it was no fun fighting an enemy who was 15 miles faster and had almost twice the climb." Nevertheless, he managed to score five more victories in the obsolescent D.H.2s by February 15, 1917—and still had yet to come into his full stride, when he returned to the front in an S.E.5a that summer.

Hours before McCudden survived becoming Richthofen's 15th victim, the Germans had suffered a significant loss of their own to an F.E.2b. Captain John Bowley Quested and 2nd Lt. H.J.H. Dicksee of No. 11 Squadron were returning from a recon when they were attacked by *Jasta* 1. During the melee Dicksee shot down what he and Quested described as an enemy-flown Nieuport near Wancourt. Their victim had indeed been a captured Nieuport 16 flown by nine-victory ace and *Pour le Mérite* recipient Gustav Leffers, marking the demise of yet another of Germany's pioneer *Jagdflieger*. Vizefeldwebel Wilhelm Cymera forced Quested and Dicksee's FE down in British lines, but like McCudden they lived to tell the tale— and, for that matter, to down another enemy fighter OOC on January 25, 1917, for Quested's eighth victory.

As the dashing innovators of air-to-air combat passed on, a new generation that they had nurtured was stepping up to take their places. Although these disciples of Boelcke and Hawker would continue to refine the principles that their predecessors had laid down, aerial warfare was no longer new to them. Under these hardened professionals, the game was about to enter a new round, truly fought in deadly earnest.

6

IMPROVING THE BREED

By the end of 1916, the basic configuration of fighter aircraft, which had not existed two years earlier, had been more or less established, along with doctrines and organizations for their use. By then, too, as happens in every protracted war, an accelerated arms race had begun as each of the military industrial complexes of the combatant nations strove to produce a better fighting machine that would give its side the decisive edge to control the sky.

If a pattern could be discerned in the prevailing trends among the major powers in 1917, it might have been conservatism on the part of the Allies and paradox in Germany. Although both France and Britain experimented with some innovative ideas, the designs that found their way to the production line were by and large improvements on established formulas. The two most significant fighters produced by the Germans in that year were both essentially copies of Allied designs, but one of them incorporated within its imitative exterior the most innovative structural concept of the war.

The New Year brought a new fighter to the rapidly proliferating *Jagdstaffeln*, in the form of the Albatros D.III. Upon closer inspection, however, there was somewhat less to that rakish debutante than met the eye.

Throughout 1916, the Germans had been impressed, perhaps overmuch, by the Nieuport 11 and 17. *Idflieg*'s response, not for the last time, was to urge manufacturers to emulate the Nieuport's sesquiplane wing design. Some of their products were outright copies while others, like the Siemens-Schuckert Werke's SSW D.I, incorporated that firm's rotary engine configuration in a Nieuport-like airframe.

Also caught up in the trend was the Albatros design team, but it tried to achieve the best of both worlds by applying the sesquiplane wing arrangement to the fuselage of its successful D.II. The result, which featured two wings with a curving rake at the tips, the lower of which was of considerably reduced chord, certainly looked more graceful than the D.II with its squared-off wings—and indeed it provided a better downward view, maneuverability, and climb rate compared to its predecessor. *Idflieg* ordered 400 of the new fighters in October 1916 and *Jasta* 24 reported receiving its first three D.IIIs on December 21.

On January 7, 1917, the first Albatros D.IIIs reached *Jasta* 2 and one was promptly assigned to Manfred von Richthofen, whose score stood at 16. Before he could try it out, he was reassigned to command *Jasta* 11. Formed on October 11, 1916 and based at La Brayelle, northwest of Doaui in the 6. *Armee* sector, that *Staffel*, under Oberleutnant Rudolf Emil Lang, had thus far achieved nothing. Lang was sent to organize a new unit, Royal Württemberg *Jasta* 28, while Richthofen, who was awarded the *Orden Pour le Mérite* on January 12, was expected to whip *Jasta* 11 into better fighting shape.

Upon his arrival at La Brayelle on January 20, one of Richthofen's first decisions was that camouflage really did nothing to hide his plane, and went the opposite route by having it completely overpainted in red. When his men protested that he would be singled out by the enemy, Richthofen suggested that all of them adopt some red as a unit marking, and add an additional color for personal identification. Richthofen inaugurated his all-red Albatros D.III to combat on January 23, shooting down an F.E.8 pusher scout of No. 40 Squadron over Lens and killing its Australian pilot, 2nd Lt. John Hay, for his 17th and *Jasta* 11's first victory.

On January 24, Richthofen forced an F.E.2b of No. 25 Squadron to land west of Vimy, where its wounded crewmen, Captain Oscar Greig and Lieutenant John E. Maclennan, were taken prisoner. Richthofen landed near his victims, but it was not for a chat; "one of my wings broke during the air battle at 3,000 metres altitude," he wrote his mother afterward. "It was only through a miracle that I reached the ground without going *kaput.*"

His confidence in his new plane abruptly shaken, Richthofen soon learned that he was not alone. On January 17, *Armee Oberkommando* 2 reported four cases of "Rib fractures and breakage of the leading edge" in the course of turning maneuvers and diving. While diving after a Spad VII on the 22nd, Leutnant Roland Nauck of *Jasta* 6 reported that the lower right wing of his D.III shed fabric and then the spar itself broke away, although he managed to land unhurt. On the same day Richthofen's lower wing failed, *Jasta Boelcke* reported three similar incidents, one of which killed five-victory ace Rudolf Reimann. Over the next two months Richthofen flew a Halberstadt D.II, in which he may have scored as many as 11 victories by the end of March.

Unknown to the Germans, the Nieuport 17 had also been exhibiting structural flaws intrinsic to its sesquiplane layout. For example, three pilots of No. 60 Squadron RFC reporting twisting of the lower wing spar and failures, particularly around the interplane strut's socket joint around the spar, while diving in December 1916. Given that the Albatros D.III was heavier and more powerful than the Nieuport, it is not surprising that it would be even more prone to such twisting and breakage.

Responding to the crisis, Albatros strengthened and braced the lower wing cellule, just enough for the D.III to resume operations in time for the burst of aerial activity that attended General Robert Nivelle's spring 1917 offensive. As a result of the German fighters' subsequent success during the intense air battles that April, *Idflieg* placed such a heavy order for more D.IIIs that Albatros set about building them not only at its Johannisthal factory, but at a subsidiary in Scheidemühl, the Ostdeutsche Albatros Werke (OAW).

"Bloody April," as the British had every right to call it, had come of an attempt to support Nivelle's offensive that actually preceded it, on April 9. The French belatedly got theirs underway on the 16th, culminating in the Second Battle of the Aisne, which ended four days later with 187,000 casualties and negligible gains. Aside from the Canadian seizure of Vimy Ridge, the British Expeditionary Force, too, had little to show for the 158,660 casualties it had suffered when its advance ceased on May 17.

The Allied failure both on the ground and in the air were largely the result of a change in German strategy on the Western Front following the replacement of General von Falkenhayn as Chief of the General Staff by Paul Ludwig Hans Anton von Beneckendorff und von Hindenburg on August 29, 1916. Hindenburg and his chief of staff, General Erich Ludendorff, focused German efforts for the new year against Russia, which in spite of Brusilov's victory was showing signs of political, economic, and moral strain that made its collapse an inviting possibility. Between February 21 and the end of March 1917, the Germans carried out a general withdrawal across France to a shorter front line with well-prepared defenses in depth running from Arras along the river Scarpe to the Chemin des Dames ridge, collectively dubbed the *Siegfried Stellung*.

That defensive posture eased the job of the *Jagdflieger*, who were further aided by General Trenchard's policy of having his squadrons fly constant offensive patrols over enemy territory, ostensibly to "reduce the Hun to a proper state of mind." This may have maintained the initiative in British eyes, but the outnumbered Germans had already been long accustomed to fighting on the defensive, and their application of Boelcke's tactical dicta to that end had by April been honed to a lethal state of efficiency. Far from demoralized, the Germans saw it as a means of saving precious fuel, time and effort, as *Luftschutz Offiziere* (air protection officers) stationed at the front telephoned word of major aerial incursions to colleagues in corps headquarters, who then directed their fighter assets to intercept at the time and position of their choice. To paraphrase Richthofen's thoughts on the matter, if the enemy insisted on coming to one's shop, why go out looking for customers?

The Germans were also favored by the prevailing westerly wind, which worked against Allied aircraft trying to make their way home while tending to blow damaged German aircraft toward or farther behind their own lines. This contributed to the greater number of Allied planes permanently lost, while allowing a great number of damaged German aircraft to be recovered and repaired. That in turn,

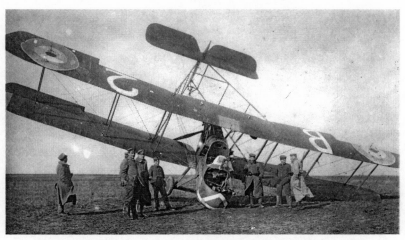

In a prelude to "Bloody April" on March 31, 1917, Leutnant Kurt Wolff of Jasta 11 shot down F.E.2b 7691 of No. 11 Squadron, which the Germans had to tip over in order to extricate the mortally wounded observer, 2nd Lt. W. G. T. Clifton. The pilot, 2nd Lt. L. A. T. Strange, was taken POW. (*Greg Van Wyngarden*)

combined with Allied reliance on front-line troops or other airmen to provide eyewitness statements that were often imprecise or overoptimistic, resulted in inflated Allied claims over enemy planes that left them with a far less accurate picture of how much damage they were actually doing than the Germans could ascertain from the planes downed in their territory.

The statistics for the month reflect that discrepancy. The RFC admitted to the loss of 245 aircraft and kite balloons, as well as 316 airmen killed or missing, while claiming 160 German aircraft destroyed, 206 OOC and 24 balloons burned. In that same period, the French lost 55 aircraft, while claiming 70 Germans. The *Luftstreitskräfte*, by comparison, reported the loss of 76 aircraft and seven balloons, with 12 airmen killed, six missing and six wounded, while claiming 298 Allied planes and 34 balloons.

One more factor that made April 1917 so costly to the British was the very inconsistency of their fighter force. Never before or since did so many different types coexist in a single aerial struggle against enemies who by then were reasonably familiar with their own relatively homogenous collection of scouts. April was in fact a month of transition in the RFC, with outdated fighters such as the D.H.2, F.E.8, F.E.2b and F.E.2d, soldiering on alongside scouts in the process of being eclipsed, such as the Sopwith Pup and Nieuport 17, two squadrons of imported French Spad VIIs, and harbingers of a new generation: the Sopwith Triplane, S.E.5 and Bristol F.2A.

Pleasant as the Sopwith Pup had been to fly, the Triplane had won accolades since test pilot Harry Hawker first flew it on May 30, 1916, and proceeded to loop three minutes after takeoff. Dividing its wing area between three relatively short wings with an aileron on each had given it a fast roll rate, and the wings' narrower chord gave them a high aspect ratio that improved their efficiency and countered drag, as well as endowing the plane with a rapid climb rate. The prototype's front-line evaluation on July 1 had been similarly successful, with Roderic Dallas claiming two victories in it. The Triplane's impact on the front was delayed, however, because the first fully equipped unit, No. 1 Squadron, RNAS, was on the then-quiescent Flanders front.

In February 1917, Naval 1 was sent south to Chipilly aerodrome, south of Albert and east of Amiens, to relieve Naval 8, which was withdrawn to exchange its Pups for Triplanes. Naval 1 pilots such as Dallas, Theodore F.N. Gerrard, Herbert Victor Rowley, and Richard Pearman Minifie made the most of the new, target-rich environment to ring up substantial tallies. Naval 8, soon joined by Nos. 9 and 10 Squadrons, would follow suit.

Even allowing for inflated claims, the Triplanes made a startling impression on their adversaries. The first to fall into German hands was brought down near Lagnicourt by *Flakbatterie* 505 on April 6, Flight Sub-Lieutenant N.D.M. Hewitt of Naval 1 being taken prisoner. After an indecisive combat on April 23, Flight Commander Anthony Rex Arnold of Naval 1 reported, "The fight lasted about 20 minutes and the German pilot showed great skill in manoeuvring his machine, but was at a disadvantage, as the Triplane could out-manoeuvre and out-climb the hostile machine."

On April 29, Triplanes of Naval 1 and 8 literally took on *Jasta* 11's best over its home turf. By that date, now-Hauptmann Manfred von Richthofen had exceeded the score of his mentor, Boelcke, and made his all-red Albatros D.III a familiar and feared sight to his enemies. Under his tutelage *Jasta* 11, too, had developed into the deadliest fighter unit in the *Luftstretskräfte*. The 29th saw *Staffel* and *Staffelführer* at the top of their game, starting about noon with an ambush on three Spad VIIs of No. 19 Squadron, RFC, that ended in 2nd Lt. Richard Applin being killed by Richthofen; Lieutenant W.N. Hamilton brought down a POW by his brother, Leutnant Lothar von Richthofen; and the flight leader, Major Hubert D. Harvey-Kelly—the same Harvey-Kelly who had claimed the RFC's first victory back in August 1914—become the 24th victim of Leutnant Kurt Wolff with a head wound from which he died three days later. At 1655 Richthofen destroyed an F.E.2b, killing Sergeant George Stead and Corporal Alfred Beebee of No. 18 Squadron, while Wolff claimed another whose pilot, 2nd Lt. George H.S. Dinsmore, managed to force land in British lines with his observer, 2nd Lt, G.B. Bate, mortally wounded. Wolff then went on to shoot down a B.E.2f of No. 12 Squadron.

The brothers Richthofen struck again at 1925 hours, each downing a B.E.2e of No. 12 Squadron and killing all four crewmen. Soon afterward, *Jasta* 11 encountered what Manfred reported as "a strong enemy one-seater force of Nieuports, Spads and Triplanes." Certainly both Nos. 1 and 8 Squadrons RNAS had Triplanes up at that time, and it seems to have been six of Naval 8's planes, flown by Flight Commander Rex Arnold leading Flight Sub-Lieutenants Robert A. Little, A. R. Knight, Philip A. Johnston, Roderick McDonald and Albert Edward Cuzner, that first engaged the Germans between Fresnoy and Gavrelle.

"We flew on," Richthofen later wrote, "climbing to higher altitude, for above us some of the Anti-Richthofen Club had gathered together. Again, we were easy to recognize, the sun from the west illuminated the aircraft and let their beautiful red color be seen from far away. We closed up tightly, for each of us knew we were dealing with 'brothers' who pursued the same trade we did. Unfortunately, they were higher than we were, so we had to wait for their attack. The famous Triplanes and SPADS [were] completely new machines, but it is not a matter of the crate as much as who sits in it; the 'brothers' were wary and had no spunk."

In fact, the Triplanes did engage the Germans, but their formation broke up and 26-year-old Canadian Flight Sub-Lieutenant Cuzner, who had flown 15 patrols since joining Naval 8, made the error of giving up his height advantage to square off with Richthofen, whose experience prevailed over the Triplane's innate superiority. In his after-action report, Richthofen stated, "The plane I had singled out caught fire and after a short time, burned in the air and fell north of Henin Liétard."

Cuzner was the Red Baron's 52nd victory and his only one over a Sopwith Triplane. It was also the only victory credited to *Jasta* 11 in the course of a more involved combat that resulted in some further British casualties. Separated from their flight, Arnold and Little spotted Naval 1's patrol and a formation of five Albatros below them. As both Triplanes dove, Little lost track of Arnold, only to see fellow Australian Richard Minifie of Naval 1 attacking an Albatros east of Douai. Little joined in and saw the German crash land on his aerodrome. Little then reported seeing the other Albatros attack Minifie and "although he put up a splendid fight, was forced down by numbers to about 50 ft, where I last saw him. I was then attacked by more scouts."

Little fought his way out of this melee right above *Jasta* 11's base, to share his 10th victory with Minifie—who also returned. Interviewed later in life, Minifie explained, "Yes, they nearly had me down on Douai aerodrome, about 200–300 feet off it. But luckily my Triplane was just that little shade faster than they were. I was going low for home, and they let me go and get a lead of about 500 yards on them. So that was that—they just couldn't catch me." Minifie, Naval 1's youngest ace at age 19, went on to be the squadron's top Triplane pilot, scoring 17 of his 21-victory total in that type.

Victor Rowley claimed a red Albatros OOC—his first of nine victories—before three others shot up his motor, but he managed to glide over the lines to force-land south of Bapaume. Flight Sub-Lieutenant H.M.D. Wallace of Naval 1 was wounded in the arm and also force landed south of Bapaume, where he burned his Triplane to prevent its falling into German hands—only later learning that he had, in fact, come down in British territory! Flight Sub-Lieutenant A.P. Haywood was wounded, but also came down on the British side.

Although *Jasta* 11's pilots had managed to drive off the cheeky "Tommies" who had violated their airspace, the overall performance of the Triplanes left many of them stunned and *Idflieg*, when it read reports on the new fighters, concerned. The RNAS, on the other hand, was pleased to let word of its new heroes leak to the outside world. After Bloody April, Naval 8's exploits would be joined by a collective claim of 87 enemy planes by five Canadians of "B" Flight, No. 10 Squadron RNAS, whose names became associated with the legends they inscribed below the cockpits of their black-cowled Triplanes: "Black Roger" flown by Gerald Ewart Nash, "Black Death" by John Edward Sharman, "Black Prince" by William Melville Alexander, "Black Roger" by Ellis Vair Reid, and "Black Maria" by their leader, Raymond Collishaw.

While the RNAS's Triplanes were offering the most visible glimmer of hope to the British during Bloody April, two other fighters were making their debuts with the RFC that month. The first was the less-than-auspicious beginning to one of the great success stories of British military aviation: the Bristol Fighter.

In 1916, the RFC began seeking a replacement for the intolerably vulnerable B.E.2c. The Royal Aircraft Factory responded with the R.E.8, another slow corps observation plane that at least put the observer behind the pilot with a Scarff ring so he could make better use of his machine gun. At the same time Bristol engineer Frank Barnwell designed the R.2A, a two-seater which had the fuselage raised above the lower wing by struts, in order to improve the pilot's view over the upper wing. A revised version with unequal-span wings and a 150-hp Hispano-Suiza engine, designated the R.2B, was quickly superceded by another with equal-span wings and a new Rolls-Royce Falcon I engine. At that point, the Bristol design was being regarded as a reconnaissance-fighter, and by the time prototype A3303 flew on September 9, 1916, it had been redesignated as the F.2A. With its side-mounted "ear" radiators replaced by a circular nose radiator, A3303 underwent its official tests between October 16 and 18, using both a two and four-bladed propeller. The RFC, already impressed with the plane's potential, ordered 50.

If there was anything truly innovative about the Bristol, it was the CC gear synchronizing the Vickers machine gun within its cowling that fired through a hole in the radiator. This system had been designed by Major George E. Colley and George Constantinesco, a Romanian physicist who had come to England in 1910, and who had made a name for himself with his Theory of Sonics, now known as continuum mechanics, by which power could be transmitted by vibrations or pressure pulses in liquids, solids or gases. The CC gear applied Constantinesco's theory to a hydraulic system called Fire Control Timing Gear. This early version, which used oil as its medium, was introduced in de Havilland D.H.4s of No. 55 Squadron in March 1917, and was prone to chronic failure. A later development, using a mixture of 90 percent paraffin (kerosene) and 10 percent oil, proved to be more reliable and in fact superior to mechanical interrupter gear, since it freed the gun's rate of fire from dependence upon the varying revolutions per minute of the engine. The F.2A's rear observer manned a single Lewis gun on a Scarff ring.

The first operational F.2As were delivered in December 1916 to No. 48 Squadron, which after training deployed to Bellevue, France, in March 1917. There it waited for the Battle of Arras, in hopes of surprising the enemy. The squadron's crews were led by a cadre of veteran flight and deputy flight leaders. Captain A.T. Cull had seen considerable action, and Captain Alan M. Wilkinson had already claimed 10 victories in D.H.2s with No. 24 Squadron. Captain William Leefe Robinson, who had been awarded the Victoria Cross for destroying Schütte-Lanz airship *SL-11* over north London on the night of September 2, 1916, was the most famous of 48 Squadron's flight commanders, but also the least experienced in combat over the Western Front. "Robinson did not appreciate the fact that the Bristol could be used as an offensive weapon by the pilot, and that it was not necessary to provide one another with protection," said Wilkinson. "We were not bothered about Robinson's VC, only that he seemed to dislike any opinion other than his own in matters [of] which, I might say, he had no experience."

As fortune would have it, No. 48 Squadron's first offensive patrol, on April 5, would be over Douai—home to Richthofen and *Jasta* 11—and Robinson was slated to lead it. Ignoring the higher speed and greater maneuverability that the Bristol offered over other two-seaters, Robinson adhered to the standard tactic of closing up the flight when attacked, so that the rear gunners could provide each other with mutual support. He also disregarded advice not to fly at the low altitude of 4,000 feet. To top things off, when told that the lubricating oil in the machine guns froze at high altitude, Robinson's alleged reply to the gunnery officer was, "If the guns are freezing up through the freezing of the oil, stop oiling the guns and therefore there will be nothing to freeze."

Captain William Leefe Robinson, who had received the Victoria Cross for destroying Schütte-Lanz airship SL-11 over north London on the nights of September 2–3, 1916, led the first combat patrol of Bristol F.2A two-seat fighters on April 5, 1917—straight into disaster at the hands of Manfred von Richthofen and Jasta 11. (Raymond L. Rimell)

By the time Robinson's flight neared Arras at 1100 hours, German ground observers had reported them to *Jasta* 11 at Brayelle, which dispatched five Albatros D.IIIs to intercept. As the Germans closed in, Robinson's six Bristols closed up, but their gunners barely had a chance to fire before the Albatros scouts tore into them, twin guns blazing. F.2A A3340 fell out of formation and force landed near Lewaarde, Manfred von Richthofen's 35th victory. Its wounded pilot, 2nd Lt. Arthur N. Lechler, set fire to his plane with his flare pistol before being taken prisoner; the observer, 2nd Lt. Herbert D.K. George, died in Douai hospital soon afterward.

While Richthofen climbed to rejoin the chase, the Bristol gunners tried to engage their darting assailants, only to find their weapons, left unlubricated at Robinson's orders, seizing up. Vizefeldwebel Sebastian Festner drove down Robinson and his observer, 2nd Lt. Edward D. Warburton, both of whom became POWs. Catching up with Bristol A3343 near Cuincy, Richthofen drove down Lieutenants H. T. Adams and D.J. Stewart, who were also wounded and taken prisoner. A fourth Bristol was brought down by Leutnant Georg Simon, placing another wounded aircrew, Lieutenant Horace A. Cooper and 2nd Lieutenant A. Boldison, in German captivity.

The remaining two F.2As limped home full of holes. One was crewed by Lieutenant P. Pike and Canadian 2nd Lt. Hugh Bradford Griffith, the latter of whom reported that their plane became separated from the formation and in a lone rearguard action he had driven down an assailant. Griffith also stated that he saw a Bristol diving emitting smoke and three others were heavily engaged by a superior number of enemy fighters, but not before Robinson and Warburton had driven one down out of control. The two claims were officially credited as No. 48 Squadron's first victories, but the sad truth was summed up by Richthofen, "After the attack, which was similar to a cavalry charge, the enemy squadron lay demolished on the ground. Not a single one of us was even wounded."

Although Richthofen had reasonable cause to dismiss the new two-seater, he could not have known that he and his paladins had been unwittingly abetted by an enemy flight leader who had done things about as wrong as he possibly could. The next patrol of the day, aggressively led by Captain Wilkinson, corrected those initial errors when it encountered three Albatros near Douai, two of which Wilkinson and his 24-year-old observer, Lieutenant Laurence William Allen, drove down. The flight claimed another enemy "driven down" before it returned safely. While leading the day's third patrol Captain David M. Tidmarsh, another 24 Squadron D.H.2 veteran, engaged a two-seater east of Douai, only to see it escape into the clouds. Second Lieutenant Oswald W. Berry attacked an enemy plane southeast of Douai and drove it down in a steep spiral, while Lieutenant George N. Brockhurst drove down a red scout. Only Wilkinson's and Allen's victory was credited, as "out of control," but those second and third sorties did much to restore 48 Squadron's shaken confidence in its new machines.

In the days that followed, 48 Squadron's aircrews became better acquainted with their planes and learned to take advantage of the F.2A's outstanding speed and maneuverability by using it as one would a single-seat scout, with the added asset of a "sting in the tail." Two Bristol crews claimed enemy planes OOC northeast of Arras on April 6, one victim possibly being Unteroffizier Ludwig Weber of *Jasta 3*, who was wounded.

After a disastrous debut, Bristol F.2As of No. 48 Squadron proved to be outstanding two-seat fighters and led to the even better F.2B. F.2B A-7220 of No. 48 Squadron was piloted in September 1917 by 2nd Lt. James A.W. Binnie, who scored nine victories. (*Philip Jarrett Collection via Jon Guttman*)

When Albatros D.IIIs of *Jasta* 4 assailed a flight of F.2As on April 8, skillful mutual support by the Bristols resulted in six claims, one of which was credited as "out of control" to Tidmarsh and 2nd Lt. C.B. Holland, and 2nd Lts. Oswald W. Berry and F.B. Goodison, while a second OOC was jointly credited to the teams of 2nd Lts. George Brockhurst and C.B. Boughton; Robert E. Adeney and Leslie G. Lovell; and A.J. Riley and L.G. Hall. One of their claims was genuine—and a demoralizing loss to the enemy—as D.III 1958/16 broke up and crashed between Vitry and Sailly, killing *Jasta* 4's commander, Leutnant Wilhelm Frankl, a *Pour le Mérite* recipient who had scored his 20th victory the day before. Any celebrating at 48 Squadron that evening would be muted, however, by a second attack on the patrol east of Arras by *Jasta* Boelcke, in which Leutnant Otto Bernert forced F.2A A-3330 down near Remy with Berry dead and Goodison mortally wounded.

Patrolling continued without letup, with the team of Wilkinson and Griffith having shares in three Albatros D.IIIs and a two-seater on April 9. Tidmarsh and Holland, Brockhurst and Boughton shared in another victory on April 10, and on the 11th Tidmarsh was leading three other Bristols on patrol when some of *Jasta* 11's men dived on them over Fampoux. Tidmarsh, Holland, Brockhurst, Broughton, Adeney, Lovell, Riley, and Hall were jointly credited with two

Albatros D.IIIs, but again *Jasta* 11 recorded no casualties, while hitting 48 Squadron hard for the second time in a week. Adeney and Lovell were killed by Leutnant Karl Emil Schäfer, while Brockhurst and Boughton were slain by Lothar von Richthofen. Tidmarsh and Holland were brought down alive by Kurt Wolff, to spend the rest of the war as POWs. That left Wilkinson the only original flight leader still flying, but he brought his total up to 19 by April 22. He was then put in command of Spad VII-equipped No. 23 Squadron, where administrative tasks kept him from further action. Still, he had done much to show what the Bristol Fighter could do and how to do it.

Having recovered from their poor first showing, another 200 Bristol Fighters were ordered for the RFC, modified with longer-span tailplanes and a slope to the upper fuselage longerons. The first 150 F.2Bs, as the altered Bristols were called, used Hispano-Suiza engines, but the next 50 were powered by the 220-hp Rolls-Royce Falcon II, with radiator shutters to help control the engine's temperature. Most Bristols would come fully into their stride with the 275-hp Falcon III. Applying the tactics pioneered by No. 48 Squadron during Bloody April, Bristol crews of Nos. 11, 20, 22, 62, and 88 squadrons would give the F.2B one of the most formidable reputations over the Western Front.

Just days after the Bristol Fighter's debut of dramatic mixed fortunes, the single-seat S.E.5 commenced operations. Even while the Spad VII was entering production in France and capturing the RFC's interest, in June 1916 Royal Aircraft Factory engineers John Kenworthy, Henry P. Folland and Frank W. Goodden were working on two Hispano-Suiza-powered designs of their own. One, designated the F.E.10 (fighter, experimental No. 10), had the pilot and his machine gun perched in front of the propeller in a nacelle braced to the undercarriage and upper wing in a manner similar to that of the unsuccessful Spad SA.1. The other, designated S.E.5 (scouting experimental, No. 5), was similar in overall layout, but with the engine in front and the pilot seated aft of the wings. Not surprisingly, the latter was chosen for further development, but the F.E.10's vertical tail surfaces were retained in lieu of the original S.E.5's smaller fin and rudder.

When the first 21 French-made Hispano-Suiza 8A engines were delivered to the RFC on September 20, most were slated for British-built Spad VIIs, but two were used to power the first and second S.E.5 prototypes. On November 28, the R.A.F. received its first example of the new geared 200-hp Hispano-Suiza 8B, which it subsequently installed in the third prototype, A'4563—thereby creating the first S.E.5a.

S.E.5 A'4562 broke up during a test flight on January 28, 1917, killing Major Goodden. Simple modifications corrected the plane's structural problems, however, and the first production S.E.5, A'4845, cleared its final inspection on March 2, 1917. The first production batch of S.E.5s did not make a promising impression on their pilots, who complained of poor lateral control—a shortcoming that was alleviated somewhat, but never entirely, by reducing the wingspan and the rake of the wingtips. Early production S.E.5s also featured an overhead gravity tank, a large half-canopy that pilots called the "greenhouse," and a mechanism that could raise or lower the pilot's seat. Armament consisted of one .303-inch Vickers machine gun in the fuselage, synchronized by the new CC hydraulic gear, and a .303-inch Lewis gun on a Foster mount above the upper wing.

The first S.E.5s were assigned to No. 56 Squadron under Major Richard Graham Blomfield, a new unit that nevertheless, like 48 Squadron, had the benefit of a hand-picked veteran cadre. The most famous of the "old hands" was A Flight's 20-year-old leader, Captain Albert Ball, whose own suggestions for an ideal fighter led to the Austin-Ball A.F.B.1, which was tested at Martlesham Heath on June 1, 1917, but not put in production. Ball had high expectations for the S.E.5, but after giving the first prototype a 10-minute test flight on November 23, 1916, he remarked with bitter regret that the new scout had "turned out a dud."

On April 7, 13 S.E.5s of No. 56 Squadron landed at Vert Galant, joining the Spad VIIs of No. 19 and Sopwith Pups of No. 66 Squadron. Ball made no secret of his dislike for the SE and when General Trenchard visited the sector, Ball flew to Le Hameau and entreated him to replace the new fighters with Nieuports. While Trenchard lent him a sympathetic ear, Ball had already taken the liberty of modifying his S.E.5, A'4850, back at London Colney. He replaced the "greenhouse" with a small Avro windscreen, which reduced drag and gave the pilot better access to the upper Lewis gun. He removed the adjustable armored seat and replaced it with a board until a simpler seat could be installed. He altered the Lewis gun mounting, lengthening the slide by two inches to make it easier to replace the ammunition drums. Ball discarded his synchronized Vickers gun and replaced it with an obliquely mounted downward-firing Lewis. He also removed the fuel and water gravity tanks from the upper wing and installed long Spad-type exhaust pipes. Ball noted that his weight-saving, drag-reducing alterations considerably improved performance, but he still regarded the SE "a rotten machine."

As with Hawker's field modifications to the D.H.2, most of Ball's, apart from the downward-firing Lewis gun, were adopted on production S.E.5s with RFC approval, and the scout was the better for it. In addition, the wheels were moved farther forward and the external overwing tank replaced by internally fitted fuel and water gravity tanks behind the leading edge of the upper wing center section, which was also strengthened and covered with plywood to better withstand the Lewis gun's recoil. While snow and bad weather delayed test-flying in the altered S.E.5 until April 13, that afternoon Ball learned that Trenchard had authorized him a Nieuport for his personal use, although he still had to fly S.E.5 A'4850 on squadron patrols.

Ball, in A'4850, led five S.E.5s on their first operational patrol at 1018 hours on April 22. The pilots' enthusiasm was tempered somewhat by orders not to cross the front lines, and neither Ball nor South African Captain Henry Meintjes, leading C Flight that afternoon, reported any decisive results.

Captain Cyril Crowe led B Flight the next morning, encountering no enemy activity. Meanwhile, at 0600 hours Ball had taken off alone to patrol between Douai and Cambrai in his Nieuport 17, B1522, hoping to catch a German en route to or from one of those aerodromes. Two Albatros two-seaters appeared over Cambrai, and Ball carried out his usual tactic—a dive, a pullout underneath his quarry and a volley into its underside from his elevated Lewis gun. The first

Captain Albert Ball of A Flight, No. 56 Squadron, at London Colney just before taking off for France on April 7, 1917. S.E.5 A4850 shows the simple Avro windscreen Ball installed in place of the drag-producing "greenhouse," as well as a headrest. Those and most of the other modifications he'd made—excepting the replacement of the synchronized Vickers with a downward firing Lewis—were incorporated into the succeeding S.E.5a, turning what Ball initially condemned as a "rotten machine" into a winner. (*Imperial War Museum*)

German evaded him, but Ball slipped under the second, fired half a drum into it and then pursued it until it crashed into the roadside between Tilloy and Abancourt. Thus, No. 56 Squadron's first official victory was not scored in one of its assigned aircraft.

Ball found and attacked another Albatros a few minutes later, but its evidently experienced pilot throttled back, causing him to overshoot, and put 15 bullets in the Nieuport's lower spars. Ball dived away and landed safely at 0845, but until a new lower wing could be installed he would have to make do with his unloved S.E.5.

Taking off at 1045 and climbing to 12,000 feet, Ball spotted an Albatros C.III over Adinfer, dived, pulled up and opened fire—only to suffer a gun jam. After landing at at Le Hameau to rectify the jam and taking off again, at 1145 he sighted five Albatros scouts over Sevigny and again dived, firing 150 rounds into one opponent that fell out of control and burst into flames before reaching the ground. The other four Germans put some rounds into Ball's plane, but he used the S.E.5's superior diving speed to escape. Three-quarters of an hour later, Ball encountered another Albatros C.III north of

Cambrai, dived underneath and fired half a drum of Lewis into it. The German pilot, Vizefeldwebel Egert of *Fl. Abt.* 7, dived away, made a good landing and then helped his observer, Leutnant Berger, who had suffered a severe neck wound in Ball's attack.

Meintjes led a five-plane patrol at 1315 that afternoon, but half an hour later Lieutenant William B. Melville turned back with engine trouble and his S.E.5, A'4852, overturned while landing. The rest of the flight unsuccessfully pursued a German two-seater south of Lens. In a final sortie, Ball led Lieutenants Clarence R. W. Knight and John Owen Leach in search of enemy balloons, but they returned empty handed at 1735.

So ended the S.E.5's first day. Only the redoubtable Ball had shot anything down, but all in all the modified aircraft had not performed badly. Even Ball came to appreciate the S.E.5, scoring 11 victories in it.

Inevitably 56 Squadron suffered its first fatality on April 30, when 2nd Lt. Maurice A. Kay was shot down east of Fresnoy by Leutnant Edmund Nathanael of *Jasta* 5, after which Leach claimed his killer in flames—in spite of *Jasta* 5's suffering no losses that day. A far more serious blow to morale occurred on May 7, with the loss of two flight leaders. After downing an Albatros D.III in concert with Lieutenants Melville, Cecil A. Lewis and Reginald T. C. Hoidge, followed by a solo victory that probably wounded Leutnant Wolfgang Plüschow of *Jasta* 11, "Duke" Meintjes was outmaneuvered by a third D.III pilot who shot off the top of his control column and wounded him in the wrist. Meintjes dived away and managed to land near the headquarters of the British 46th Division before passing out from loss of blood. Meintjes's score stood at eight, but he was out of the war.

Soon after that, Ball went missing. Although early German propaganda credited him to Lothar von Richthofen—in spite of Lothar himself claiming a Sopwith Triplane that day—German eyewitnesses reported seeing Ball's SE emerge from a thick cloud at 200 feet, inverted with its propeller stationary, before crashing. Ball suffered a broken neck and leg, but no wounds. It is possible that he had become disoriented in the cloud and while flying inverted the Hispano-Suiza's large float chambered carburetor flooded the air intake, causing the engine to stall. To top off a melancholy day 2nd Lt. Roger M. Chaworth-Musters was shot down and killed by Leutnant Werner Voss of *Jasta* B.

In June, No. 56 Squadron began to receive its first examples of the S.E.5a, powered by the 200-hp Hispano-Suiza 8B, along with further refinements. Fast, rugged, and almost viceless, the S.E.5a became a mainstay of the RFC and later of the Royal Air Force right up to the end of the war. The first unit to employ it, "Fighting Fifty-Six," was also the most successful, being credited with 401 victories and producing numerous famous aces, two of whom—Ball and James T.B. McCudden—were awarded the Victoria Cross.

The RFC had taken longer than any other air service to fully embrace the tractor fighter, but by August 1917 Bristol F.2B Fighters were replacing the Beardmore-engine F.E.2bs and Rolls-Royce Eagle-powered F.E.2ds in Nos. 11, 20 and 22 squadrons. During that time, nevertheless, the ungainly looking pushers managed to get in some last jabs at the *Jadgstaffeln*.

On January 7, 1917, Vizefeldwebel Walter Göttsch of *Jasta* 8 scored a hit in the fuel tank of F.E.2d A'39 of No. 20 Squadron over Ploegsteert Wood. With flames literally at his back the FE pilot, Corporal Thomas Mottershead, dived for Allied lines while his observer, Lieutenant W.E. Gower, played a hand fire extinguisher over him. As it alighted on a flat field in British territory, A'39's undercarriage collapsed, throwing Gower clear but pinning Mottershead in the cockpit. Gower and nearby troops managed to extricate him from the wreckage, but Mottershead died of his burns and injuries five days later.

On February 12, Motterhead was posthumously gazetted for the Victoria Cross, the only noncommissioned airman in the RFC so honored, while Gower received the MC. Meanwhile, on February 3, another 20 Squadron team, 2nd Lt. C. Gordon-Davis and Captain R. M. Knowles, had claimed a "Halberstadt OOC" over Wervicq. Their victim turned out to be Göttsch, whose wounds kept him out of *Jasta* 8 until April.

On the evening of April 5—the same day Richthofen and *Jasta* 11 had turned the first Bristol sortie by No. 48 Squadron into a fiasco—

18 F.E.2bs of No. 100 Squadron departed Izel-le-Hameau on the RFC's first night bombing mission, which would become the F.E.2b's primary duty from August 1917 until roughly a year thereafter. Their target was Douai, where Richthofen and his men, alerted by their front-line *Schutzoffiziere*, took up defensive positions and fired up at any plane that entered a searchlight beam. The British later recorded that "Four hangars were completely destroyed, and other damage was done," though it certainly didn't stay *Jasta* 11 from its Bloody April depredations for long. "It was a wonderful display that the 'brother' had put on for us," Richthofen wrote afterward. "Only a frightened rabbit would have been impressed by it. I find that, in general, bombing at night had significance only on morale."

Amid this period of decline, one F.E.2d team amassed the highest tally of enemy planes credited to anyone who flew pusher aircraft. Born in London on October 20, 1894, Lieutenant Frederick James Henry Thayre was piloting a B.E.2c with No. 16 Squadron when he and his observer, Lieutenant C. R. Davidson, managed to shoot down a Fokker E.III on March 18, 1916. Thayre was later posted to No. 20 Squadron, where he was assigned Lieutenant Francis Richard Cubbon as his observer.

Also born in London on November 26, 1892, Cubbon had scored his first victories over Albatros D.IIIs as observer to Lieutenant R.E. Johnston on April 24, 1917. Together with Thayre and F.E.2d A6430, however, Cubbon forged a formidable triumvirate of men and machine, starting with two enemies in flames on the 29th. On May 1, they destroyed an Albatros two-seater in flames, killing Unteroffizier Karl Gottwald and Leutnant Erich Heckmann of *Fl. Abt.* 6. After forcing a two-seater to land on May 3—which was not credited—they came under attack from 26 Albatros D.IIIs, two of which they shot down. Late in that fighting retreat they ran out of Lewis ammunition and were fending off attackers with their automatic pistols when the Germans finally disengaged.

Thayre and Cubbon shared in three victories on May 5, during a fight with 20 Squadron's old enemy *Jasta* 8 in which Walter Göttsch—back and commissioned a Leutnant—brought down an

Jasta 11 at the top of its game at Rocourt aerodrome on April 23, 1917, with Rittmeister Manfred von Richthofen seated in his all-red Albatros D.III. Standing from left are: Leutnant Karl Allmenröder, Leutnant der Reserve Hans Hintsch, Vizefeldwebel Sebastian Festner, Leutnant Karl-Emil Schäfer, Leutnant Kurt Wolff, Leutnant Georg Simon and Leutnant der Reserve Otto Brauneck. Sitting: Leutnants Karl Esser, Lothar von Richthofen, and Konstantin Krefft. Two days after this photograph was taken Festner, with 12 victories, was killed by Lieutenant C.R. O'Brien and 2nd Lt. J.L. Dixon, a Sopwith 1-1/2 Strutter team of No. 43 Squadron. (Jon Guttman)

F.E.2d, killing Air Mechanic 2nd Class G. Worthing and taking the wounded pilot, 2nd Lt. G. Bacon, prisoner. Of the total of nine D.IIIs credited to 20 Squadron's crews, one cost *Jasta* 8 the life of Vizefeldwebel Peter Glasmacher.

Thayre and Cubbon added steadily to their score throughout May, with an Albatros D.III on the 12th, followed by 'doubles' on the 13th, 23rd and 25th. Cubbon was promoted to captain and both men were awarded the MC and Bar before finishing the month by destroying a two-seater and a D.III on the 27th.

Fighting continued almost daily throughout June as Lt. Gen. Herbert C. O. Plumer's Second Army prepared to assault Messines Ridge. On the morning of June 5, No. 22 Squadron was beset by Albatros D.IIIs of *Jasta* 5, which forced one of its F.E.2bs down at Vaucelles where its wounded crew, Captain F. P. Don and 2nd Lt. H. Harris were taken prisoner and credited as victory number *33* for

Leutnant Werner Voss. On the other hand, 21-year-old Canadian Captain Carleton Main Clement and his Glaswegian observer, 2nd Lt. Llewellyn Crichton Davies, claimed two D.IIIs northwest of Lesdains. One of their victims was *Jasta* 5's acting commander and 15-victory ace Leutnant Kurt Schneider, who suffered a thigh wound that became infected, resulting in his death on July 14. The morning's bag brought Davies's tally to five, for which he received the MC. Clement, whose score stood at eight, would claim another six in Bristol Fighters before he and his observer, Lieutenant R. B. Carter, were killed by flak on August 19, 1918.

The Germans lost a second ace to a "Fee" that same day, when Albatros D.IIIs attacked No. 20 Squadron over the Ypres-Menin road. Seeing one F.E.2d diving away with its pilot, Lieutenant W.W. Sawden, mortally wounded by a red Albatros, Lieutenant Harold Leslie Satchell and 2nd Lt. Thomas Archibald Mitford Stewart Lewis went to Sawden's assistance and engaged the German in a 15-minute duel before a close-range burst from Lewis caused the Albatros to break up and crash near Zandvoorde. The pilot proved to be Leutnant Karl Emil Schäfer, a former *Jasta* 11 member with 30 victories and the *Orden Pour le Mérite*, who had just taken command of *Jasta* 28. Thayre and Cubbon were also credited with an Albatros in that fight, as were Captain Donald Charles Cunnell and his observer, Sergeant Edward H. Sayers.

On June 7, the Battle of Messines commenced with a bang—from 19 mines laid under the German trenches by British sappers—and that evening Captains Thayre and Cubbon sent an Albatros down shedding its wings over Houthem. Their victim, Leutnant Ernst Wiessner of *Jasta* 18, had just downed an R.E.8 for his fifth victory earlier that day. It was Thayre's 20th victory, Cubbon's 21st.

During a patrol two days later, Thayre dived on an Albatros two-seater east of Ploegsteert and Cubbon's fire sent it diving vertically, streaming smoke, though nobody saw it crash. Just as Thayre was pulling up to rejoin his flight, F.E.2d A6430 suddenly took a direct shell hit from *K Flak* 60, and crashed hear Warneton. The Germans subsequently dropped a message confirming Thayre's and Cubbon's deaths, but their graves were never found.

On June 29, four F.E.2ds of No. 20 Squadron had dropped some bombs and took 10 photographs when they came under attack by their old enemy, *Jasta* 8, over Houthulst. Lieutenant Henry George Ernest Luchford and 2nd Lt. W.D. Kennard were credited with one of their assailants in flames, as were Lieutenant H. W. Joclyn and Private F. A. Potter. In addition, 2nd Lt. Reginald M. Makepeace and Lieutenant Melville W. Waddington got an Albatros OOC. *Jasta* 8 became reluctant to press its attacks after that, for the Fees had brought down two of its aces. Leutnant Alfred Ulmer, with five victories, crashed in flames, dying of his injuries soon after. Leutnant Göttsch's Albatros D.V spun down trailing smoke and though unhurt he was understandably shaken up—this was not his first rough handling by 20 Squadron.

While the FEs fought their last air battles over the Western Front, two pushers were playing an equally surprising role in home defense. On the night of June 16, the Germans struck at London with their newest class of high-altitude Zeppelin airships, called "Height Climbers" by the British. High cross winds and engine trouble kept all but *L42* and *L48* from reaching England, and with a thunderstorm threatening to the west *L42*'s commander, Kapitänleutnant Martin Dietrich, judged it prudent to attack Dover instead. Even then, a south-southeast wind caused his bombs to fall on Ramsgate, were one 660-lb. bomb struck a naval ammunition depot, killing three civilians and wounding 14 civilians and two servicemen.

L42 returned safely to base, but *L48*, serving as flagship for the raid with Korvettenkapitän Victor Schutze aboard, was plagued by a frozen compass and a malfunctioning starboard engine by the time it made landfall south of Orfordness. Schutze tried to bomb Harwich, but *L48*'s 13 bombs fell on a field at Kirton, five miles to the north. While the Zeppelin made for home at an altitude of 17,000 feet three Home Defense aircraft that had been struggling up attacked it simultaneously at 0325 hours on June 17. The defenders were 2nd Lt. L. P. Watkins in B.E.12 6610 of No. 37 Squadron, based at Goldhanger, Essex, and two aircraft from the Experimental Station, RFC, Ordfordness: D.H.2 A5058 flown by Captain R. H. M. S. Saundby, and F.E.2b B401, crewed by 2nd Lt. Frank Douglas Holder and

Sergeant Sydney Ashby. Their combined gunfire set *L48* ablaze and it fell to earth near Theberton, Suffolk. Of its 18-man crew only Leutnant-zur-See Otto Meith and Machinist's Mate Heinrich Ellerkamm survived, the latter cushioned by the Zeppelin's collapsing aluminum structure as it hit the ground.

Saundby, Holder, and Watkins were awarded the MC and Ashby the Military Medal—and Saundby, who had previously flown D.H.2s with No. 24 Squadron and F.E.8s with No. 41 Squadron, had finally scored his fifth victory. Serving in Iraq, Aden, and Egypt in the interwar years, and as Deputy Commander-in-Chief, Bomber Command during World War II, the belated ace retired in 1946 as Air Vice-Marshal Sir Robert Saundby, KCB, KBE, MC, DFC, AFC, and died on September 25, 1971.

Lieutenant William C. Cambray gives a disturbing demonstration of how an F.E.2d observer dealt with an attack from the rear in F.E.2d A6516 of No. 20 Squadron at Clairmarais in July 1917, shortly before the hard-fighting unit began replacing its pushers with Bristol F.2Bs. The pilot, Captain Frank Douglas Stevens, had an extra Lewis gun fixed to the right side of the nacelle. (*Greg Van Wyndarden*)

A month after eliminating Richthofen's man in *Jasta* 28, No. 20 Squadron claimed the Red Baron himself. At about 1030 hours on July 6, the unit was attacked over Wervicq by *Jasta* 11 and claimed seven enemy planes, four of which were credited to Lieutenant Donald C. Cunnell and 2nd Lt. Albert Edward Woodbridge. Woodbridge later recalled:

> Cunnell handled the old FE for all she was worth, banking her from one side to the other, ducking dives from above and missing head-on collisions by bare margins of feet. The air was full of whizzing machines, and the noise from the full-out motors and the crackling machine guns was more than deafening. . . . Cunnell and I fired into four of the Albatroses from

as close as thirty yards, and I saw my tracers go right into their bodies. Those four went down. . . . Some of them were on fire—just balls of smoke and flames—a nasty sight to see. Two of them came at us head-on, and the first one was Richthofen. There wasn't a thing on that machine that wasn't red, and how he could fly! I opened fire with the front Lewis and so did Cunnell with the side gun. Cunnell held the FE on her course and so did the pilot of the all-red scout. With our combined speeds, we approached each other at 250 miles her hour. . . . I kept a steady stream of lead pouring into the nose of that machine. Then the Albatros pointed her nose down suddenly and passed under us. Cunnell banked and turned. We saw the all-red plane slip into a spin. It turned over and over, round and round, completely out of control. His engine was going full on, so I figured I had at least wounded him. As his head was the only part that wasn't protected by his motor, I thought that's where he was hit.

Richthofen's recollection of the incident suggests that the "all-red" Albatros that Woodbridge saw was someone else's. First, his D.V 4693/17 only had the nose, wheel hubs and tail painted red. Second, the Baron was still approaching at 300 meters and recalled being astounded to see the observer in the lead FE stand up and open fire at him at such a distance when, "Suddenly there was a blow to my head! I was hit! For a moment I was completely paralysed throughout my whole body. My hands dropped to the side, my legs dangled inside the fuselage. The worst part was that blow on the head had affected my optic nerve and I was completely blinded."

Instinctively switching off his engine to minimize the fire hazard, Richthofen descended to 800 meters before his vision began to return, at which point he restarted his motor and, noting that two of his men—Leutnante der Reserve Alfred Niederhoff and Otto Brauneck—had followed him down, landed in a field of high grass outside Wervicq. With a 10-centimeter-wide section of bone laid bare and a severe concussion, the *Rittmeister* was rushed to Field Hospital 76 at Courtrai, and subsequently convalesced at St.

Nicholas Hospital until July 25, when—though not fully healed—he rejoined his unit at Marckebeke.

The medical examination suggested that the round that glanced off Richthofen's skull may in fact have come from behind, from one of his own men reacting to Wainwright's long shot, thereby giving the English gunner a more indirect role in temporarily depriving the Flying Circus of its "ringmaster." Aside from that, *Jasta* 11 recorded no casualties to remotely match the seven Albatros D.Vs credited to 20 Squadron that day.

Promoted to captain after the action, Cunnell—with Lieutenant A.G. Bill as his observer—was credited with an Albatros in flames on July 11, for his ninth victory. During another combat over Wervicq the next day he was killed by anti-aircraft fire, but Lieutenant Bill managed to take control of the F.E.2d and fly it back to base.

Woodbridge survived to sit in the back seat of a Bristol Fighter, claiming three more victories in concert with 2nd Lt William Durrand. After the war Woodbridge became a pilot and after some time in civil aviation, rejoined the Royal Air Force, but fatally crashed during a night landing attempt at Jask, Persia, on September 7, 1929.

In August 1917, Bristol F.2Bs began arriving at No. 20 Squadron. Given the aggressiveness with which so many of its veterans had handled their Fees, their transition to the faster and more agile Bristol was remarkably smooth. The same could be said for the squadron mechanics, already experienced with the Roll Royce engines that the F.E.2d and the F.2B had in common. By that time, too, 20 Squadron was credited with 203 enemy planes. It would raise that total to 619 in Bristols, making it the highest-scoring squadron of World War I, although only a fraction of its claims, in FE and Bristol alike, can be matched by postwar documentation of enemy losses.

Although the F.E.2bs and F.E.2ds saw about another year of service as night bombers, and a few D.H.2s turned up for a time in Palestine and Macedonia, as of August 1917 the era of the pusher fighter was at an end—at least until 1944, when a new type of "pusher" fighter, propelled by jet power, resumed their saga anew.

7

IMITATIONS AND
INNOVATIONS

While the RFC was adding the S.E.5a and Bristol Fighter to its arsenal, the RNAS was getting its own more powerfully armed fighter that June. Good as the Sopwith Pup and Triplane were, their firepower left something to be desired compared to their German opposition. Lieutenant Arthur Stanley Gould Lee spoke for the Pup pilots of No. 46 Squadron in a diary entry for June 29:

> The Sopwith-Kauper interrupter gear with which the Pup is fitted is complicated mechanically, and sometimes goes wrong, and then the bullets go through the prop. It's this gear which slows down the Vickers. In the air, when you press the trigger, instead of getting the fast rattle of a ground gun, you have a frustrating pop! pop! pop! The Huns have a much more efficient gear, for the Spandau fires very fast.

In December 22, 1916, Sopwith, together with R.J. Ashfield, Herbert Smith, F. Sigrist, and Harry Hawker, unveiled the prototype of their own twin-gun fighter, the F1, for flight testing. The F1 had a shorter, deeper fuselage than the Pup, with the engine, cockpit, and guns concentrated within the foremost seven feet of fuselage. To facilitate production, Sopwith eliminated the dihedral on the upper wing and compensated by doubling the dihedral of the lower one, to five degrees. The twin Vickers installation was partially covered by a fairing that sloped upward from the nose, and which was initially thought to protect the pilot from the slipstream effect sufficiently to make a conventional windscreen unnecessary.

Similar though all the Sopwiths were in construction, the F1's altered configuration gave it a pugnacious appearance and equally aggressive flight characteristics that differed radically from those of the docile Pup and manageable Triplane. The first F1 was powered by a 110-hp Clerget 9Z engine when Harry Hawker got in its cockpit and, as he put it, "bounced into the air" from Brooklands aerodrome on December 26. The torque of the rotary engine, combined with the concentration of weight up front, endowed it with breathtaking maneuverability but Hawker noted the sensitivity of the controls, which required a judicious hand, especially during takeoff.

Two subsequent unserialed prototypes were designated the F1/2, a naval prototype, and the F1/3, which was flown with the 130-hp Clerget 9B, 110-hp Le Rhône 9J and the experimental Clerget LS (Long Stroke), later rechristened the 140-hp Clerget 9Bf. It was allegedly when the latter was delivered to Martlesham Heath on March 24, 1917, that one of the Testing Squadron's pilots said, "Just to look at the beast gives me the hump at the thought of flying it." That remark, recorded by RFC technical officer Sir Harry Tizard, along with the gun fairing's appearance, led to the sobriquet "Camel," which, though no more official than "Pup," soon became just as universally used.

One feature to be added as the F1 developed was a cutout in the upper wing center section to alleviate the pilot's restricted view upward and forward—a significant weakness that would lead to larger apertures being made on production Camels by pilots in the field. May 1917 also saw the second naval prototype, N518, test flown at Martlesham Heath with a new 150-hp A.R.1 ('Admiralty Rotary No.1'), an improvement over the Clerget with steel-lined aluminum cylinders designed by RNAS engineering liaison officer Wilfred Owen Bentley. The engine gave such outstanding performance that it was put into production as the Bentley B.R.1, which became the best of the Camel's many power plants.

In early June 1917, No. 4 Squadron RNAS began replacing its Pups and on the 4th Flight Commander Alexander M. Shook, in Camel N6347, attacked an enemy plane 15 miles off Nieuport, which dived and escaped in a dense sea haze. Engaging 15 German aircraft between Nieuport and Ostende at the next evening, Shook sent a scout crashing on the beach and drove a two-seater down out of control 10 minutes later. The first front-line loss occurred on June 13, when Flight Sub-Lieutenant Langley F.W. Smith, an American volunteer with eight victories previously scored in Pups, was killed in N6362. Some witnesses said his Camel broke up while he was stunting above the German naval aerodrome at Neumünster.

A prelude of somewhat different things to come occurred on the early morning of July 4, when five of Naval 4's Camels encountered 16 Gotha bombers, which were then attacking London and other cities in England, flying at an altitude of between 12 and 15,000 feet, 30 miles northwest of Ostende. Shook attacked one of the Gothas and last saw it diving and trailing black smoke. He then attacked a second bomber until his guns jammed. Shook was subsequently awarded the Distinguished Service Cross for his part in the action, but his fellow pilots were equally keen to come to grips with the twin-engine giants. Flight Sub-Lieutenant Sydney E. Ellis dove into the center of the enemy formation and fired 300 rounds into a Gotha that stalled and fell away erratically, with brown smoke spewing from the rear gunner's cockpit. Flight Sub-Lieutenant Albert J. Enstone claimed to have damaged one Gotha in the fight and forced a second down low over the Netherlands.

The Camels of Naval 4, joined by those of Naval 3, chalked up several more successes in July. On July 10, however, Flight Sub-Lieutenant E.W. Busby was killed in action and two days later Naval 4 was reminded of the new plane's unforgiving nature when Ellis, a Canadian with two victories in Pups and three in the Camel, fatally spun into the ground. Notwithstanding that cautionary mishap, it had been a satisfactory first month for the touchy but nimble debutante. In the next few months Camels proliferated not only in RNAS, but RFC squadrons, where they and the S.E.5a were destined to serve side by side as mainstays of the British fighter force for the rest of the war.

Two less conventional British fighter designs of 1917 were doomed to less successful careers. Late in 1916, Geoffrey de Havilland built a tractor-engine successor to his D.H.2, powered by a 110-hp Le Rhône 9J radial and armed with a synchronized Vickers gun that could be elevated as high as 60 degrees. The most unusual feature of the D.H.5, however, was the placement of the pilot forward of a back-staggered upper wing, intended to give him as good a forward view as a D.H.2 pilot had enjoyed. Although its 100 mph speed at 10,000 feet was a distinct improvement over the D.H.2's 77, the D.H.5 was slower and climbed less rapidly than the Pup, and its service ceiling of 14,300 feet was less than the Pup's 17,500 feet. In spite of that, 400 D.H.5s were ordered on January 15, 1917.

The first D.H.5s reached No. 24 Squadron on May 1, and their first success came on May 25, when 2nd Lt. Stanley Cockerell, a D.H.2 veteran, shot down an Albatros D.III over Ligny for his sixth victory. Only 19 other claims were to be made by the squadron, however, before it was re-equipped with S.E.5as, and in only two cases were the enemy aircraft seen to crash.

D.H.5s also equipped Nos. 32, 41, 64 and 68 (Australian) squadrons, but their successes were far exceeded by the frustration of enemy aircraft outrunning or outclimbing them. The ruggedly built D.H.5s performed yeoman service as ground strafers during the Battle of Cambrai in November 1917, but attrition to ground fire and enemy fighters was inevitably high. Even while No.64 Squadron was bringing its new D.H.5s to the front in October 1917, No. 41 Squadron was beginning to replace its D.H.5s with S.E.5as. By January 1918, the last D.H.5s had been withdrawn.

Less deserving of obscurity than the D.H.5 was the Bristol M.1A, a monoplane designed by Frank Barnwell, creator of the redoubtable F.2B. The M.1A's misfortune began with its first flight on July 14, 1916—just when No. 60 Squadron's Morane-Saulniers were souring Hugh Trenchard's attitude toward monoplanes in general.

That was unfortunate for the RFC, because the Bristol had none of the Morane-Saulnier's faults. Although its thin wings were wire-braced to the fuselage underside and to a rounded pylon above the cockpit, they proved sturdy enough to withstand the stresses of combat and had ailerons rather than wing-warping. The Bristol's tail surfaces had horizontal and vertical stabilizers, making it easier to handle than the Morane-Saulnier, and its single Vickers machine gun had interrupter gear, not metal deflectors. The most remarkable feature of the Bristol monoplane was the performance it achieved with a mere 110-hp Clerget 9Z rotary engine—130 mph and the ability to climb to 10,000 feet in 8 1/2 seconds, as compared to the 109.4-mph top speed of a Morane-Saulnier I, which took twice as long to reach 10,000 feet. Test pilot Oliver Stewart rated the Bristol M.1's maneuverability as superior to that of the later S.E.5a and Sopwith Snipe.

Bristol took steps to remedy the prototype's principal shortcoming—a complete lack of downward visibility—by removing a section of fabric from the right wing root of the M.1B, which also featured a pyramidal bracing pylon above the cockpit. The first M.1B, A5139, went to France and on the 23rd it was flown by three veteran pilots, including Lieutenant D'Urban V. Armstrong and Captain Roderic Hill, both of whom had flown Morane-Saulniers in No.60 Squadron. Hill and the third pilot, Captain A.M. Lowery of No. 70 Squadron, wrote favorable reports about the Bristol, but Trenchard had made up his mind before he even read them, citing its limited downward view as the official excuse to reject it out of hand. Front-line fighter pilots who had heard about the M.1B were flabbergasted. "It is true that the downward and forward view was slightly restricted," Oliver Stewart wrote, "but there was not a fighting pilot of experience who would not have exchanged that view for the speed and climb of the Bristol Monoplane with alacrity and enthusiasm."

Although no Bristol monoplane ever fought over the Western Front, three M.1Bs served with No. 111 Squadron in Palestine from June 1917 through March 1918. On August 3, 1917, the War Office ordered 125 Bristol M.1Cs, which had panels cut out of both wing roots and were powered by 110-hp Le Rhône engines, but they, too, were destined to see action only in sideshows. On March 2, 1918, No. 72 Squadron arrived at Basra, equipped with D.H.4s, S.E.5as, Spads, Martinsydes, and eight M.1Cs, the latter primarily for ground attack. The monoplanes got off to a unique start in Mesopotamia when two of them gave an aerobatic display before some Kurds, resulting in the entire tribe switching its allegiance from the Turks to the British.

Banished to the sidelines, this Bristol M.1C served with C Flight of No. 72 Squadron from Mirjana airfield in Mesopotamia in 1918. (Jon Guttman)

Another sideshow that gave British pilots their best chance to put the Bristol monoplane through its paces was Salonika, the scene of intermittent fighting since October 1915, when Bulgaria joined the Central Powers and aided Austria-Hungary's invasions of Serbia and Macedonia. As British and French ground and air units were shipped to Salonika to assist Serbia's army-in-exile, the Germans likewise lent support to the Bulgarians. The air war produced its share of distinguished aces, the most successful being Germany's Rudolf von Eschwege, who scored 20 victories, mostly with *Fl. Abt.* 30, until his death on November 21, 1917, while attacking a British balloon whose basket had been packed with explosives specifically to eliminate him. The Germans also based two *Jagdstaffeln* there, *Jasta* 25 since its formation on November 28, 1916—whose leading ace, Gerhard Fieseler, scored 19 victories—and *Jasta* 38, formed on July 1, 1917.

Early in January 1918, a handful of Bristol M.1Cs were shipped to Nos. 17 and 47 squadrons in Macedonia, whose fighters were amalgamated on April 1 to form a single unit, No. 150 Squadron. Again in mixed company with S.E.5as, Nieuports and Camels, the Bristol finally got the opportunity to show its worth in aerial combat on April 25, when Lieutenant Arthur E. de Montainge Jarvis fired 150 rounds at a DFW C.V, which he last saw diving steeply toward Rupel Pass.

Later that same morning, Jarvis in his M.1C and Lieutenant Acheson
G. Goulding in an S.E.5a attacked another DFW near Nihor and in
spite of an attempt by two Albatros D.IIIs to intervene, they shot it
down, apparently on fire over Angista. On the next day Jarvis in his
M.1C and Lieutenant J.J. Boyd Harvey in a Nieuport sent a DFW
crashing into Hristos Gully. Captain Frederick D. Travers managed
to claim five of his wartime total of nine victories flying M.1Cs over
Macedonia. Nevertheless, no more than 35 Bristol monoplanes saw
any combat use, the rest being used as trainers.

Like Britain's Albert Ball, France's Georges Guynemer used his ace
status to influence the progress of fighter aviation. A fundamental
believer in the Spad VII, but keen to see it improved, he wrote Louis
Béchereau in December 1916, "The 150-hp Spad is not a match for
the Halberstadt. Although the Halberstadt is probably no faster it
climbs better, consequently it has the overall advantage. More speed
is needed; possibly the airscrew could be improved."

One answer to Guynemer's prayers came later that month in the
form of the first Spad VII using the 180-hp Hispano-Suiza 8Ab
engine. Back on June 11, 1916, however, Mark Birkigt had successfully bench-tested a new V-8 engine, the 8B, which could produce
208-hp at 2,000 rpm, and used a spur reduction gear to transfer that
power to the propeller. After testing the 8B in a Spad VII, Béchereau
concluded that it would require a somewhat larger, more robust airframe. In addition to its size, the Spad 13.C1, which was ordered into
production in February 1917, had rounded wingtips, forward-staggered cabane struts with a frontal bracing wire, and was armed with
twin .30-caliber Vickers machine guns with 380 rounds each.

Sous-Lieutenant René Dorme, one of the many aces in
Guynemer's *Escadrille* N.3, test-flew one of the new Spad XIIIs at
Buc on April 4, 1917, and at least one was undergoing evaluation in
a front-line escadrille on April 26. On that same day, General
Trenchard instructed Captain William J.C. K. Cochran-Patrick of
No. 23 Squadron to go to La Bonne Maison Aerodrome and

inspect—but not fly—the Spad XIII. On May 1, Cochran-Patrick and accompanying British officers drafted a report on the new fighter that included locally recorded performance figures of 120 mph at 13,120 feet, a climb to that altitude in 11 minutes, and climb to 22,965 feet in 28 minutes. "The machine is said to be less handy near the ground," the report stated, "but considerably handier at a height than the 150-hp Spad."

At the end of May, the British Aviation Supplies Depot received Spad XIII S498. Given the British serial number B3479 and tested at Candas, it exceeded expectations, reaching a speed of 140 mph at 15,000 feet and climbing to that altitude in 16 minutes, 18 seconds. On June 9, B3479 was sent to No. 19 Squadron for front-line evaluation and on June 13, Captain Frederick Sowry drove down a German two-seater for his third victory. Lieutenant G.S. Buck destroyed an Albatros the next day, and Fred Sowry became an ace in B3479 on July 21, when he drove an Albatros D.III down OOC northeast of Ypres. It would seem, then, that the British may actually have drawn first blood in the Spad XIII, before its French creators.

Another suggestion that Guynemer had made to Béchereau at the end of 1916 was for a fighter capable of mounting a cannon. By developing a variant on his geared engine, the 220-hp Hispano-Suiza 8Cb, which raised the propeller above the cylinder heads, Birkigt was indeed able to mount a 37mm Puteaux cannon with a shortened barrel firing between the cylinders through a hollow propeller shaft. Bechereau installed that weapon system in an enlarged version of the Spad VII, which was designated the 12Ca.1 (for type XII, cannon-armed single-seater).

In spite of its unusual armament, the Spad XII did not look like a freak—in fact, with its lack of bulged fairings on the cowling and slightly forward-staggered wings, it was one of the most elegant-looking Spads ever built. Inside the cockpit, however, the cannon's breech protruded between the pilot's legs, necessitating Deperdussin-type elevator and aileron controls on either side of the pilot instead of a central control column.

When Capitaine Guynemer flew the Spad XII in the spring of 1917, he recorded a maximum speed of 137 mph at ground level and

Few of the Spad XII, armed with a 37mm cannon and a single Vickers machine gun, reached the front, and were flown by the most proven pilots. In June 1918, S454 went to Lieutenant Georges Félix Madon of Spa.38, who painted the fuselage, tail, undercarriage, and wheels red. Credited with 41 victories, Madon was also a mentor to other aces, such as André Martenot de Cordoux and David E. Putnam. (*SHAA B78.1512*)

a maximum ceiling of 23,000 feet. The main shortcoming he saw in what he called his "*avion magique*" was in the 37mm cannon being a single-shot weapon, but the Spad XII also had a synchronized .30-caliber Vickers machine gun, which could be used to help sight the cannon on a target before it was fired—or help the pilot fight his way out of trouble after it had been.

Spad XII S382 arrived at N.3, then based at St. Pol-sur-Mer to support the British Passchendaele offensive, in July 1917. Guynemer used it to attack a DFW C.V on the 5th, but it was damaged by the enemy observer and was sent back for repairs until the 20th. On July 27, Guynemer used S382 to shoot down an Albatros scout with eight machine-gun rounds and one cannon shell, killing Leutnant der Reserve Fritz Vossen of *Jasta 33*. He downed a DFW over Westroosebeke the next day using two shells and 30 bullets, but damage from its return fire forced him to send S382 back to the shop until August 15.

Guynemer scored a double victory on August 17. The first, an Albatros dispatched with his machine gun near Wladsloo at 0920, carried Leutnant Ernst Schwartz and Oberleutnant Robert Fromm of *Fl. Abt. (A) 233* to their deaths. Five minutes later, he used his cannon to destroy a DFW in flames south of Dixmuide, killing Unteroffizier

Johann Neuenhoff and Leutnant Ulrich von Leyser of *Fl. Abt.* 40. An inconclusive fight with an aggressive two-seater crew the next day put Guynemer's Spad XII out of action once more, but the plane's overall performance encouraged the *Aéronautique Militaire* to order 1,000. It is doubtful that more than 20 were completed, though, before production problems with the engine and cannon arrangement led to the contract being canceled and full priority placed on Spad XIII production.

Guynemer's successes notwithstanding, the average pilot would have found the Spad XII a handful—or, literally, two handfuls. Aiming the cannon while using the Deperdussin controls required considerable dexterity. The cannon had a heavy recoil, fumes filled the cockpit after each firing and reloading it by hand was easier said than done in the heat of combat. On top of the cannon's problems, the geared Hispano-Suiza engine proved to be as troublesome in the Spad XII as it did in the early XIIIs. In consequence, the few Spad XIIs to reach the front were generally allocated one or two per escadrille, to be flown by its best pilots. A few French aces added to their scores in them, most notably Lieutenant René Fonck of Spa.103, who got two Spad XIIs in May 1918, and claimed 11 victories in them, of which seven were confirmed.

August had also seen the delivery of Spad XIII S504 to Guynemer, who used it to shoot down a DFW near Poperinghe on the 20th. His total of 53 victories was now second only to Richthofen's 61, and to cap off the day General Trenchard visited St. Pol to present Guynemer with the DSO.

In September Lieutenant Albert Deullin, a former N.3 ace now commanding N.73, received Spad XIII S501. N.3's Capitaine Heurteaux also got one and while test flying it on the 3rd, he spotted an enemy plane near Ypres and he dived to attack. Heurteaux's guns jammed, however, and as he broke away the German—possibly Leutnant Otto Kunst of *Jasta* 7, whose claim that day was not confirmed—punctured his oil line and pierced his femoral artery. Heurtaux would have bled to death in the air, but the incendiary bullet that passed through his thigh cauterized the wound. As it was, his war was over with 21 victories.

Lieutenant Albert Deullin, commander of Spa.73, 20 victory ace and writer of a hand-
book on air tactics for the Aéronautique Militaire, prepares for a flight before his new
Spad XIII S501 in September 1917. (SHAA B91.5584)

Meanwhile, Guynemer had gone on leave on August 24, but typically had spent much of it visiting the Spad representative at Buc,
making further suggestions to improve its fighters. After returning to
St. Pol, Guynemer's attempts to return to action were frustrated by
bad weather and engine malfunctions. At 0825 hours on September
11, he took off in S504, accompanied by Sous-Lieutenant Benjamin
Emmanuel Bozon-Verduraz. At 12,000 feet, the Frenchmen spotted
a DFW C.V northeast of Ypres, which they attacked from above and
behind. Bozon-Verduraz missed and had pulled up to prepare for
another diving pass when he noticed eight enemy planes approaching and went after them. The Germans turned away, so Bozon-
Verduraz went back to rejoin Guynemer, only to find no trace of him
or the DFW.

Upon returning to St. Pol at 1020, Bozon-Verduraz's first words
were, "Has he landed yet?" Guynemer had not, and one month later,
the Germans announced that Leutnant Kurt Wissemann of *Jasta* 3
had killed him for his fifth victory. A sergeant of the German 413th
Regiment certified that he had witnessed the Spad's crash and identified the body, noting that Guynemer had died of a head wound, one
of his fingers had been shot off and a leg was broken. An Allied
artillery barrage drove the Germans back before they could bury the

body, which thus vanished amid the chaos that was the Western Front.

Although Wissemann claimed a Spad over the right location, he never stated it was Guynemer's. By the time the *Luftsteitskräfte* made its pronouncement, he was no longer available for comment, having been killed on September 28 by S.E.5a pilots Captain Geoffrey H. Bowman and Lieutenant Reginald Hoidge of No. 56 Squadron. Another possibility is that Guynemer was shot down by a Rumpler C.IV from *Fl. Abt. (A)* 224w, whose crewmen, Flieger Georg Seibert and Leutnant der Reserve Max Psaar, were subsequently killed near Oudekapelle, 17 kilometers north of Poelkapelle, by Sous-Lieutenant Maurice Medaets, a Spad VII pilot of the Belgian *5e Escadrille*.

The Spad XIII would go on to be the principal French fighter for the rest of the war, but its front-line introduction in force would be hindered by problems with the Hispano-Suiza 8B's spur reduction gear. In November 1917, for example, some escadrilles reported their Spad XIIIs being grounded two days out of three because of engine trouble.

While the Sopwith Camel was able to coexist with the S.E.5a and Bristol F.2B in the RFC, France's general satisfaction with the Spad VII and commitment to the Spad XIII as its successor undermined the prospects of numerous other creditable fighter designs finding acceptance. Nieuport produced some refined variants on its 17—the 17bis, 23, 24, 25 and 27—but they served primarily as a supplement until enough Spads were available to replace them. By late 1917 the sesquiplane, with its structural limitations, clearly had no future and Nieuport's engineers devoted themselves to developing a biplane, the 28. That too would fail to find favor with the *Aéronautique Française*, but would find a moment of glory in 1918, as the first fighter to see action with the U.S. Army Air Service.

Morane-Saulnier had also been striving to keep its once-ubiquitous monoplanes in service. Late in 1916, it had produced a monoplane similar to the Type V, with ailerons and a rigid wing braced from underneath by a trestlework of struts, called the Type U. A more refined version, with a fuselage rounded by stringers ending in a conical tail, and a spinner over the cowling, was tested by the both the

One of the few Morane-Saulnier AC monoplanes to reach the front, MS682 bears the blue-gold pennant of N.76 and the legend Viking II of its pilot, Danish volunteer Sous-Lieutenant Leith Jensen. (*Musée de l'Air et l'Espace*)

French and British in January 1917. Designated the AC, this monoplane offered a speed of 125 mph at 10,000 feet and excellent visibility in all directions but down. Its single Vickers machine gun was faired over, making it all but impossible to reach in the event of a jam. Although General Trenchard had no interest in any more Morane-Saulnier monoplanes, 30 ACs were built for the French as a rotary engine hedge against the problems being experienced in the geared Hispano-Suiza 8B engine. They appeared in various units in the spring and summer of 1917, but never equipped an entire escadrille and were eventually withdrawn.

Another noteworthy French fighter, long assumed by aviation historians to have been yet another rejected Spad competitor, was in fact conceived with an entirely different client in mind. Lacking a suitable indigenous fighter design when it entered the war, Italy had used Nieuports, mostly license-built by Macchi. In the autumn of 1916, Capitano Ermanno Beltramo, a member of the Italian Military Aviation Mission in Paris, contacted René Hanriot and his chief engineer, Emile Eugène Dupont. Years later, Beltramo wrote, "Of my own initiative I asked Mr. Hanriot if he were willing to build, without obligation, a single-seat fighter following the concepts which I would suggest in order to create a type better suited than the Nieuport to the fighter needs of our theater of operations." By November, Dupont had created the HD.1, which underwent flight testing at Villacoublay on December 20.

Structurally conventional, with the usual wood and canvas aside from aluminum cowl panels, the HD.1 was notable primarily for its W-shaped cabane strut arrangement, similar to that of the Sopwith 1-1/2 Strutter that Hanriot was then license building for the *Aéronautique Française*, and for the greater span and dihedral of its upper wing in relation to the lower. Powered by a 120-hp Le Rhône 9J engine, the HD.1 was angular but well-proportioned and stands alongside the Sopwith Pup, Pfalz D.IIIa and Nieuport 28 among the war's most aesthetically pleasing airplane designs.

By February 1917, the Hanriot was being test-flown in Italy, where it was praised by Maggior Generale Giovanni Battista Marieni of the General Direction of Aeronautics for its superiority to the Nieuport 17 in speed, handling, the view from the cockpit, and "automatic stability which prevents it from spinning and overturning." Fifty HD.1s were ordered from France while Macchi negotiated an initial order to license-produce 200 in June 1917. Italy ended up purchasing a total of 360 H.D.1s from Hanriot, and of the 1,700 it ordered from Macchi, 831 were delivered by the end of the war, with another 70 completed by February 1919.

The first Hanriot-built HD.1s arrived at the 76a *Squadriglia* at Borngano in July 1917, but deliveries from France were slow and by October 25, only the 78a *Squadriglia* had likewise converted—just as the Austro-Hungarians, with German assistance, were achieving a decisive breakthrough at Caporetto. In consequence, both squadrons had to destroy 16 of their new fighters and retreat to Istrana. Meanwhile, as Britain and France sent land and air contingents to help the Italian army's retrenchment along the Piave River, the RFC shipped two R.E.8 and three Sopwith Camel squadrons to northern Italy. The Camel, whose reputation was by then well established among the Germans, would be perpetually misidentified alongside its

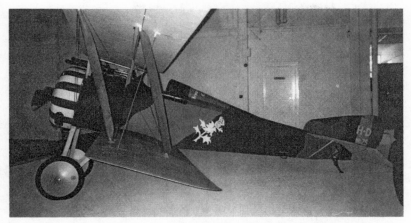

Designed for the Italians, the Hanriot HD.1 also distinguished itself in Belgian service. This one at the RAF Museum at Hendon wears the markings of Sous-Lieutenant Jan Olieslagers (six victories) of the 9e Escadrille. (Jon Guttman)

radial-engine stablemate, the Hanriot HD.1, for the rest of the conflict in Italy.

At that point, Macchi was producing its own HD.1s, which it delivered to the 82a *Squadriglia* in early November, followed by the 70a and *80a* by the end of the month and the 72a in December. Sergente Alessandro Contardini of the 82a scored the first HD.1 victory on November 6. The first loss was Aspirante Vittorio Aquilino of the 78a, shot down near Maser on the 14th, probably by Leutnant Bussmann of *Jasta* 1, even though his claim on a "Sopwith" at Il Montello, a little northeast of Maser, was not officially confirmed.

German aid to the Austro-Hungarians had included a balloon section, seven *Flieger Abteilungen* and *Jastas* 1, 31 and 39, which arrived in Italy in September 1917, playing a prominent role in the Battle of Caporetto. It was also the Germans who gave the HD.1 its first real test on December 26. On Christmas day, Captain William G. Barker and Lieutenant Harold B. Hudson of No. 28 Squadron had strafed the Austro-Hungarian aerodrome at Motta di Livensa, and it may have been in reprisal for that that the Germans launched a "Boxing Day" raid on Trevignano field, near Istrana. If the Germans were indeed seeking revenge on 28 Squadron, they had pinpointed the wrong target—all three Camel units were based at Grossa. Upon being alerted at about 0900 hours, at least 16 Hanriots of the *70a*, *76a*, *78a* and *82a Squadriglie* took off from Istrana to engage the 30 raiders.

Attacking in an untidy formation, the Germans dropped one bomb on a hangar of the *76a Squadriglia*, wrecking or damaging a few HD.1s, killing six ground personnel and injuring some others. The Germans paid for those modest results with eight DFW C.Vs shot down by the Italians and some 28 Squadron Camel pilots who joined in the melee.

Sottotenente Silvio Scaroni of the *76a* had taken off and barely completed a circuit of his field when he saw three DFWs swooping at 500 feet to scatter their bombs around the hangars. "I attacked the closer one, which was engaged in strafing the airplanes of my squadron lining the field," he wrote in a letter to his family. "With two short, well-aimed bursts I brought it down just at the border of the airfield. It crashed and caught fire."

Scaroni and Sottotenente Giorgio Michetti attacked a second two-seater, whose crew, Scaroni wrote, "fought us back with admirable ability and tenacity making our attacks difficult and ineffective." As they drove it lower, Scaroni noticed the observer cease firing and remove a cartridge belt from around his waist to reload his gun. Taking advantage of the respite, the two Italians bore in and drove the plane to the ground, where it turned over. "As we flew around it we saw the passenger crouching and getting out," Scaroni wrote, "then with a special explosive device he torched the wreck without worrying about the pilot who died miserably in the fire. The explosion of the fuel tanks splashed with burning fuel the passenger also, who started thrashing and rolling on the ground. Some artillery men reached him and helped him removing his burning clothes, then they captured him." Leutnant der Reserve Johann Edelbohle of *Fl. Abt. 2* had been the unfortunate pilot, while Leutnant Pallasch survived as a POW. Sergente Andrea Theobaldi, one of six *82a* pilots involved in the fight, reported:

> I took off at 0915 under a hail of bullets, when I reached a ceiling of 600 meters, I found myself in the middle of a group

of enemy fighters flying in the direction of our airfield....I
tried to attack them, but I soon realized that they were encir-
cling me....An enemy machine detached itself from the
group and I flew straight after it and, with just two quick
bursts, I saw it go down and land in a field northeast of
Camalò. The enemy aircraft turned over and started to
burn....I could see one of the airmen crawl out of the airplane as quickly as he could...his legs were on fire.

Theobadi had only fired 45 rounds when he landed at 0955, with
credit for one of the two DFWs whose crews were captured alive that
morning.

At 1230 a second wave of Germans came in, this time including
the first bombing strike in Italy by twin-engine AEG G.IVs, courtesy
of newly arrived *Kasta* 19, *Kagohl* 4. Two DFWs and one of the
AEGs were shot down this time, the latter having run a gauntlet that
resulted in it being credited to Captain James H. Mitchell of No. 28
Squadron, Sottotenente Scaroni of the 76*a* and Sergente Giacomo
Brenta of the 78*a Squadriglia*.

In a letter to aviation historian Rinaldo d'Ami decades later,
General Brenta recalled:

I can simply tell you that I was able to draw closer to it, but
nobody else was near me, except Scaroni, who was coming
on very fast. I fired some 50 rounds and I presume I hit the
pilot, as the huge twin-engine machine immediately went
down in a vertical dive....However, if a British officer made
a claim on the enemy aircraft, then he must have attacked it
before I did....The sky was very crowded that morning.

Killed in the AEG were the pilot, Unteroffizier Franz Hertling,
and his crewmen, Leutnant Georg Ernst and Leutnant der Reserve
Otto Niess. The Germans claimed three enemy fighters in the raids,
but the Italians and the British denied having lost any.

One curious conclusion to the day was a heated dispute that
ensued when Scaroni and Michetti met the observer they had
brought down that morning, who insisted that it was British pilots

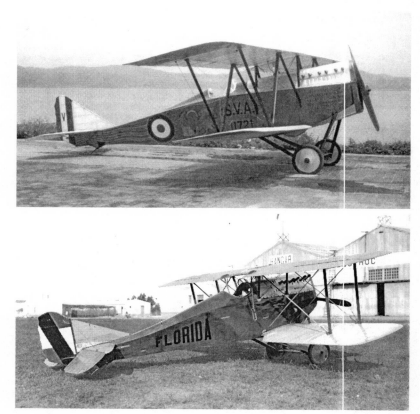

Top: An SVA-5 in markings of the 87a Squadriglia, famed for its overflight of Vienna on August 9, 1918, at the Museo Storico Dell'Aeronautica Militare in Vigna di Valle, Rome. Although not accepted as a fighter, the SVA-5 excelled as a high-speed, long-range reconnaissance plane. (*Museo Storico Dell'Aeronautica Militare*) Bottom: Another Italian design that failed to find favor with its own fighter pilots, the Ansaldo A.1 Ballila served the Poles well in their 1920 war against Bolshevik Russia and saw much postwar service in other air arms, such as Uruguay's as seen on April 24, 1925. (*Jon Guttman*)

who had brought him down. Aside from the similarities between the Camel and the unfamiliar HD.1, Scaroni and Michetti attributed Pallasch's attitude to Prussian arrogance that could not accept being bested by Italians. The stereotyping was mutual, however, for upon learning that all of the downed raiders were German, Scaroni remarked, "This explained their aggressiveness and their daring," reflecting *his* low opinion of the Austro-Hungarian airmen.

By mid-1918, the Hanriot HD.1 was Italy's fighter mainstay, with Spads and Nieuports playing a supplementary role in the squadrons. Among its many successful exponents was second-ranking Italian ace Scaroni, at least 19 of whose 26 victories were obtained in HD.1s.

In June 1917, the exiled *Aviation Militaire Belge* also ordered 125 HD.1s from the Hanriot firm. The first was assigned on August 22 to the 1e *Escadrille* at Le Möeres, whose pilots had already declined an offer to replace their Nieuport 17s with Spad VIIs. They likewise rejected the first HD.1 out of hand, starting with their leading ace, André de Meulemeester, followed by Jan Olieslagers and so on down the line to the most junior member, Willy Coppens. Coppens was still flying the escadrille's last Nieuport 16, and willing to try any alternative to its treacherous flight characteristics. His enthusiasm upon discovering how well the Hanriot handled soon won over his squadron mates. Three of Belgium's five aces flew HD.1s in the redesignated 9e *Escadrille* in 1918—de Meulemeester, Olieslagers and Coppens.

The closest Italy came to producing indigenous land fighters were two relatively large single-seaters built by the Societa Ansaldo. Both had deep wooden fuselages of boxlike structure that converged into a knife-edge along the lower rear, were powered by a 220-hp SPA 6A straight-six engine, and were armed with twin .303-inch Vickers machine guns whose placement on either side of the fuselage made them inaccessible to the pilot in the event of jams. The SVA, designed in 1917 by Umberto Savoia, Rodolfo Verduzio and Celestino Rosatelli, featured a W-shaped Warren truss of interplane struts that would appear in Rosatelli's Fiat fighter designs after the war. Although the SVA-4 and longer-ranging SVA-5 were capable of 143 mph, they were judged unsuitable as fighters due to inadequate maneuverability and poor visibility from the cockpit. The SVA-5's outstanding speed and six-hour endurance made it a highly successful photoreconnaissance plane, however. Produced and entering service in February 1918, its overflights deep in enemy territory, most famously a 625-mile propaganda leaflet-dropping flight over Vienna on August 9, 1918, became legendary.

At a recommendation from 12-victory ace Luigi Olivari, Ansaldo chief engineer Luigi Brezzi tried to improve the basic SVA design with a more conventional single-bay strut-and-wire layout. Olivari was looking forward to test-flying the resultant Ansaldo A.1 Ballila, but before he could he was killed when his Spad VII stalled and crashed on October 13, 1918. The Ballila was put into production and entered service in July 1918, but Italian pilots still thought its maneuverability inferior to that of their French planes and it saw little use outside of home defense. Its only air-to-air success occurred on October 8, 1918, when Tenente Leopoldo Eleuteri of the 70a *Squadriglia* shot down an Oeffag-Albatros D.III near Santa Lucia di Piave, for his sixth of seven victories. After the war Ballilas were exported to a number of air arms, most notably being used for ground attack by the Polish air force, including American volunteers of the 7th *Eskadra* "Kosciuszko," during its 1920 war with Bolshevik Russia.

With Bloody April seeming to prove the Albatros D.III's worth and further orders coming in, Germany's Albatros Werke spent spent that month further refining what seemed a winning formula. One refinement was the by-product of a failed testbed for reduction gear intended to allow the Mercedes III engine to be repositioned within a fully enclosed cowling while increasing the airscrew's propulsive efficiency. Three Albatros D.IVs had been ordered by *Idflieg* in November 1916, but the airscrew vibration they produced during ground testing rendered them unflyable. Later tests with three and four-bladed propellers at least got the plane off the ground, but its lackluster climb rate and still-unacceptable vibration led to the D.IV's abandonment in April 1918.

While the D.IV's geared engine was a failure, Albatros decided to adapt its finely streamlined fuselage of elliptical cross-section, along with its more rounded rudder profile and altered tailskid fairing, to the D.III's engine layout. The D.III's sesquiplane wing was retained with the gap reduced by some 110mm and, more significantly, a less substantial fuselage-wing joint than the D.III's and the aileron cables rerouted through the upper wing, rather than the lower. The resultant "lightened Albatros D.III airframe," designated the D.V, weighed 50 kilograms less than the D.III. Strangely, considering its previous D.III experience, *Idflieg*'s engineers tested the new plane's fuselage and rudder but failed to static-test the wings before ordering 200 D.Vs.

The first D.Vs began arriving at the front in May and almost from the onset reports came in of wingtip flutter and structural failure. The lightened fuselage structure also proved to be prone to crack and break during rough landings.

Within the month *Idflieg* was doing belated stress testing and concluded to its dismay that the D.V's wing layout was even more vulnerable than that of its predecessor, while its performance was virtually the same. A call for better fighters was issued, including a triplane inspired—much as the Albatros sesquiplanes had been inspired by the French Nieuports—by the remarkable performance displayed by the Sopwith Triplane.

Circumstances conspired against the complete abandonment of the Albatros D.V, however. On April 6, 1917 the United States declared war on Germany and recognition of the industrial potential of that new adversary led to a drastic expansion of German air power on June 23. Among other things, the so-called *Amerika-Programm* called for the formation of 40 new *Jagstaffeln* and a second *Jastaschule* to help train the new fighter pilots selected from 24,000 new recruits. Pending the appearance of a suitable replacement in the face of the impending American threat, *Idflieg* saw no alternative to placing production orders for more Albatros D.Vs—400 in May and 300 in July.

The D.V's arrival at the front coincided with the first German attempts to create what the Allies already had had for the past year. In the face of Allied offensives some *Jagdstaffeln* had been gathered in temporary local *Jagdgruppen* whose constituent squadrons changed as shifting front-line priorities required. On June 24, however, Crown Prince Rupprecht of Bavaria announced the formation of a permanent fighter wing, *Jagdgeschwader* I, in his 4. *Armee*, to comprise *Jastas* 4, 6, 10 and 11. Although the Russians and French had already had such fighter groups since 1916, *Luftstreitskräfte* com-

Albatros D.Vs of *Jasta* 15 line up for inspection at La Selve aerodrome in July 1917.
Intended as a refinement over the proven D.III, the Albatros D.V was deemed "lousy" by
a profoundly disappointed Manfred von Richthofen. (*Johan Visser*)

mander, Generalleutnant Ernst von Hoeppner, stated in his postwar
memoirs that JG.I had been formed in response to another enemy:

> Due to his number and his sporting spirit, the Englishman
> was always our most dangerous enemy and the British Front
> required, as a matter of course, the main force of the German
> air service.
>
> The ever-increasing number of aircraft which the opposition
> deployed to reach a target made it seem desirable for us to
> combine several Jagdstaffeln into a Jagdgeschwader...In the
> personage of Rittmeister [Manfred] von Richthofen....the
> Geschwader received a Kommandeur whose steel-hard will
> in relentlessly pursuing the enemy was infused in every
> member of the Geschwader. His refined lack of pretension,
> his open, gallant manner [and] his military skill secured for
> him amongst the Army an unshakable trust that, despite his
> young age, was matched with great respect.

On the following day Richthofen, flying with Leutnant Karl
Allmenröder, to whom he would pass command of *Jasta* 11, blooded
JG.I by sending an R.E.8 of No.53 Squadron crashing into the
trenches near Le Bizet. In Richthofen's hands JG.I would travel to

wherever the need for local air superiority beckoned. Like Boelcke, Richthofen would send up patrols in response to telephoned reports from officers stationed at the front, only this time in anywhere from two to four of his *Staffeln* at a time, their identities easily discernable by the winding black ribbon around the fuselages of *Jasta* 4 aircraft, black and white tail bands of *Jasta* 6, yellow noses of *Jasta* 10 and red noses of *Jasta* 11. Richthofen also made a practice of establishing satellite airfields closer to the front to allow faster responses when necessary. These tactics made the most of his assets and, combined with their peripatetic nature and the colorful livery of their planes, earned his collection of star pilots a sobriquet from their opponents that became as famous as the one he had acquired by then: The Red Baron's Flying Circus.

That such tactics helped his "gentlemen" hold their own against the British in no way blinded Richthofen to the sobering fact that they did so in spite, not because of, the fighters they flew. In a letter to a friend on the *Luftstreitskäfte* staff, Oberleutnant Fritz von Falkenhayn, on July 18, the Baron complained of the inadequate quality, as well as numbers, of the aircraft he led, "The D.V is so far surpassed by and so ridiculously inferior to the British single-seaters that one can't begin to do anything with this aircraft. But the people at home have not bought anything new for almost a year, except for these lousy Albatroses, and have remained stuck with the D.III, in which I fought in the autumn of last year."

On August 1, Oberleutnant Adolf Ritter von Tutschek, commander of *Jasta* 12, expressed similar feelings in a letter home, "In the past four weeks three new types of enemy aircraft have appeared. They are without a doubt far superior in their ability to climb than the best D.V.

"They are the new English S.E.5 one-seater, the 200-hp Spad, and the very outstanding Bristol Fighter two-seater. While the Albatros D.III and D.V come near in their ability to climb with the Sopwith and Nieuport and even surpass them in speed, it is almost impossible for them to force an S.E.5 or a 200-hp SPAD to fight because the enemy is able to avoid it by the ability of his craft to out-climb the Albatros."

After describing the Bristol as "our most dangerous opponent," von Tutschek spoke for virtually every German fighter pilot on the Western Front:

> In my opinion a machine superior to these three would be more important than an increase in the number of the present ones. I can achieve more with three pilots and planes which are completely trustworthy, as good or better than the opposition in climbing, maneuverability, and sturdiness, than I can with 20 pilots in D.Vs of whose ability and performance I am not convinced, and must watch with apprehension while diving during air battle.

As of August 31, Albatros products—424 D.Vs, 385 D.IIIs and even 56 D.IIs and D.Is—made up 84 percent of the 1,030 fighters in front-line inventory. Nevertheless, the pilots' complaints had not gone completely unaddressed, as evidenced by the two new fighter types, the Pfalz D.III and Fokker F.I, which made their front-line debuts at that very same time.

The Pfalz D.III was a product of the Pfalz Flugzeugwerke GmbH at Speyer, Bavaria, which had previously built Roland D.IIs under license. A single-seat version of Roland's two-seat C.II "*Walfisch*" (whale), the D.II "*Haifisch*" (shark) was a biplane whose fuselage was constructed in two halves from three-ply veneer strips. Sleek looking but overweight and underpowered, it never matched the Albatros's appeal and only achieved limited production and use. When *Idflieg* called for a fighter to match the Nieuport 11 and 17, the Pfalz engineering team, headed by Rudolf Gehringer, produced an original design that, significantly, was not really a sesquiplane, but a biplane with a smaller lower wing, supported by U-shaped cabane and interplane struts. The wood veneer fuselage, which incorporated a compound wing root along with integral fin and tailplane surfaces, was based on Pfalz's previous experience with the Roland D.II.

Accepted and put into production in mid-1917, the sleek-looking Pfalz D.III was more elegantly sharklike than the original *Haifisch*. When the first three reached the front, however, the reception was less than enthusiastic. Leutnant Werner Voss, now com-

Pfalz D.III 1386/17 was flown by Leutnant Alfred Lenz, commander of Jasta 22. Although more robust than the Albatros D.V, the Pfalz's performance failed to live up to its racy appearance. (Johan Visser)

manding *Jasta* 10, flew his on a few missions, but is said to have still preferred his Albatros D.V's superior climb rate and maneuverability to the newer plane's stronger wing structure and better diving characteristics.

Similar complaints of relatively sluggish handling characteristics and performance indicative of an unfavorable power-to-weight ratio undermined the Pfalz's popularity as more arrived at *Jastas* 4 and 10, as well as Bavarian *Jastas* 16, 32, 34 and 35, during the fall of 1917. On top of that, Pfalz's attempt to reduce drag by enclosing of the D.III's twin machine guns within its fuselage was bitterly criticized by pilots who found them inaccessible if they needed to correct a jam.

Voss and Richthofen were more appreciative of the two Fokker F.Is they received for evaluation at the end of August. These were preproduction specimens of Anthony Fokker's response to *Idflieg*'s request, made in June 1917, for a fighter to counter the Sopwith Triplane.

At that time Fokker, whose fortunes had been eclipsed by the Albatros fighters, had been developing a new series of aircraft based on a box spar wing structure pioneered by Swedish-born engineer Villehad Forssman. Fokker also knew of the all-metal cantilever wing structures developed by Dr. Hugo Junkers and proven when his J.I monoplane took to the air on December 12, 1915. Fokker, however, decided that Forssman's wooden structure offered a lighter weight airframe for the power that engines of the time could provide.

The first of Fokker's experimental *Verspannungslos* ('without external bracing') designs, the V1 and V2, were sesquiplanes with plywood covered wings and fuselages, respectively powered by air-cooled rotary and water-cooled inline engines. Tested in early 1917, they showed great potential, but when he learned of *Idflieg*'s pending requirement, Fokker, hardly one to pass up an opportunity to regain his prominence in the industry, decided that if a triplane it wanted, a triplane it would have. He therefore took the fuselage of a V3, a rotary engine biplane fighter he'd been building for the Austro-Hungarian air service, and reconfigured it as a triplane, the V4. To save weight the V4 used a canvas, rather than plywood covering over a steel tube fuselage frame and plywood box spar wing structure. It originally featured simple non-balanced elevators and ailerons and no interplane struts on the wings, but as the latter were slightly lengthened they required a set of I-shaped interplane struts and balanced control surfaces were added. The V4 was powered by a captured 110-hp Le Rhône engine, but its successor was given a German-built copy, the Oberursel Ur.II.

While the improved V4 version—later redesignated V5—was undergoing testing late in June, Fokker also produced the V6 with a 160-hp Mercedes water-cooled inline engine, but it proved to be heavy, slow and sluggish. Fokker therefore proceeded with the rotary engine concept, in the form of three pre-production F.Is (the 'F' designator being the lowest letter in the alphabet not being used by the *Luftstreitkräfte* thus far). The first, F.I 101/17, was tested to destruction on August 11, but on the 28th the other two arrived at JG.I's aerodrome at Marcke. F.I 102/17 went to Richthofen, whose score then stood at 59. The other, 103/17, went to Voss, who with 38 victories was engaged in an amicable but nonetheless earnest rivalry with his *Geschwaderkommandeur*.

The two aces differed considerably in technique and temperament. Richthofen was never the natural pilot Voss was, but a superb tactician with murderously efficient hunting instincts and, as testified by his men, uncanny vision. Voss, high-strung and impulsive, was master of any plane he flew and a deadly shot. Richthofen saw the F.I, with its advanced structure, agility and climb rate, as the hoped-for panacea to the fragile Albatros D.V and sluggish Pfalz D.III. Voss, equally disillusioned with both machines, embraced his F.I as made just for a man of his talents.

On September 1, as Richthofen reported: "Flying the triplane for the first time [in combat], I and four gentlemen of *Staffel* 11 attacked a very courageously flown British artillery-spotting aircraft. I approached [until] it was 50 meters below me and fired twenty shots, whereupon the adversary went down out of control and crashed on this side near Zonnebeke.

"Apparently the adversary had taken me for a British triplane, as the observer stood up in his machine without making a move to attack me with his machine gun."

The Baron's 60th victim was R.E.8 B782 of No. 6 Squadron. The wounded pilot, Lieutenant J.B.C. Madge, was taken prisoner and the hapless observer, 2nd Lt. Walter Kember, was killed.

Two days later *Jasta* 11's morning patrol attacked a flight of Pups from No. 46 Squadron over Menin. One of the British, Lieutenant Arthur Stanley Gould Lee, described the action in a letter whose text he must have altered in the process of compiling it into his autobiography, *No Parachute*, since both F.Is wore streaky greenish camouflage with light blue undersurfaces, with no overpainted colours at the time:

> The first patrol ran quickly into trouble, five of 'A' Flight…
> met Richthofen's Circus and had a hectic scrap. The Pups
> were completely outclassed by the D.Vs and most of their
> share of the fighting consisted of trying to avoid being rid-
> dled. Mac [2nd Lt. K.W. McDonald] and [2nd Lt. Algernon
> F.] Bird were seen to go down in Hunland. [Lieutenant
> Richard] Asher might have reached the Lines. The two
> chaps who got away, badly shot about, said that one of the
> Huns was flying a triplane, coloured red. It must be a cap-
> tured naval Tripe, I suppose.

Leutnant Werner Voss and Fokker F I 103/17 proved to be a pairing of man and machine that put the seal of approval on the triplane. Even the *Jasta* 10 ace's spectacular death on September 23, 1917, made him and his fighter the talk of the Western Front. (*Jon Guttman*)

McDonald was killed for Leutnant Eberhardt Mohnicke's sixth victory. Richthofen drove the other Pup down south of Bousbecque, though not without a fight, as he reported, "I was absolutely convinced that in front of me I had a very skillful pilot, who even at 50 meters altitude did not give up, continued to fire and, even when flattening out [before landing] fired at an infantry column, then deliberately steered his machine into a tree. The Fokker F.I 102/17 is absolutely superior to the British Sopwith."

At the crash site Anthony Fokker, who was visiting Marcke to promote his new fighter, photographed Richthofen beside his captive— who in spite of his misfortune looked quite pleased to have done his duty as best he could and survived his run-in with the Red Baron. Meanwhile, at 0955 hours Voss downed a Camel north of Houthem, killing Lieutenant A.T. Heywood of No. 45 Squadron.

After that day's success, Richthofen went on three weeks' leave, placing Leutnant Kurt von Döring in acting command of JG.I and his triplane in the care of Kurt Wolff, who assumed command of *Jasta* 11 on September 11, and was promoted to Oberleutnant the next day. Wolff, who had not scored since his 33rd on July 7, was keen to resume his winning streak in the new triplane.

Voss got a Pup on September 5, driving Lieutenant Charles W. Odell of No. 46 Squadron down in Allied lines, unhurt. "They were patrolling north-east of Ypres when Odell, who had seen a triplane coming down from behind, but taken no notice, thinking it was a Nautical, was amazed to find it firing at him," Arthur Gould Lee wrote. "He turned, assuming the R.N.A.S. pilot had gone off his rocker, than saw the black crosses. The others turned too, and a brisk little scrap followed, the Hun being joined by a D.V. The triplane, which was painted red, had a tremendous performance, and when he decided he'd had enough he lifted up above everybody like a rocket. He was a pretty hot pilot, for he holed most of the Pups, but nobody could get a bead on him." Again, Lee referred, perhaps retrospectively, to a color that neither F.I had, but the German's flying style clearly suggests Voss, who also destroyed a Caudron G 6 of French *Escadrille* C.53 that day and an F.E.2d of No. 20 Squadron on the next.

Voss destroyed two Camels on September 10, killing 2nd Lts. A.J.S. Sisley and O.C. Pearson of No. 70 Squadron, and claimed a Spad VII of Spa.37 20 minutes later. He downed two more Camels the next day, one of whose pilots, six-victory ace Lieutenant Oliver L. McMaking of No. 45 Squadron, died east of St Julien. Voss in turn was credited to McMaking's squadron mate, Captain Norman MacMillan, as not one but two triplanes driven down "out of control" east of Langemarck, the sixth and seventh of his nine victories. In fact, through the violent maneuvers that caused the misperception among his enemies (MacMillan believed there were three triplanes involved in the fight), Voss emerged unscathed, having raised his tally by nine in about as many days.

On September 15, *Jasta* 11 dived on four Camels of No. 10 Squadron RNAS over Moorslede. Although attacked from above, the British managed to dodge the Germans' fire and a general engagement ensued, during which Flight Sub-Lieutenant Norman M. Macgregor fired into a triplane at 25 yards' distance, saw it fall in a steep dive and claimed it as "out of control" for his fifth victory. This time the OOC represented genuine "first blood" for the Camel against its soon-to-be classic counterpart: Wolff's body was found in the wreckage of F.I 102/17 near Nachtigal, north of Werwicq.

At 0930 hours on September 23, Voss destroyed a D.H.4 of No. 57 Squadron south of Roulers. His score now stood at 48, but a *Staffel* mate, Leutnant Aloys Heldmann, noticed the toll the past month's activity was taking on him, "He was on edge; he had the nervous instability of a cat. I think it would be fair to say that he was flying on his nerves. And such a situation could have but one end." Joining his brothers Otto and Max for lunch, Werner Voss discussed plans for his upcoming leave. At 1800 hours he led five other fighters on the day's last patrol, but when he spotted a patrol of S.E.5as from No. 60 Squadron over Poelkapelle, Voss, undoubtedly eager to raise his score to an even 50, dove on it. Voss was in turn jumped by the S.E.5as B Flight, No. 56 Squadron.

The epic 10-minute dogfight that followed was documented by the testimonies of some of Britain's most seasoned fighter pilots, and they were all awed by the virtuosity of Voss, his triplane, and by the damage they inflicted. Of 60 Squadron's flight, Captain Harold A. Hamersley came down with his engine shot up and Captain Robert L. Chidlaw-Roberts returned with his rudder bar shot through. In "Fighting 56," Lieutenant Keith K. Muspratt retired with a bullet in his radiator and 2nd Lt. Verschoyle P. Cronyn limped home with his wings so badly riddled he spent that night in a sweaty funk, unable to sleep.

That left Voss and an Albatros D.V that had come to his aid to tackle such 56 Squadron champions as Jimmy McCudden, Arthur P.F. Rhys Davids, Reginald Hoidge, Richard A. Maybery and C Flight's leader, Captain Geoffrey Hilton Bowman. Among the many who marveled at Voss's and the triplane's performance, Bowman reported, "I put my nose down to give him a burst and opened fire, perhaps too soon; to my amazement he kicked on full rudder, without bank, pulled his nose up slightly, gave me a burst while he was skidding sideways, and then kicked on opposite rudder before the results of this amazing stunt appeared to have any effect on the controllability of his machine."

Eventually Rhys Davids drove down the Albatros, whose pilot survived, and then shot down F.I 103/17 at Plum Farm, 700 meters north of Frezenburg. Voss's body, hastily buried under fire, was obliterated in the battle being fought there, but his last fight was the talk of 56 Squadron that night. The two F.Is' overall performance that month—at least six victories by Voss, including four Camels, and two by Richthofen—put the seal of approval on Fokker's new fighter.

The production model, redesignated Dr.I (for *Dreidecker*, or triplane) differed from the F.I by having a modified cowling, a straight rather than slightly curved leading edge to the horizontal stabilizer, and the attachment of two wooden skids at the lower end of the interplane struts to protect the undersides of the wings in case of ground loops. While the F.Is and early Dr.Is had ailerons of different square meterage to compensate for the engine torque, those of later Dr Is had identical ailerons of increased area.

In the month following Voss's death, JG.I's pilots were assigned a few Fokker D.V fighter trainers to familiarize them with rotary engines. When Richthofen returned to Marcke on October 23, *Jasta* 11 had 17 of the much anticipated Dr.Is.

The Circus's elation with the new machines would be short-lived. On October 29, a German pilot mistook Vizefeldwebel Josef Lautenschlager's Dr.I 113/17 for a Sopwith Triplane and sent him crashing to his death north of Houthulst Forest. The next day, both Lothar and Manfred von Richthofen had to force-land malfunctioning Dr.Is. A more alarming mishap occurred elsewhere that day when Leutnant Heinrich Gontermann, 39-victory ace and commander of *Jasta* 15, test flew his newly delivered Dr.I 115/17 over La Neuville aerodrome, only to see the ribs break away from the upper wing spar, resulting in a crash from which he died of his injuries that evening. On October 31, Richthofen saw Dr.I 121/17 of *Jasta* 11 glide down to land and suddenly drop its left wing and crash, killing Leutnant Günther Pastor.

On November 2, an alarmed *Idflieg* grounded all Dr.Is. A crash commission examined the triplane's wing and judged the box spar structure sound, but that the ribs and aileron attachment points, neither of which was attached to the box spar, were not. At low angles of attack—as in a dive—the forces of lift moved aft on a wing, which caused the Dr.I's ribs to flex. Similar flexing occurred on the ailerons, which was more pronounced on the V5 and its production derivatives, with their increased wingspans. While the F.Is had been able to handle those stresses, the Dr Is had not because their unvarnished wing interiors had absorbed moisture, weakening the glue—already thinned as an economic measure—that helped hold them together.

The committee concluded that Fokker needed to improve his quality control, among other things using cold-water glue of more robust consistency, transverse nailing to reinforce the bond, and a more thorough application of varnish over the wing structure before applying the fabric covering. The left aileron's aerodynamic balance was reduced, but a decrease of inboard taper increased the overall aileron area, reducing stress and increasing the roll rate to the right (a particularly welcome feature when dogfighting Camels).

Deliveries of the improved Dr.Is resumed in late December and *Jasta* 11 re-equipped with them in January 1918, soon to be joined by *Jasta* 6. Until then, those units had to make due with the Albatros D.V, while *Jastas* 4 and 10 made the most of their Pfalz D.IIIs.

While the first Pfalz D.IIIs and Fokker F.Is were arriving in August, Albatros, though still unable to ascertain the cause of the D.V's wing failures, had redesigned its wings with stronger spars wrapped in aluminum for extra flexibility, heavier ribs, additional wing support cables and sometimes a small auxiliary bracing strut at the base of the interplane strut. The strengthened D.V, designated D.Va, also had the aileron cables rerouted through the lower wing as they had been on the D.III, and the fuselage structure was reinforced using a thicker gauge of plywood. An improved gun interrupter gear, devised by a Werkmeister Semmler, replaced the Hedke system in production D.Vas.

Testing was not completed until December 1917, but in late August *Idflieg*, satisfied with Albatros's modifications in spite of the fact that the reinforced airframe was now heavier than the D.III's, let alone the D.V's, placed an order for the first of an eventual 1,600 Albatros D.Vas. That and a last D.III order for OAW in September reflected the *Luftstreitkräfte*'s desperation as it tried to build itself up for the Americans' expected arrival in early 1918, even while its *Jagdflieger* strove to counter a series of Allied offensives throughout the summer and fall of 1917.

Concurrent with the introduction of the Albatros D.V and D.Va was a gradual change in the camouflage on its wings and tail surfaces, from painted-on patches of dark green and mauve to directly applied fabric panels in lozenges of four or five varying shades, dark for the uppersurfaces and lighter for the lower. These were supposed to achieve an overall camouflage effect when viewed at a distance, although that was often rendered moot by the frequent practice of decorating the aircraft in flamboyant *Staffel* colours and personal motifs. Perhaps more important, the preprinted fabric saved the weight that painting added, needing only an application of protective clear dope.

Germans were not the only airmen in the Central Powers who longed for a fighter to match those of the Allies in 1917. Like Italy, Austria-Hungary was unsuccessful in developing an effective indigenous scout in the early war years, its pilots using German designs such as the Fokker A.III (their designation for the E.III) and the Hansa Brandenburg D.I, created by a design bureau headed by Ernst Heinkel. A biplane braced by a unique junction of eight interplane struts into a starlike arrangement and featuring a deep fuselage whose rear upper decking tapered aft into a vertical stabilizer, the Brandenburg D.I or KD (*Kampf-Doppeldecker*) entered production in May 1916. Oberst Emil Uzelac, commander of the *Kaiserlische und Königlische Luftfahrtruppen*, personally test-flew the new fighter on November 7—and promptly crashed, suffering a concussion. Nevertheless, the Brandenburg D.I (series 65), fitted with a Type II VK canister holding an MG 08/15 machine gun and ammunition on the upper wing, was committed to the front. On December 3, Oberleutnant Godwin Brumowski, flying D.I 65.53 with *Flik* 12, teamed up with Linienschiffleutnant Gottfried Banfield of the Trieste Naval Air Station and Zugsführer Karl Cislaghi of *Flik* 28 to bring down a Caproni Ca.1 bomber over Mavinje.

Only two other victories would be scored by Brandenburg-built KDs. One of its pilots, Zugsführer Julius Arigi of *Fluggeschwader* 1,

Hansa-Brandenburg D.I 28.37 boasted some improvements over the standard "*Kampf Doppeldecker*," starting with the vertical stabilizer added on Phönix-built planes and a Bernatzik-synchronized Schwarzlose machine gun alongside the engine. Shown with *Fliegerkompagnie* 24 at Pergine aerodrome, it was used by Hungarian ace of aces Jozsef Kiss to score three of his 19 victories in the summer of 1917. (*Greg Van Wyngarden*)

added a vertical stabilizer and an enlarged rudder which improved the flight characteristics somewhat, and this was incorporated in the 72 D.Is (series 28) built by the Phönix firm. Phönix-built KDs took a reasonable toll on Italian aircraft, less due to the plane than the skill of its pilots.

Another improvement was the introduction of interrupter gear in place of the Type II VK canister. Anthony Fokker had been laboring to adapt his gear to the Schwarzlose machine gun, with its retarded blowback, but before he succeeded, Leutnant Otto Bernatzik, the technical officer for *Flik* 8, devised one that was actuated by an exhaust rocker arm at every second propeller revolution for his unit's Brandenburg C.Is in the spring of 1916. This was installed on some D.Is soon after. Later, Oberleutnant Eduard Zaparka developed interrupter gear for the Hiero engine that would accommodate twin machine guns, albeit at every fourth engine revolution. Daimler produced one that doubled the Zaparka's rate of fire and in October 1917, Oberleutnant Guido Priesel came up with a variation on Fokker's cam system that was superior to the Daimler gear and became standard on Oeffag Albatros fighters in 1918.

After scoring his fifth victory in a Brandenburg C.I two-seater on January 2, 1917, now-Hauptmann Godwin Brumowski was given command of a new, specialized fighter (or *Jagd*) unit, *Flik* 41/J. Before commencing operations, however, he was sent to observe developments over the Western Front, flying four combat missions with *Jasta* 24 from March 19 to 27, and meeting Manfred von Richthofen. Brumowski was profoundly influenced by what he saw—after returning to Italy in April, he took steps to turn *Flik* 41/J into an elite fighter outfit like *Jasta* 11 and even painted some of his own planes red in emulation of Richthofen, with the personal addition of a skull on the fuselage. In June, Brumowski—displaying an outspokenness worthy of the Red Baron's—reported to his superiors that, "the KD is absolutely useless...the best pilots (and only they can fly the type) are shackled, ruin their nerves and perish in crashes over the airfield, without their expert skill achieving anything."

One result of Brumowski's appeal was the replacement of the Brandenburg D.I in his and other *Jagdfliegerkompagnien* with Austrian versions of the Albatros D.II and D.III, license-built by the Oesterreichisches Flugzeugwerke A.G. (Oeffag) in Wiener-Neustadt and powered by 185-hp Austro-Daimler engines. In an ironic sidebar to the decline of the German Albatros sesquiplanes, later versions of the Oeffag D.III, constructed with greater care and a better grade of wood than its German cousins, held up well in combat. While the Oeffag's construction seems to have reduced, if not eliminated, the sesquiplane curse, pilot complaints of spinners coming off led to their being done away with on late production series 153 and all 253 series D.IIIs, which featured a spinnerless propeller in front of a rounded nose cowl with no ill effect on performance. The series 253, powered by a 225-hp Austro-Daimler with a maximum of 125 mph, proved to be the most successful fighter to serve in the *Luftfahrtruppen*—and best of all the Albatros sesquiplanes. Equally significant, however, are the production figures of these excellent machines: at least 203 Series 253, out of a grand total of about 550 Oeffag D.IIIs. For comparison, in Germany Albatros produced about 900 D.Vs and 1,012 D.Vas, to which OAW added another 600 D Vas. Austria-Hungary offered superior quality, but at what proved to be a fatal sacrifice in quantity.

The first truly Austrian-designed land fighter was almost rejected out of hand before it reached the drawing board. On June 8, 1916, Julius von Berg of the Oesterreichisch-Ungarische Flugzeugfabrik "Aviatik" GmbH proposed a fighter to use a 160-hp Daimler engine and a similar single-seat scout powered by a 120-hp Daimler. Both were rejected by the *Luftfahrtruppen*'s *Fliegerarsenal* (Flars) because it wanted Aviatik to license-produce Knoller C.II two-seaters, rather than pursue its own projects. In August, however, Oberst Uzelac learned of Berg's idea and authorized him to proceed.

Just two months later, on October 16, Aviatik fighter prototype serial 30.14 was ready for its test flight at Aspern. Combining a flat-sided wooden fuselage with Knoller-style wings featuring a reflex curvature, the 30.14 was coming in from its first flight when it suddenly plunged into the ground, killing its test pilot, Feldwebel Ferdinand Könschel. Aviatik engineer Julius Kolin was convinced that the center of pressure shift had been responsible for the crash and set about redesigning the wing. Several follow-up prototypes were built and tested, until success was finally achieved with 30.19, which first flew on January 24, 1917. After test-flying the plane on March 31, Oberleutnant Oszkar Fekete praised its "fabulous climb and enormous maneuverability," and the Aviatik D.I was accepted for production.

On May 15, 30.19, retro-fitted with an improved one-piece upper wing, was sent along with the first production Aviatik D.I, 38.01, to *Fluggeschwader* 1 on the Isonzo front for combat evaluation. Flying 30.19 with an unsynchronized machine gun mounted on the upper wing, Hauptmann Karl Sabeditch shot down a Caproni Ca.1 on the 23rd.

The Aviatik, also called the Berg D.I, was produced by a number of sub-contractors and appeared in equally numerous forms, using a succession of increasingly powerful engines, a variety of radiators and different armament, ranging from single guns firing over the upper wing to synchronized weapons buried in the cowling and finally twin guns in front of the cockpit as pilots favored. Although extraordinarily nimble for an airplane powered by an inline engine, the Aviatik D.I occasionally suffered wing failures due to shoddy construction,

Oberleutnant Fritz Pisko of Flik 60/J soberly surveys the wing damage to his Lohner-built Oesterreichischer Aviatik D.I 115.26 on March 18, 1918, having survived a similar incident in 115.05 just two days earlier. An inspection revealed that Lohner had substituted a lighter rib design and applied the fabric contrary to Aviatik specifications. (*Antal Boksay album via Jon Guttman*)

depending on the manufacturer, and in spite of the ubiquity it achieved by the end of 1917, Austria's first fighter never achieved a significant level of ascendency over its Allied counterparts.

In June 1917, Phönix, having already improved the Brandenburg D.I it had built under license, unveiled two prototypes of its proposed successor. One, bearing the serial 20.14, introduced a wireless variation on the Nieuport sesquiplane wing cellule, designed by Leo Kirste, which combined a "V" interplane strut with a third strut that braced the lower wing to the middle of a somewhat elongated Brandenburg D.I fuselage. The 20.15, designed by Edmund Sparmann, utilized a more conventional, wire-braced wing based on his observations of German aircraft—and the pros and cons of the sesquiplane layout as employed on the Albatros. Test flights showed the 20.15 wing to be more robust than that of the 20.14, in addition to which it provided a climb rate and flight characteristics that were vastly superior to those of the Brandenburg D.I. The 20.15's speed was not significantly higher than the Brandenburg's, but that was remediable by installing a more powerful engine than the 185-hp Daimler—which it got in the form of a 200-hp Hiero. Production of

Phönix D.IIa 422.14 flown by Feldwebel Sandor Kasza, a six-victory Hungarian ace of Flik 55/J, at Pergine in early May 1918. The plane inside the hangar at right was flown by Feldwebel István Kirják (3 victories). (*Greg Van Wyngarden*)

the Phönix D.I began in August, with two Zaparka-synchronized machine guns installed on either side of the engine.

Austria-Hungary had a more poorly developed industrial capacity than Italy, and once again it took Oberst Uzelac to personally expedite the Phönix D.I's delivery to the front. By December, Phönix D.Is were entering the inventories of *Fliks* 4/D, 15/D, 17/D, 48/D, 54/D, and 66/D, where they were to serve as escorts to those units' reconnaissance aircraft, and at fighter *Fliks* 14/J 30/J, 60/J, 61/J, and 63/J.

Activated in November 1917, *Flik* 60/J was sent to Grigno in the mountainous Val Sugana, about 60 miles north-northwest of Venice. *Flik* 60/J was led by Oberleutnant Frank Linke-Crawford, with six enlisted pilots and a complement of series 128, 228 and 328 Phönix D.Is. Linke-Crawford was already credited with 13 victories while flying Brandenburg D.Is and Oeffag-Albatros D.IIIs in *Flik* 41/J under Brumowski's tutelage, and it may have been he who first blooded the Phönix. On January 10, 1918, he took off in D.I 228.16, accompanied by Stabsfeldwebel Kurt Gruber, another veteran with five victories, in D.I 228.24. Over Val Stagna, they encountered what Linke described as a "Sopwith two-seater" accompanied by

Nieuports, and attacked. In short order, they sent the two-seater, a SAML of the 115a *Squadriglia*, down just within Italian lines, followed by one of its escorts. Since Austria-Hungary credited shared victories in the French manner, two were added to both Linke-Crawford's and Gruber's personal tallies. The SAML crew, Sergente U. Lenzi and Sottotenente S. Achenza, survived unhurt, as did Sergente Antonio Reali of the 79*a Squadriglia*, who upon returning to Istrana aerodrome with 20 bullet holes in his Nieuport 27, made a claim of his own for an unidentified enemy fighter over Primolano. That went rightly unconfirmed, but Reali would be credited with 11 victories by the end of the war.

Opinions varied regarding the Phönix D.I's merits. During a flight comparison in September 1917, it was judged to be superior in speed and climb rate to the Oeffag-Albatros D.III and to have better flight characteristics than the Aviatik D.I. A German report in October stated that the Phönix, "possesses totally amazing qualities, especially the quickness of maneuver and stability when throttled down. The pilot can stall the aircraft virtually on the spot and drop several hundred meters without losing control." In February 1918, however, *Flik* 60/J reported that the, "D.I is not favored by pilots because the speed and climb are inferior to the Nieuport, Spad and Sopwith fighters." *Flik* 30/J complained that it was too slow and "almost too stable for quick combat maneuvers." Whatever its faults, the Phönix D.I and its successors, the D.II, D.IIa and D.III, acquired a reputation for ruggedness, especially in a dive, akin to those of the S.E.5a, the Spad XIII, and the Pfalz D.IIIa. It also did much to provide Austria-Hungary's small but spirited air arm with a competitive fighter of its own design.

8

THE RIGHT TOOLS
FOR THE JOB

Specialized Fighter Categories

As the war itself widened, so did the exigencies that called for the development of aircraft to fulfill special requirements. This often involved modifying fighters to exploit the aerial control they had acquired, both in their original role as scouts, and as photoreconnaissance planes with the addition of cameras in the fuselage, as was done on Spads and SVA-5s.

As aircraft performance improved, their more aggressive use over the battlefield increased, with fighters being called upon to strafe enemy troops, communications, or logistical targets behind the lines in support of their own soldiers. Such duties were never popular among fighter pilots, since they brought the planes low to the ground, exposed to every enemy soldier holding a gun and tempting the law of averages until that one bullet marked "to whom in may concern" hit a fuel tank, a radiator, an oil line, or the pilot. To D.H.5 pilots, ground attack and close support duties seemed less a case of playing the plane's strengths so much as punishment for its shortcomings as an air superiority fighter.

The close-support fighter went from casual adjunct to regular requirement in the late summer of 1917. At that time the Germans introduced a class of smaller, lighter, more agile two-seaters to equip *Schutzstaffeln*, meant to "protect" reconnaissance planes, the first of which was the Halberstadt CL.II. Arming their planes with trays of

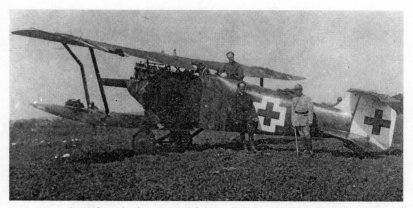

A Hannover CL.IIIa brought down in French lines shows the robust, relatively compact airframe and back-to-back seating of pilot and observer that made it an effective ground strafer and, if need be, a formidable two-seat fighter. (*SHAA B76.911*)

anti-personnel grenades as well as their two machine guns, the Halberstadt units quickly evolved into *Schlachtstafflen* or "battle flights," with ground attack their primary mission.

Amid Britain's protracted Passchendaele offensive, on September 3, 1917, the Germans were forced to evacuate Péronne, before which British reinforcements were reported massing along the Somme River at Bray and St. Christ. When the British began crossing the bridges, 24 Halberstadt CL.IIs swooped in, shooting and hurling down grenades from as low as 100 feet. As the Germans hoped, panic ensued, with Tommies throwing themselves over the parapets of the bridges to escape the punishment. Further back, artillery troops and their horses were also attacked. Only two Sopwith scouts intervened and, in a demonstration of the agility and aggressive teamwork that the CL.II shared with the Bristol Fighter, the Germans shot one of them down. All told, the Germans estimated that their 24 Halberstadts had left the better part of a division in disarray.

Often fitted with a thin sheet of armor under the communal pilot-observer's position, Halberstadt CL.IIs figured prominently in the counterattacks that retook much ground from the British around Cambrai on November 30. By that time they were being joined by a similar product of the Hannoverische Waggonfabrik A.G., the Hannover CL.II, which featured a compact, biplane tailplane to maintain maneuverability while reducing the chance of it being hit by the observer's gun. Later refinements, the Halberstadt CL.IV and Hannover CL.III and CL.IIIa, played prominent roles in the *Schlastas* for the rest of the war.

Although the CL types were not used in the fighter role to the full extent that the British used their Bristol F.2Bs, they earned the respect of Allied fighter pilots as tough opponents and a handful of German crews accumulated aces' scores in the course of defending themselves. Most famous—or notorious—was Hannover CL.IIIa pilot Unteroffizier Johann Baur of *Fl. Abt.* 295b, who with Leutnant Georg Hengl as his observer was credited with six French aircraft downed in 1918, and subsequently became Adolf Hitler's personal pilot in the 1930s.

By the Battle of Cambrai, the British were responding to the German ground strafers by fitting small racks under fighters like the Camel and S.E.5a to carry up to four 25-pound Cooper bombs. Captain Arthur Gould Lee of No. 46 Squadron described bomb-dropping practice in mid-November 1917:

> You dive at the target until you're at about 100 feet, meanwhile judging the exact moment to release the bomb with the control on the joystick. Pretending you're on the real job, you then flatten out and swerve quickly aside to get clear of the upward burst of the explosion. Dropping dummies on the aerodrome target, with no bullets to bother me, I found it surprisingly easy to get close results, in fact mine were much the best in the squadron. My proudest four, dropped one at a time, were all within a yard or two of the target, compared with other people's 100 yards, and one man's 170 yards. I hope this unexpected skill doesn't land me into any awkward jobs....It was a thrilling experience to shoot with two guns for the first time—the whole machine shudders with the rapid rate of fire and the double explosions.

"But imagine after waiting all those months for Camels," he added later, speaking for a good many of his colleagues, "striving not to be shot down in Pups, and looking forward to toppling Huns two at a

Camel H828 was flown by Canadian Lieutenant Floyd W. Wells of No. 80 Squadron, RAF, which specialized in low-level strafing and ground support for most of its combat career. (*Floyd W. Wells album via Jon Guttman*)

time with my two Vickers, to find myself switched to ground straf-ing!" Whereas some specialized close support aircraft carried armor plate—and the Germans evolved an entire "J" class of armored ground attackers—fighters could not afford to sacrifice their perform-ance for the protection it offered at the cost of added weight, leaving them vulnerable to every infantryman holding a firearm. For similar reasons to balloon busting, ground attack was universally unpopular among the fighter pilots, but when duty called they carried it out and Camels, S.E.5as and Bristol Fighters, among others, came to give much useful and thoroughly appreciated ground support to the troops, as did Spad XIIIs fitted with similar Cooper bomb racks flown by French and American pilots.

Among the most devastating tactical uses of British fighters in the ground support role—in conjunction with what was arguably their greatest success in achieving air superiority—occurred during General Sir Edmund H. H. Allenby's last drive toward Damascus. In mid-March 1918, as German and Turkish *Flieger Abteilungen* with their attached Halberstadt and Albatros fighters proved insufficient to master the growing numbers of British aircraft in Palestine, the Germans shipped the newly formed *Jasta* 55 to Palestine, where it was attached to Marshal Erich von Falkenhayn's Heeresgruppe F,

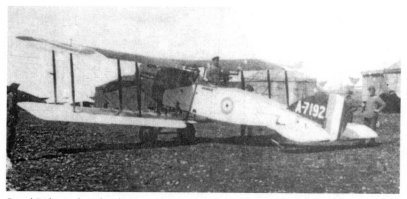

Bristol Fighters played a decisive role in seizing control of the air over Palestine and using it to help annihilate the enemy on the ground. F.2B A-7192 was crewed by Lieutenant Charles R, Davidson and 2nd Lt. A. Simmons of No. 111 Squadron, RFC to down German two-seaters on December 17 and 22, 1917, and an Albatros D.III on the 29th-bringing Davidson's total to six. In early 1918, all of 111 Squadron's Bristols were transferred to No.1 Squadron, Australian Flying Corps, which flew them to final victory outside Damascus. (*Philip Jarrett*)

commanded since February by Marshal Otto Liman von Sanders, and thus redesignated *Jasta* 1F. The day after *Jasta* 1F settled in for operations from Jenin, however, No. 1 Squadron, Australian Flying Corps, was brought fully up to strength with 18 Bristol F.2Bs, many acquired from No. 111 Squadron, RFC when it became a single-seater unit. In the months that followed, the two Allied fighter units steadily whittled away at their opponents, a relatively high ratio of the results being borne out by German loss records. The Bristols, aggressively crewed by teams such as Captain Ross M. Smith and Lieutenant Ernest A. Mustard, established such an ascendancy that by late August they were reporting whole flights of German fighters they encountered spinning down to land, where the Aussies finished off the abandoned planes on the ground. After the war, the Ottoman command attributed much of the Damascus campaign's outcome to the virtual elimination of Turkish and German aircraft by British and Australian fighters, preventing them from tracking changes in British deployment before the offensives on September 19.

The climax came on September 23, when Allenby's forces smashed through Turkish lines, and his fighters bombed and strafed

Turkish transport and soldiers as they fled along the Jordan Road toward Wadi Beidan. By the 24th, at the end of what came to be known as the Third Battle of Megiddo, the area west of Amman had been cleared of enemy troops and the Turkish Seventh and Eighth Armies ceased to exist as viable fighting forces. The Turks abandoned Damascus on the 30th.

Like ground attack, destroying enemy kite balloons was a task disliked by normal fighter pilots for similar reasons. The would-be "balloon buster" had to go deep in enemy lines through a gauntlet of ground fire and anti-aircraft artillery, attack the target as the ground crew's power winch rapidly pulled it down through an intensifying cone of fire. If he succeeded in setting the gasbag afire, the pilot still had to get home as every enemy fighter in the vicinity who noticed the blaze converged to cut off his escape route. Success depended as much on luck as on tactics and skill. A handful of pilots became specialists in that dangerous game, in a seemingly obsessive combination of pyromania and death wish that their comrades called "balloon fever." Whether a squadron had such fearless eccentrics or not, however, the frontline intelligence-gathering and artillery directing that balloons performed often made them strategic targets of vital importance, especially when an advance was in the offing.

No airplane is known to have been specifically developed for balloon busting, although some came to be regarded as better than others for the task. The Sopwith Camel and Hanriot HD.1 were both rugged and nimble, but generally aircraft that combined good diving speed and durability, such as the S.E.5a, Spad XIII and Pfalz D.IIIa, offered the best odds of survival.

A unique exception to that rule was exhibited by Sottotenente Giovanni Ancilotto, the most successful Italian balloon specialist of the war. Although his unit, the 77a *Squadriglia*, was equipped with Spad VIIs when he decided to go after Austro-Hungarian balloons or "Drachen" in November 1917, he chose to fly his sorties in Nieuport 11 No.2265 because it was expendable. Equally obsolescent was the plane's armament, an above-the-wing Lewis gun and wing mounted Le Prieur rockets. Yet "Gianni" Ancilotto destroyed two balloons on November 30 and December 3, and crowned his brief rampage by flying through his third and final victim on December 5, returning to Marcon aerodrome with sections of burnt fabric draped over his flying wires. Ancilotto survived the war with 11 victories, only to be killed in an automobile accident on October 18, 1924, at age 27.

At least three other balloon aces are known to have survived coming too close to their targets for comfort. On May 15, 1918, Adjutant Willy Coppens of the Belgian 9e *Escadrille* was just pulling up when the German balloon he attacked snapped its moorings and surged up, catching his Hanriot from underneath. Coppens had the presence of mind to shut off his motor so his propeller would not tangle in a line, waited until his plane slithered down the side of the deflating gasbag, restarted his engine and pulled up and away just before it burst into flame for his fourth victory.

All five victories credited to Maréchal-des-Logis Pierre Cardon of Spa.81 in 1918 were over balloons. His last, shared with Lieutenant Jacques Leps and Sergent Maurice Rouselle northwest of Soissons on June 6, was also the most memorable. "We were all so intent on the Drachen," he stated, "that it was only at the last moment I looked around and saw that Leps and Rousselle were converging on me! I took evasive measures with the result that we did not collide, but I went through the flames and smoke of the exploding balloon. I emerged with my carburetor full of gum and burnt rubber. The rubbery stuff choked the engine and I had to glide in. My plane was in a pitiful state, but I managed to reach our side of the lines."

Eight of Leutnant der Reserve Friedrich Theodor Noltenius's 21 victories were over Allied balloons. While flying a Fokker D.VII with *Jasta* 27 on September 14, 1918, he attacked a British balloon near Vitry-en-Artois, later remarking: "I only wanted to press the attack home when suddenly, while I was a mere 50 meters away, a gigantic flame rose, which completely engulfed me! The shock hurled me away. I at once took course for the lines after I had discovered that the machine was still in flying condition. But what a shambles she was! The cloth covering had become completely slack all over the machine

Kite balloons such as this German Type AE "Drachen," based on the French Caquot model, remained mainstays of front-line observation and artillery spotting throughout World War I. That also made them frequent fighter targets, although the locations of their nests were well inside their lines and the ring of anti-aircraft fire that surrounded them made "balloon busting" an extremely hazardous specialty. (*Jon Guttman*)

and billowed. Large shreds of balloon cloth hung in the struts and in the empennage. The controls acted perfectly different. To movements of the rudder, the plane did not react at all. In addition, the plane was excessively tail-heavy. In this condition I would have been unable to survive in a dogfight. Fortunately the strong western wind carried me home to our lines very quickly and I was able to land safely on our field."

Although the aircraft used in balloon busting were standard, their armament was not. Wing-mounted Le Prieur rockets proved too erratic, even at close range, to hit a balloon with any measure of reliability. Incendiary bullets proved effective, provided the attacker persisted long enough to allow the hydrogen escaping from the balloon to mix with oxygen in the atmosphere in order to ignite. Such ammunition had been developed as early as 1902, when John Pomeroy produced a nitroglycerine-based explosive round for use against airships, which was further refined alongside the work of Royal Navy officer Frank Arthur Brock. In 1914, James Buckingham came up with a phosphor-tipped round, a flat-nosed version of which was later produced to tear larger holes in a Zeppelin's skin. All were used against balloons, some 26 million Buckingham Mark VII rounds being produced in total.

Carrying anti-balloon ammunition came with a caveat. Although incendiary rounds were less accurate at long range than standard bullets, many German fighter pilots, including Manfred von Richthofen, mixed them with standard and tracer rounds for use against heavier-than-air craft. Albert Ball employed early Buckingham bullets against airplanes prior to the appearance of the flat-nosed round. Such ammunition had been prohibited at the Geneva Peace Conference of 1899, but the ban was not renewed at the next conference in 1907. Even so, the horrific damage and injury such bullets could cause made them a bone of contention in the accepted articles of war.

In 1916, the Germans threatened to court martial any Allied aircrews they captured with Brock-Pomeroy or Buckingham ammunition as war criminals. By 1918, it had become an officially expressed British policy that "Flat-nosed Buckingham ammunition is on no account to be used against any aircraft other than balloons or airships." Anyone ordered on an anti-balloon sortie was issued a blue card indicating the nature of his mission, in case he was brought down and taken prisoner.

Regardless of whether it was legal or not, most airmen did not want to contribute to a mutually escalating usage of balloon ammunition against airplanes. When Lieutenant William Maclanachan of No. 40 Squadron, RFC, added anti-balloon rounds to his Lewis gun magazine in intended reprisal for the German use of incendiary bullets against a squadron mate, it was his friend Lieutenant Edward Mannock who earnestly persuaded him to abandon the idea.

While the vast majority of balloon attacks were made using standard 7.92mm, .303-inch or .30-caliber machine guns, the French produced an 11mm Vickers gun specifically for the task, which saw use by selected personnel in French and American Spad and Nieuport 28 squadrons. Willy Coppens was also delighted when the

French presented him with an 11mm Vickers after scoring his ace-making fifth victory on May 19, 1918. Using both that and the more usual .303-inch Vickers on his Hanriots, he brought his total to 35 balloons, as well as two airplanes, by October 14, when a wound serious enough to necessitate the amputation of his left leg terminated his combat career. Notwithstanding that, the Belgian ace of aces and history's most successful balloon specialist proved to be an extraordinary survivor among his breed. His many honors included ennoblization as Willy Coppens, Baron d'Houthulst, when he finally died on December 21, 1986, at age 94.

The development of aerial operations by night, especially bombing, led to a fighting response. Zeppelin raids on England led to the establishment of RFC Home Defence squadrons that were initially equipped with modified reconnaissance planes, such as the B.E.2c, obsolescent fighters like the B.E.12 or F.E.2b, or even training aircraft such as single-seat, armed Avro 504s. When Gotha and Zeppelin-Staaken bombers began to eclipse the airships, the British initially withdrew front-line units such as Nos. 56 and 66 squadrons to reassure the public, before expanding its home defense force with a new breed of night fighters. S.E.5as and Bristols had flame dampers installed over their exhausts, but the most specialized were Camels, unofficially nicknamed Sopwith Comics, with the pilot's seat relocated further aft so he could use two Lewis guns on Foster mounts above the wing in place of the synchronized Vickers. This seemingly retrograde step was meant to prevent the flash of the gunfire from ruining the pilot's night vision.

By 1918, the French CRP units were employing Nieuport 27s with flares under the wings to be lit during the landing approach for the defense of Paris from night raiders. In October 1918, the American 1st Pursuit Group added the 185th Aero Squadron, with flare-equipped Camels for night interception and strafing, to its four Spad XIII squadrons. The Germans, too, made use of Albatros D.Vas, Roland D.VIs, and later, Fokker D.VIIs to oppose nocturnal

Allied bombing raids, *Jasta* 73 racking up a particularly impressive record against French Voisin 8s and 10s.

One other aspect of night fighting pioneered during World War I began with the formation of No. 151 Squadron, Royal Air Force, at Hainault Farm on June 12, 1918, and its deployment to Marquise and Famechon aerodromes in France on the 21st. With the Germans bombing Britain less, but with nocturnal strikes behind Allied lines increasing, the job of 151's Camel pilots was to either intercept the night raiders or attack them en route back to their bases, using searchlights or moonlight to find their targets—in essence a night intruder unit. First blood was drawn when South African Captain D'Urban Victor Armstrong claimed an LVG OOC near Estrée on June 29. On August 10, Captain A.B. Yuille shot down a Zeppelin-Staaken R.VI of *Riesenflugzeugabteilung* (Rfa) 501 over Doullens, killing the entire crew. Another giant, from Rfa.500, fell to Lieutenant F.C. Broome on September 15, only the pilot surviving to be taken prisoner. By the end of the war, 151 was credited with bringing down 16 enemy planes on the Allied side of the lines, five on the German side, and five unconfirmed. Its South African commander, Major Christopher J. Quinton-Brand, scored five of his 12-victory total by night, and Armstrong had accounted for four among his wartime total of six; tragically, the latter, renowned for his aerial dexterity, was killed while stunting two days after the armistice.

In addition to the evolution of aerial dominance over the battlefield, World War I produced a variety of waterborne aircraft meant to achieve the same goal over the sea. While floatplanes were the principal scouts and fighters to operate from the coasts of Western Europe, the most notable seagoing fighters developed by Russia, Austria-Hungary, and Italy were flying boats.

Russian naval airmen often made aggressive use of the versatile flying boats designed by Dmitry Pavlovich Grigorovich since 1913. The M.9, which first flew on January 9, 1916, and featured a 150-hp Salmson engine driving a pusher propeller, was the most successful.

Major Gilbert W. Murlis-Green, commander of No. 44 Squadron, lands Sopwith Comic B5192, a night fighter version of the Camel with twin overwing Lewis guns, at Hainault Farm, where a Zeppelin-shaped wind vane on the hangar symbolized the home defence unit's purpose. Murlis-Green, formerly an ace with No. 17 Squadron in Salonika, brought down a Gotha G III on the night of December 18, 1917, for his eighth victory. (*Greg Van Wyngarden*)

It led to smaller versions intended as flying boat fighters, the two-seat M.11—for which Aleksandr de Seversky designed a set of skis for use on land or from frozen lakes in winter—and the single-seat M.12.

The most successful Russian flying boat pilot, Aleksandr Nikolayevich Prokofiev de Seversky, was born in Tiflis on June 7, 1894, and learned to fly in 1908, prior to entering the Naval Academy at St. Petersburg. In June 1915 he was assigned to the 2nd Bombing and Reconnaissance Squadron of the Baltic Fleet, but while returning from his first sortie, an unsuccessful attack on a German destroyer in the Gulf of Riga, his French-built FBA flying boat crashed and its bombs exploded, killing his observer and injuring his leg, requiring an amputation below the knee.

Upon recovery, Seversky defied an order relieving him of front-line flying duties by engaging in an unauthorized aerobatic display that got him arrested, but which also caught the attention of the tsar, who arranged for his return to his squadron on July 1. Three days later, flying a Grigorevich M.9, he downed a German scout over the Gulf of Riga. On August 13, he claimed three German seaplanes, earning the Golden Sword of St. George.

After breaking his other leg in another crash and again recovering, Seversky scored two more victories while flying a Nieuport 21 on October 10. He was subsequently sent to serve as naval attaché to the United States in March 1918, and as a result of his disillusionment with the Bolshevik Revolution, he would remain there. He became an American citizen in 1927 and embarked on a career as an airplane designer for his own company, which would later be reorganized as Republic Aviation.

In 1916, while Austria-Hungary still had yet to produce a land-based fighter, one of its naval officers was improvising its first flying boat fighter. Born in Castelnuovo (now Boka Kotorska, Montenegro) on February 6, 1890, Godfrey Richard Banfield was of Irish ancestry and British citizenship, but became an Austrian citizen in 1903, and followed his father's career in the *Kaiserlische und Königlische Kriegsmarine*. Renamed Gottfried Banfield, he earned his pilot's certificate in August 1912, and the outbreak of war found him stationed at the Pola naval base. Following Italy's entry in the war, in June 1915, Banfield helped establish a naval air base at Trieste, located 70 miles from Venice, 10 miles from the mouth of the Isonzo River, 60 from the Piave, and just 18 miles from the Italian naval base at Grado. Given those distances from the battle lines, Trieste's aircrews frequently operated in support of the army and were in constant action against Italian ships and aircraft over the northern Adriatic Sea. While patrolling the mouth of the Isonzo in Lohner flying boat *L.47* on June 27, Fregattenleutnant (lieutenant) Banfield and his observer, Seekadett Herbert Strohl Edler von Ravelsburg, spotted an Italian kite balloon and put it out of commission with 500 rounds. It was credited as Banfield's first victory.

In February 1916, Banfield was appointed to command at Trieste and on April 5, he made his first flight in *L.16*, a Lohner Type M flying boat that he had modified into a single-seater with a Schwarzlose MG 07/12 machine gun bolted to the hull in front of the cockpit. He flew many, varied missions thereafter and was promoted to Linienschiffsleutnant (lieutenant commander) on May 1.

On the evening of June 23, Banfield attacked a French FBA Type C flying boat over the Gulf of Trieste, fatally striking its Italian

Left, Austria's leading naval ace, Linienschiffsleutnant Gottfried Freiherr von Banfield, scored all nine of his victories in flying boats, whose development as fighters he personally influenced. Right, In February 1916, Banfield converted Lohner L.16 into a single-seat fighter by bolting a forward-firing machine gun to the hull, and proceeded to shoot down four Allied planes with it. (Jon Guttman)

observer, a Mate 2nd Class Grammaticopoulo, in the head and heart. The French pilot, Enseigne de Vaisseau de 1e Classe André Victor Vaugeois, landed and tried to taxi toward Grado until another 100 rounds from Banfield killed his engine. Vaugeois then manned the observer's machine gun, forcing Banfield to fire again until the weapon was disabled and Vaugeois finally surrendered. The FBA, riddled with 120 bullets, was towed by the motor boat *Primula* to Trieste, from whence it was transported to Vienna for display in the War History Museum. After his minor neck wounds were attended to, Vaugeois was invited to dine with Banfield, who toasted his tenacious courage. The next day Banfield sent another FBA crashing into the Gulf of Trieste, but this time Italian motor boats arrived and towed the plane and its wounded crew back to Grado.

On August 1, Banfield in *L.16* intercepted a formation of Caproni Ca.1s en route to bomb Fiume naval base and drove one down to crash-land at the Volasca parade grounds, where the crew was taken prisoner. On August 6, Lohners *L.16* and *L.99* attacked another Caproni of the 4a *Squadriglia da Bombarda* at about 9,000 feet over Miramare. A bullet through the radiator forced *L.99*'s crew to glide back to Trieste, but Banfield, in *L.16*, shot out all three of the Ca.1's engines and it crashed into a house southeast of Sistiana, where its pilot, Sottotenente Valentino Zannini, died of his wounds. His co-pilot, Sergente Mario Broghi and observer, Sergente Biagio Mantieri, emerged wounded but alive. On August 15, Banfield shot two down French-flown FBA Type H flying boats. The crew of the first was wounded, while the second's crewmen, Enseigne de Vaisseau Baron Jean Roulier—commander of the French navy flyers on the Isonzo front—and Méchanicien A.H. Cousterousse, were killed.

Banfield's month of success said much for the soundness of the Lohner flying boats' design. It also encouraged the development of single-seaters such as the Hansa-Brandenburg CC, a small, speedy flying boat whose biplane wing cellule was supported by the same "star strut" arrangement as used in the D.I. Banfield flew a Hansa-Brandenburg CC to bring down an Italian Farman over the Sdodda Estuary on October 13, 1916, although it was not confirmed. His next confirmed victory, over a Caproni on December 3, also involved the CC, given the *Abwehr* number (for defense interceptors) A.12, in concert with army pilots Cislaghi and Brumowski.

Banfield did not score again until 1917, by which time both Austria-Hungary and Italy had introduced more flying boat fighters to their naval arsenals. Hansa-Brandenburg followed up its CC with the W.18, a single-seat flying boat fighter that dispensed with the star-strut arrangement in favor of more conventional interplane struts. Josef Mickl designed a unique single-seat flying boat specifically for Banfield, the Oeffag Type H, which received the *Abwehr* serial A.11, and which its recipient painted blue. "It seemed to be a good color for camouflage for flying over water," Banfield explained. "More than this, however, it seemed a very good color for night flying, which I did a lot of in the 'Blue Wonder.'" Indeed, at 2330 hours on May 31, 1917, Banfield used A.11 to shoot down an enemy flying boat near the mouth of the Primero River, from where the Italians towed it back to Grado the next morning. It was the first nocturnal victory by any Austro-Hungarian pilot and Banfield's ninth—he would make further claims thereafter, but none were confirmed. Citing A.11 as the favorite of all the aircraft he flew, he said, "It was so good that I repeatedly suggested that it be built in quantity, but this was never done."

Awarded the Knight's Cross of the Military Order of Maria Theresa, the Hapsburg Empire's highest honor—and with it a baron's title—Gottfried Freiherr von Banfield lived in Trieste for the rest of a successful life in shipping salvage, dying on September 23, 1986.

Austria-Hungary produced a floatplane fighter, based on Ernst Heinkel's less-than-stellar "star-strutter," the D.I. In spite of its shortcomings, Phönix built some 60 D.Is with twin floats as the KDW (*Kampf Doppeldecker, Wasser*) for use by both the Austro-Hungarian and German navies.

The KDW inspired Ernst Heinkel to develop a far better two-seat biplane reconnaissance fighter, the Hansa-Brandenburg W.12, whose rudder extended below rather than above the fuselage to give the observer a less obstructed field of fire. Powered by a 160-hp Mercedes D.III or 150-hp Benz Bz.III engine and armed with one or two LMG 08/15 machine guns forward and one flexible Parabellum gun aft, the W.12 entered German service in 1917 and 146 would be built. The Dutch, after interning one, obtained a license to build another 35 for their navy. The W.12's speed of 100 mph and an endurance of 3 1/2 hours suited it well for patrolling the North Sea from the naval bases of Ostende or Zeebrugge, which became as dangerous to Allied aircraft patrolling the North Sea as Trieste, Pola, and Fiume were to the allies in the Adriatic.

The W.29, a monoplane variant using struts extending from the floats to support the wing, first flew on March 27, 1918, and offered even better performance than the W.12's, with a speed of 109 mph and a four-hour endurance. Oberleutnant zur See Friedrich Christiansen led Zeebrugge's floatplane unit in both W.12s and W.29s against British shipping and flying boats off the Flanders coast, shooting down British airship *C27* and 12 airplanes, as well as damaging a British submarine, *C.25*, for which he became the only German floatplane pilot to be awarded the *Orden Pour le Mérite*.

So successful were Ludwig Lohner's flying boats that when a broken engine shaft caused a Type T boat, *L40*, to come down near Volano on May 27, 1915—just three days after war had been declared—the Italians ordered Macchi to built 10 copies of the plane for its own *Regia Marina*. Macchi had no previous experience in flying boats, but technical co-director Carlo Felice Buzio and his staff managed to reverse-engineer a copy using a 150-hp six-cylinder

Isotta-Fraschini V4 engine, designated the L.1, which went into production in September. That led to a series of successful flying boats
including a fighter, the M.5.

Tested in May 1917, the M.5 was a downsized single-seater based
on the Lohner boats with a sesquiplane wing inspired by the
Nieuports that Macchi also built. Powered by a 190-hp Isotta-
Fraschini V4B engine with two .30-caliber Vickers machine guns
mounted inside the hull, the M.5 had a maximum speed of 117 mph,
a ceiling of 20,340 feet and an endurance of 3 hours, 40 minutes. The
best flying boat fighter of the war, it was also the most-produced, with
348 built. Three Italian aces flew it, headed by Tenente de Vascello
Orazio Pierozzi with seven victories.

M.5s also equipped a U.S. Navy contingent based at Porto Corsini
under the command of former *Escadrille Lafayette* member
Lieutenant Commander Willis B. Haviland. During an encounter pit-
ting four M.5s and a larger two-seat M.8 of the Porto Corsini
squadron against four Phönix D.I land fighters of the Pola naval station on August 21, 1918, Ensign George M. Ludlow was shot down
by Fregattenleutnant Stephan Wollemann. Ludlow alit with a
smashed magneto and a punctured radiator and crankcase just five
miles from the enemy naval base at Pola, but Landsman for
Quartermaster Charles Hazeltine Hammann landed his own damaged Macchi alongside and rescued Ludlow. For that deed,
Hammann became the first U.S. Navy combat pilot to be awarded the
Medal of Honor, but he was tragically killed in a postwar air crash in
Langley, Virginia, on June 21, 1919.

Of all the navies, Britain's was unique in operating wheeled fighters at sea. Some were launched from platforms built over a warship's
guns, although their only recourse for a landing was to ditch at sea in
hopes of the plane being recovered by crane. . . or at least the pilot
being rescued. In 1917, the Royal Navy built a 228-foot deck on the
bow of the battlecruiser *Furious*, and off Scapa Flow on August 2, a
Sopwith Pup flown by Commander Edwin Harris Dunning became
the first wheeled airplane to land on the deck of a moving ship. After
five days of more takeoffs and landings, on the 7th a burst tire caused
Dunning's plane to pitch over the side. He drowned in the cockpit
before rescuers could reach him.

Landsman for Quartermaster Charles H. Hammann poses before a Macchi M.5 of the U.S. Navy contingent at Porto Corsini. During a fight between four M.5s and four Phönix D.Is on August 21, 1918, Ensign George M. Ludlow was shot down with a smashed magneto and a punctured radiator and crankcase, just five miles from the enemy naval base at Pola, but Hammann landed his own damaged Macchi alongside and rescued Ludlow. For that deed, Hammann was promoted to Ensign and became the first U.S. Navy combat pilot to be awarded the Medal of Honor, but he was tragically killed in a postwar air crash in Langley, Virginia, on June 21, 1919. (*National Museum of Naval Aviation*)

In 1918, *Furious* went to war with further decking aft, although the smokestack and superstructure in between presented a problem that would be solved later in the year with the first all-deck carrier, HMS *Argus*. *Furious* came equipped with a specialized Sopwith Camel variant, the 2F1, which featured shorter-span wings, a narrower-track undercarriage, a hinged, folding tail for shipboard storage, slim steel tube cabane struts and a single synchronized Vickers gun, supplemented by a Lewis gun above the upper wing on a Foster-type mounting.

On June 18, 1918, two of *Furious*'s Camels carried out the first carrier-launched interception when they attacked two oncoming bomb-armed German floatplanes, driving one into the North Sea and chasing off the other. *Furious* made history again on July 19, when six of its Camels bombed Zeppelin airships L54 and L60 in their sheds

Sopwith 2F1s—naval versions of the Camel—crowd the forward flight deck of aircraft carrier HMS *Furious* during its groundbreaking operations in the North Sea during the summer of 1918. (*Greg Van Wyngarden*)

at Tondern. After the mission, none managed to alight on *Furious*'s flight deck: Captains B.A. Smart and W.F. Dickson ditched nearby, to be rescued by the destroyer *Violent*; Captain W.D. Jackson and Lieutenants N.E. Williams and S. Dawson landed in neutral Denmark, escaped internment and returned to Britain in mid-August; and Lieutenant Walter Albert Yeulett and his Camel were lost at sea.

On August 10, 1918, another 2F1, flown by Lieutenant Stuart D. Culley, took off from a lighter towed behind the destroyer *Redoubt* to destroy Zeppelin L53. Culley's Camel, N6812, is now preserved at the Imperial War Museum.

9

AS GOOD AS IT GOT

Fighters of 1918

The year 1918 began with months of precarious promise for the Central Powers. Romania, which had entered the war on the Allied side on August 27, 1916, had been invaded by the Germans and, in spite of Russian efforts to assist it, was virtually neutralized by January 1917, with most of its southern regions occupied—including Ploesti, from which the Germans appropriated a million tons of vitally needed oil. The Italian army, disastrously routed at Caporetto on October 25, 1917, had retreated to the Piave River and seemed on the verge of collapse. Russia, torn asunder by the Bolshevik Revolution in November 1917, sued for peace on March 3, 1918, freeing tens of thousands of German soldiers for redeployment elsewhere. Only in the Middle East was the news bad, as the British, sometimes in alliance with Arab tribesmen seeking to rid themselves of Ottoman domination, drove Turkish forces steadily back in Palestine and Mesopotamia.

Of looming concern to the Germans was the United States's declaration of war on April 6, 1917. The *Luftstreitskräfte's* commander, Generalleutnant von Hoeppner, later recalled how, "The columns of the enemy press were crammed with fantasy-like statements [about how] thousands of American aircraft would flow over Germany and force it to seek peace." As 1918 dawned, however, only the first inexperienced contingents of the small but rapidly expanding American Expeditionary Force (AEF) had reached the front. All in all the Germans saw an opportunity—perhaps their last—to mobilize their troops on the Western Front for a final all-out push to eliminate the

British army, take Paris, and force Britain and France to sue for peace before the Americans could bring their resources fully into play.

When Operation Michael was launched on March 21, 1918, German ground forces in the West were the most powerful and efficient that they had been since the war began. The *Luftstreistkräfte* could not quite make the same claim. Although two more crack *Jagdgeschwader* had organized on February 4, and the number of *Jagdstaffeln* doubled on paper through the *Amerika-Programm*, their personnel and equipment betrayed the reality behind the rapid expansion. Most *Amerika-Programm Jastas* formed since June 1917 consisted of a veteran commander and perhaps a small cadre of veterans, surrounded by hastily trained pilots who would have to learn their trade the hard way.

The best fighter the Germans had at hand was the Fokker Dr.I, back in strength since Anthony Fokker had rectified the shoddy production techniques that lay behind the wing failures suffered in October and November 1917. The Dr.I, however, soon proved to be less than the world-beater that was needed to maintain air superiority on the offensive, being slower than all Allied fighters except the Sopwith Camel—and the Camel could match it in a dogfight.

Complementing this dubious triplane vanguard were the Albatros D.Va and the Pfalz D.IIIa, the latter a D.III with more rounded lower wingtips, an enlarged, rounder tailplane and machine guns repositioned in front of the pilot to afford him easier access. Intrinsically, neither plane would have been competitive with the latest Allied fighters had it not been for the improved power plant that was made available to them early in 1918: the Mercedes D.IIIa, essentially the D.III with a higher compression ratio and later re-engineered with oversize cylinders and pistons. Those modifications raised the engine's output from 160 to as high as 185 hp.

At best, even the up-powered Mercedes motor could only restore the Albatros D.Va's performance to that of its lighter but more fragile predecessor; maximum speed, for example, topped out at 116.81 mph. All the same, in light of the coming spring offensive, the development of the Mercedes D.IIIa—which likewise improved the Pfalz D.IIIa's performance—could not have come at a more critical juncture for the German army and naval air services, pending the arrival of something better.

In addition to improved engines, a radical proposal arose to increase firepower in the aging German fighters. Late in February 1918, an Ingenieur Kändler from the Siemens-Schuckert Werke visited *Jasta* 5's aerodrome at Boistrancourt with two Albatros D.Vas equipped with a pair of motor machine guns developed by his firm that he claimed could fire 1,400 rounds per minute. On February 26, Vizefeldwebel Fritz Rumey, for whom, with Vizefeldwebel Josef Mai, the upgunned fighters were intended, shot down a D.H.4 north of Busigny for his ninth victory, though it remains uncertain whether he was using the new guns at the time. In any case, they did not go into production, probably because of their complexity and the consequent maintenance problems that were anticipated.

Ironically, on the other side of the lines three new fighters were making their way to Allied front-line units. Two of them fell disappointingly short of expectations, however, while the third was never given the full utilization it deserved.

In the summer of 1917, Morane-Saulnier had produced a biplane, the AF, together with a parasol monoplane scout, the AI. The latter, like the AC, used a complex trestle of struts extending upward and outward from the lower fuselage longerons to support the upper wing, which was also slightly swept back. Static testing of the structure yielded a safety factor of 8.5. Powered by a 150-hp Gnome monosoupape 9N rotary engine, the prototype climbed to 3,000 meters (9,840 feet) in 7 minutes, 45 seconds during flight tests at Villacoublay in August, and its speed at that altitude was 134.5 mph.

On August 12, a representative on the British Aviation Commission in Paris reported on the parasol's impressive performance to RFC headquarters. None too surprising at that point, General Trenchard scribbled his verdict on the report: "I don't want it." The French, however, hedging their bets against the Spad XIII with its chronic engine troubles, ordered anywhere from 1,100 to 1,300 AIs from Morane-Saulnier, as both the MoS 27.C1 with a single Vickers machine gun and the MoS 29.C1 with twin weapons.

The Morane-Saulnier's reputation preceded it when N.156 learned that it would receive the first MoS 27s on February 4, 1918. The unit was fully equipped and redesignated MS.156 on the 9th. Two other escadrilles, 158 and 161, were re-equipped with MoS.27s by March 4 and February 21, respectively.

Jubilation gave way to trepidation on February 26, when MS.156's executive officer, Lieutenant Jean Toutary, lost his wings while performing aerobatics over his aerodrome near Châlons-sur-Marne. On March 8, two of MS.156's planes were diving on two German two-seaters when one's pilot had to pull up with a jammed weapon. The other was still diving when its wings suddenly folded and it plunged to the ground, killing Lafayette Flying Corps member Caporal Wallace C. Winter. Postwar German records revealed an anomaly—a Morane-Saulnier credited to Leutnant Julius Keller of Royal Saxon *Jasta* 21. Had he come to aid the two-seaters and fired on Winter unnoticed by his French squadron mate? Whatever the actual cause, enthusiasm for the parasol plummeted as fast as Winter's broken plane had done.

Most MS.156 pilots resumed flying in Nieuport 27s, but another of its American volunteers, Sergent David E. Putnam, was not so readily intimidated. He was apparently still flying his MoS 27 when he claimed an Albatros near Nauroy that was not credited on March 14, and a Rumpler that was, as his third victory, the next day. Dave Putnam continued to seek combat around Reims, but his tendency to fight deep in enemy territory prevented most of his claims from being confirmed.

Meanwhile, on May 15, Caporal Émile Boucheron of MS.158 crashed while landing at Maissonneuve. Twin-gun MoS.29s arrived at MS.156 on the 18th, but by then their cause was lost. Two days later, Caporal Walter John Shaffer of MS.156 wrote, "The Moranes, I am sorry to say, have been given up, owing to their weak construction, which could not stand the strain '*chasse*' work entails. I say sorry, because not only was it fast, but so small that as one pilot said, it would be maneuvered around a clothes pin."

Caporal Walter J. Shaffer of escadrille MS.156 poses in Morane-Saulnier AI MS1591 in February 1918. Though greeted with high expectation, the parasol fighter's combat career was disappointingly brief. (*Walter J. Shaffer album via Jon Guttman*)

All three escadrilles were re-equipped with Spad VIIs and redesignated Spa.156, 158 and 161. Subsequent production AIs had their wing structures bolstered with extra wires or struts, but spent the rest of the war as advanced trainers with less powerful engines, under the designation of MoS.30E-1.

Another elegant French newcomer, the Nieuport 28, represented a break at last from its series of nimble but fragile sesquiplanes. In mid-1917, Nieuport had tried a two-spar lower wing on its Nieuport 24 in an attempt to make it rugged enough to accommodate a 160-hp Gnome engine. More fundamental changes were deemed necessary, however, and on June 14, an almost completely new Nieuport took to the air—a true biplane with a longer, slimmer, stringered fuselage, although it retained the 24's and 27's tail surfaces. The leading edges of the wings were covered with three-ply laminated wood sheet and the ribs capped with tapering ply strips. Only the smaller lower wings had ailerons.

Test-flown in November 1917, the final version of the Nieuport 28.C1 was one of the best-looking aircraft of World War I, but in spite of a creditable performance, including a maximum speed of 128 mph, the *Aéronautique Militaire* did not regard it as sufficiently improved over the Spad XIII to warrant production.

That should have been the end of the story, had an ally not given the Nieuport 28 a reprieve from obscurity. In spite of a wide variety of efforts, ranging from conventional to bizarre to lethally implausible, the United States was the only major World War I power besides Japan that failed to produce a viable indigenously designed combat fighter. A few designs, notably the rotary engine Standard E-1 and Thomas-Morse S.4C scouts, saw wide use stateside as fighter trainers, and a promising two-seat fighter designed by French Capitaine Georges Lepére, the Engineering Division LUSAC-11, was about to enter front-line service when the war ended. As the AEF shipped to France in 1917, however, the U.S. government had to make a deal to supply raw materials to the French in exchange for Spad XIIIs. Engine problems and production delays slowed the Spads' delivery to the U.S. Army Air Service (USAS), so as a further interim measure the Americans also ordered 297 Nieuport 28s.

The 95th Aero Squadron, based at Villeneuve-les-Vertus, received the first of the new fighters at the end of February 1918, and the 94th Aero Squadron was fully equipped by mid-March. Due to inadequate gunnery training, the 95th's pilots were withdrawn until May 2. Meanwhile, the 94th only received enough machine guns to mount one per plane, rather than the specified two, but flew its first armed patrol on March 28.

On April 9, the 94th was transferred from Villeneuve to Gengoult aerodrome near Toul. Senior AEF officers were skeptical about the Nieuport's capabilities, but by letting them operate over the relatively quiet Toul sector, they expected the pilots to gain experience and confidence against second-line opposition, before eventually re-equipping with Spads and being turned loose against Germany's best.

Besides such relatively forgiving conditions, the 94th's pilots benefited from an extraordinary cadre of "old hands." The commander, Major John Huffer, was a Lafayette Flying Corps veteran with three aerial victories. His operations officer, Major Raoul Lufbery, was then the leading American ace with 16 victories, all scored with *Escadrille* N.124. Two of the flight leaders, Captains James Norman Hall and David McKelvie Peterson, were also veterans of the famed *Escadrille Lafayette*.

A Nieuport 28 at the Udvar-Hazy annex of the National Air and Space Museum, restored in the markings of 1st Lt. James A. Meissner, 94th Aero Squadron. *(Jon Guttman)*

The Nieuport 28's first day of combat began memorably on April 14, when Dave Peterson led 1st Lts. Edward V. Rickenbacker and Reed Chambers over the lines. Thick fog compelled Peterson to abort the mission, but Rickenbacker and Chambers, thinking he was turning back with engine trouble, continued with the patrol. The duo came under anti-aircraft fire and as they turned back toward Gengoult, two fighters were dispatched from Royal Württemberg *Jasta* 64's aerodrome at Mars-la-Tour to intercept them.

Evidence has since surfaced to suggest that one of the German pilots, Vizefeldwebel Antoni Wroniecki, had a hidden agenda when he led Unteroffizier Heinrich Simon against the intruders. Of Polish extraction, Wroniecki secretly hated the Germans and was seeking an opportunity to switch sides, hoping an Allied victory would lead to the resurrection of his partitioned and occupied homeland. In any case, both *Jasta* 64w pilots also became lost in the fog until they emerged over Gengoult.

Upon seeing an Albatros D.Va and a Pfalz D.IIIa materialize over their field, two Americans scrambled up to engage them. Just five minutes later, 2nd Lt. Alan F. Winslow was officially credited with bringing down Simon's Albatros intact, while 1st Lt. Douglas Campbell was credited with downing the Pfalz in flames, its pilot, according to some accounts, dying of his burns and injuries shortly afterward. That official report may, in fact, have been a deliberate exchange of aircraft and pilot identities to give the impression that Wroniecki was dead, lest he face a charge of treason if he later fell into German hands. Adopting the pseudonym Wrobelewski, he joined General Jozef Haller de Hallenburg's "Blue Army," a Polish force forming under the French, then transferred to an *Escadrille Polonaise* being organized at Sillé-le-Guillaume. The war ended before the unit could get into action, and Wroniecki, after trying and failing to establish an airline in Poland, enjoyed greater success in Germany during the late 1930s—as a Polish spy.

Doug Campbell's victory on April 14 was the first scored by an American-trained USAS fighter pilot (Winslow was a Lafayette Flying Corps man with prior service in *Escadrille* N.152). The Nieuport 28's place in history was assured, and it would later make more, as Campbell, Rickenbacker and several other pilots went on to become aces in it. The Nieuport 28 would figure in the dramatic death of Raoul Lufbery while trying to bring down a German two-seater on May 19. It would also give two prominent aces some hair-raising experiences when the wing fabric tore away on the aircraft flown by 1st Lt. James A. Meissner on May 2, and on Rickenbacker's on the 17th. A poor grade of glue and structural failure of the front plywood wing panels was found to be the cause of those mishaps, but a more serious problem was found with the single-valve Gnome monosoupape engine, which required a "blip switch" to slow down by cutting the ignition to some of the cylinders. While the ignition was off, fuel leaked from the valves and accumulated under the cowling, often resulting in a fire when ignition was restored to all cylinders. A tendency of the engines' improperly annealed copper-tube fuel lines to crack due to engine vibration was acute enough for Brig. Gen. Benjamin Foulois to ground all Nieuport 28s until more flexible fuel lines could be installed.

In spite of those faults, the Nieuport 28s impressed their pilots with their excellent handling characteristics. The 94th and later 95th established a good record over the Toul sector and two more squadrons, the 27th and 148th, had been equipped with the type when all four were finally transferred on June 28 to Touqin aero-

First Lieutenants Edward V. Rickenbacker, Douglas Campbell and Captain Kenneth Marr of the 94th Aero Squadron pose before a Nieuport 28. (*Douglas Campbell album via Jon Guttman*)

drome, 20 miles south of Château-Thierry, in anticipation of a new German offensive along the Marne. There, harsh reality set in as the four squadrons, newly organized into the 1st Pursuit Group, suffered heavy losses at the hands of *Jagdgeschwader* I, II, and III, along with other first-string *Jastas*, equipped with Fokker D.VIIs. By late July, sufficient Spad XIIIs were available to re-equip the American units and by early August the Nieuport 28 had disappeared from the USAS front-line roster.

While the Morane-Saulnier AI and Nieuport 28 fell short of expectations, a British fighter was exceeding them. First flown at Martlesham Heath in June 1917, the Sopwith 5F.1 Dolphin was a back-staggered biplane with a relatively deep fuselage and the center section placed directly over the pilot's head, with the intention of improving his view from the cockpit. In order to further improve forward visibility, the 5F.1 prototype's frontal radiator was replaced with a tapered cowling and radiators in the wing roots, later moved to the fuselage sides. Tail surfaces were modified and the original armament of two synchronized Vickers guns was doubled by mounting two Lewis guns on the forward spar of the center section. After testing with both four-and two-bladed airscrews in September 1917, the lat-

ter was standardized for the Dolphin, whose 200-hp Hispano-Suiza
engine gave it a performance comparable to the S.E.5a's.

By December 31, 1917, 121 Dolphins had been accepted by the
RFC, and the first examples were delivered to No. 19 Squadron in
January 1918. Many pilots looked askance on the new fighter's nega-
tive wing stagger reminiscent of the D.H.5, which had proven a poor
performer in air-to-air combat. The fact that the pilot's head protruded above the upper wing did not sit well with them, either—if the
plane turned over on landing, which given the waywardness of its
Hispano engine, was a distinct possibility, the pilot risked a cracked
skull or a broken neck. Sopwith addressed that concern by adding a
protective steel framework over the center section and break-out panels on the fuselage side as an emergency exit.

Things got off to a poor start at 19 Squadron when 2nd Lt. A.A.
Veale was killed in an accident. Nevertheless, the squadron's pilots
practiced away at their new machines and came to regard the
Dolphin's maneuverability and general flight characteristics as superior to those of their old Spads. They also found its cockpit warmer
and more comfortable than that of the average open-cockpit scout.

The Dolphin's baptism of fire came over Comines on February
26, when Dolphins and Spad VIIs of 19 Squadron engaged an equally mixed German flight that included a Fokker Dr.I and three Pfalz
D.IIIs. The triplane was attacking Lieutenant J.L. McLintock's Spad
when Canadian Lieutenant John D. de Pencier, in Dolphin C3841,
got on the German's tail. A quick burst drove it down out of control,
but the Fokker had already done its damage—McLintock was lost,
credited to Leutnant der Reserve Richard Plange of *Jasta Boelcke*.

The Dolphins' next fight occurred over Gheluwe on March 8,
when Captain Patrick Huskinson turned the tables on one of five
attacking Albatros D.Vas and shot one down. Another Albatros got
onto Captain G.N. Taylor's tail, but Captain Oliver C. Bryson got
behind it and sent it spinning down with its wings breaking up for
his 12th and final victory. The squadron's only casualty, 2nd Lt. F.J.
McConnell, was wounded but made it back to the aerodrome.

By mid-March, No. 19 Squadron was "sold" on the Dolphin. In
addition to being nimbler than the Spad, it could sustain even more

Sopwith Dolphin C3879 of No. 79 Squadron undergoes repair. New Zealand ace Captain Ronald B. Bannerman scored 14 of his 17 victories in this plane. (*Vernon G. Snyder album via Jon Guttman*)

punishment. A second Dolphin unit, No. 79 Squadron, arrived in February, while in April No. 23 Squadron exchanged its Spad XIIIs for Dolphins and No. 87 Squadron brought its Dolphins to the front. All four units gave outstanding accounts of themselves throughout the war and the most successful of the many outstanding Dolphin pilots, Baltimore-born Captain Frederick Warrington Gillette of No. 23 Squadron, was also the second ranking American ace of the war with 20 victories. Yet no further Dolphin squadrons saw service over the front and the type disappeared soon after the Armistice. In spite of its unusual appearance, no satisfactory reason has been ascertained for such scant utilization of what may have been the most underrated fighter on the Western Front.

Although it was never officially designated as such, for all intents and purposes a fourth fighter entered Allied service in February 1918 in the form of the Caudron R.11. Designed by Paul Deville as an improved version of the R.4, the R.11A.3 first flew in March 1917, powered by two 215-hp Hispano-Suiza 8Bda engines, carrying two Lewis machine guns in a front turret, two in the rear, and a fifth firing downward from under the front gunner's position. Capable of 114 mph with the later installation of 235-hp Hispano-Suiza 8Beb engines, the R.11 equipped six escadrilles of 15 each, while others were parceled out to reconnaissance units.

A Caudron R.11 of R.46 in the summer of 1918, when these nominal reconnaissance planes were escorting Breguet 14B.2 bombers as three-seat gunships. (*Valentine J. Burger*)

In addition to its primary reconnaissance mission, the R.11 revived the "flying fortress" idea as aircraft of *Escadrilles* R.46, R.239, R.240, R.241 and R.242 escorted formations of Breguet 14.B2 bombers, adding their formidable armament to their defense against German interceptors. Their success in that role kept the concept of the twin-engine, multi-purpose fighter alive through the postwar years.

In contrast to these promising Allied products, the German pilots got little more than rumors of better fighters under development when Operation Michael commenced on March 21, 1918. Over the next month, the *Jagdflieger* did their best with what they had and spent at least some of their time between missions wondering when the new planes would finally arrive.

Idflieg had in fact been seeking the answer to their prayers with a fighter competition held at Berlin's Adlershof airfield in January 1918. The 31 aircraft entered ranged from improved versions of current mainstays, such as the Albatros D.Va and Pfalz D.IIIa, to original, innovative, and often imaginative designs. Although most of the fighters were built around the Mercedes D.III or D.IIIa engines, a few entries used rotaries, including the Siemens-Schuckert Werke's SSW D.III.

The Siemens-Schuckert electrical corporation had been involved in aviation since 1907, but its first production fighter, built in mid-

1916, was essentially a Nieuport 11 copy. Only 65 SSW D.Is were built before the original 150-plane order was discontinued in June 1917, but a modified variant, the D.Ib, achieved an eye-opening climb rate of 5,000 meters (16,404 feet) in 20.5 minutes by use of an over-compressed, 140-hp version of the nine-cylinder Siemens-Halske Sh.I. This and other Siemens-Halske engines were counter-rotaries, in which the propeller and cylinders rotated in an opposite direction to the crankshaft. This resulted in greater propeller and cooling efficiency, better fuel economy, reduced drag, lower weight, and a greatly reduced gyroscopic effect. With SSW working on a 160-hp 11-cylinder counter-rotary engine, the Sh.III, *Idflieg* ordered a fighter based on the new power plant as early as November 1916. The engine was not ready for flight-testing until June 1917, but on August 5, Leutnant Hans Müller test flew the D.IIb prototype to an altitude of 7,000 meters in a record-setting 35.5 minutes. Further experiments ultimately led to the D.III, which featured wings of unequal chord and a four-bladed propeller to allow for a shorter undercarriage.

On December 26, *Idflieg* ordered 20 pre-production SSW D.IIIs, of which four were entered in the First Fighter Competition in January 1918. Again, Müller put his plane through some impressive paces, displaying exhilarating maneuverability and climbing 6,000 meters in 21.5 minutes on January 21. Pilots unused to the D.III's high rpm and unusual handling characteristics found it a hot handful, especially when it came to landing, but SSW modified the D.III further to address their complaints, and in response to Manfred von Richthofen's general lament that "all aircraft at the Competition were too slow," new wings of shorter span and equal chord (based on the D.III's lower set) were installed on a new version, the D.IV, which sacrificed climb rate for higher level speed. Encouraged by the fighter's overall performance, *Idflieg* ordered 30 D.IIIs on March 1, 50 more on March 23, and 50 D.IVs on April 8.

The first six SSW D.IIIs were delivered to *Jagdgeschwader* III on March 16, but the principal recipient, *Jagdgeschwader* II, got its first nine machines on April 6, and its overall complement was up to 35 by May 18. At that time *Jastas* 12 and 19 of JG.II were equipped with Fokker Dr.Is, and consequently their pilots' experience with rotary engines would help in making the transition to their assigned SSWs. *Jasta* 19's commander, Leutnant der Reserve Walter Göttsch, received D.III 8346/17 on April 6, but was still flying his Fokker Dr.I four days later, when he was killed in action with an R.E.8 of No.52 Squadron, crewed by Lieutenants H.L. Taylor and W.I.E. Lane. Göttsch was posthumously credited with the R.E.8 for his 20th victory, but while Lane was wounded in the leg, Taylor landed his plane intact in British lines.

As the German offensive proceeded, the SSWs were kept discretely over their own side of the lines while the pilots familiarized themselves with them in between offensive patrols in Dr.Is or, in the case of *Jastas* 13 and 15, Albatros D.Vas and Pfalz D.IIIas. Leutnant der Reserve Hans Pippart, Göttsch's successor in command of *Jasta* 19, allegedly scored the first SSW victory on April 20, when he intercepted and destroyed a Breguet 14B.2 of *Escadrille* Br.127 west of Chauny. Flying another the next morning, Leutnant der Reserve Ulrich Neckel of *Jasta* 12 bagged another Br.127 Breguet.

During a visit by SSW engineer Bruno Steffen to JG.II's aerodrome on April 22, the *Geschwaderkommandeur*, Hauptmann Rudolf Berthold, lauded the D.III's "brilliant" rate of climb and the "faultless" combination of airframe and Sh.III engine, which had gained the trust of its pilots. The praise proved somewhat premature. After seven to 10 flying hours, the engines began suffering from overheating, spark plug ejection, faulty magnetos, bearing failure, faulty throttles, piston heads disintegrating, and complete engine seizure. By May 23, JG.II's D.IIIs had been withdrawn. Berthold, however, remained a believer and urged that, "the Siemens fighter be made available as quickly as possible for, after elimination of the present faults, it is likely to become our most useful fighter aircraft."

SSW D.IIIs and D.IVs began returning to front-line service on July 22, their engines replaced by Sh.III(Rh) engines built under license by the Rhenania Motorenfabrik A.G. (Rhemag)—which curiously suffered from none of the problems that had plagued the SSW-built originals—and portions of their cowlings cut away to allow better cooling. Generally, D.IIIs were assigned to *Kampfeinsitzer Staffeln* for home defense because of their superior climb rate, while the faster and

Typifying the ultimate fate of the Siemens-Schuckert Werke's promising fighters, SSW D.III 3025/18 was used by Kampfeinsitzer Staffel 8 at Bitsch aerodrome, for home defense. It is shown after being turned over to U.S. forces at Trier in December 1918. (*U.S. Air Force Museum*)

more maneuverable D.IVs went to *Jastas* on the Western Front. Once pilots mastered the SSW's handling characteristics, they were almost unanimous in their praise for it as the best fighter at 4,000 meters or higher. Unfortunately for the *Luftstreitskräfte*, only 136 SSWs had reached operational units by November 11, 1918.

While the SSW D.III attracted an unusual share of attention at the fighter competition, the overall star was unquestionably Antony Fokker's V11 biplane. Hastily built for the competition, the V11 was based on the fuselage and tail of the Dr.I, but employed a biplane version of the wooden box spar construction employed on the triplane. The lower wing was smaller than the upper to improve downward visibility and was built in one piece, with a cutout arranged in the steel tube fuselage frame to accommodate it. The ailerons, installed only on the upper wing, were also made of steel tube and fabric covered. Streamlined steel tubing also served as interplane and cabane struts, with no bracing wires. The V11 also featured a radiator mounted in the nose, rather than on the fuselage sides or the upper wing.

Even after its fuselage was lengthened to compensate for the Mercedes inline engine, Manfred von Richthofen found the V11 to be overly sensitive and unstable in a dive. Fokker immediately responded by lengthening the fuselage further and adding a vertical stabilizer. Both the V11 and the improved V18 were tested at the competition, and Richthofen and numerous other German fighter pilots were unanimous in their praise for the Fokker biplane's overall performance, including its ability to retain its maneuverability at high altitude and to "hang on its prop." Fokker was immediately given a 25,000-mark contract to build 400 of the new biplanes, which were given the military designation of D.VII. Of additional personal satisfaction to Fokker was an order for both the Johannisthal and Schneidemühl factories of his rival, Albatros, to manufacture the D.VII under license, with a five percent royalty going to Fokker.

Fokker D.VIIs began to reach the front in April 1918, the first examples, not surprisingly, going to Richthofen's *Jagdgeschwader* I. The Red Baron had been eagerly looking forward to flying the new biplane in combat, but he never got the chance before dying in his Dr.I on April 21. JG.I's first D.VIIs went to *Jasta* 10, and Leutnant Heldmann later claimed to have flown one in mid-April. Nevertheless, he was probably still flying his old Pfalz D.IIIa when he brought down an S.E.5a on May 4, resulting in 2nd Lt. R.A. Slipper of No. 24 Squadron being taken prisoner.

Heldmann's *Staffelführer*, Leutnant Erich Löwenhardt, is known to have flown a D.VII on May 9, as implied by Leutnant Richard Wenzl, then a Dr.I pilot of *Jasta* 11, in his description of an engagement with British aircraft that afternoon in his 1930 memoir, *Richthofen Flieger*: "To my left, Löwenhardt in his new biplane already had one in front of him." Löwenhardt claimed an S.E.5a over Hamel and No. 24 Squadron did record a 15-20 minute combat over Bois de Hangard, but it lost no planes, claimed three Albatros D.Vs, and did not report seeing any new aircraft. Löwenhardt had a less disputable success the next evening when he downed a de Havilland D.H.9 over Chaulnes, killing Lieutenants L.E. Dunnett and H.D. Prosser of No. 27 Squadron.

On May 18, Wenzl, who had just transferred from *Jasta* 11 to 6 the day before, flew to 2. *Armee Flug Park* to exchange his Fokker

Fokker D.VIIs of *Jasta 72s*, with the plane of its *Staffelführer*, Leutnant Karl Menckhoff, in the foreground. Menckhoff had scored 39 victories when much to his chagrin, on July 25, 1918, he became the first German brought down and taken prisoner by a Spad XIII of the U.S. Army Air Service. (*U.S. Air Force Museum*)

Dr.I for a D.VII. Besides the superior speed and high-altitude performance the new fighter offered, Wenzl recalled everyone being pleased to return to stationary, water-cooled engines, "The inferior Rizinus oil, the elixir of life for rotary engines, made it so apparent that on hot days there would be no end to the forced landings." By the end of the month D.VIIs were mainstays at *Jastas* 6, 10, and 11, while *Jasta* 4 operated *Jasta* 6's and 11's castoff triplanes until more D.VIIs arrived.

While its pilots familiarized themselves with their D.VIIs—and downed two Spad VIIs on May 19—JG.I's commander, Hauptmann

Wilhelm Reinhard, received orders on the 21st to depart Cappy aerodrome for Pusieux Ferme, from whence the *Geschwader* would support the 7. *Armee*'s offensive on the Chemin des Dames. JG.I arrived at Pusieux on the evening of the 26th, but poor weather limited operations when the German spring offensive's third phase, Operation Blücher-Yorck, commenced on May 27.

Amid the day's confusion a curious double mystery arose. On one hand, the British reportedly found a Fokker D.VII, serial No. 2184/18, near Achiet-le-Grand on May 27, and gave it the captured aircraft registration number G/5/12. The only matching German loss was that of Leutnant der Reserve Rudolf Windisch, commander of *Jasta* 66, brought down while attacking a French aerodrome, probably by Sous-Lieutenant Souleau and Maréchal-des-Logis Cavieux of Spa.76. Adding to the day's anomalies were conflicting reports that Windisch was a prisoner and that he had been killed—shot while trying to escape, perhaps? In any case, the Fokker D.VII did not remain secret for long.

Meanwhile, at JG.II's base at Le Mesnil-Nesle, Hauptmann Rudolf Berthold had been looking forward to getting D.VIIs also, but deliveries were delayed. On May 28 JG.I lent him one of its machines and he took to it instantly. "It flies very comfortably," he noted. "Above all, the controls are so light that I can even handle them with my right arm." Given the fact that a neglected, still-festering wound rendered his right arm all but useless, Berthold's comments speak volumes for the D.VII's handling characteristics—as does the fact that he used it to shoot down a Breguet 14 over Crouy that very morning.

The next afternoon Berthold was leading *Jasta* 15's Albatros D.Vas in his "borrowed" Fokker when they were jumped north of Ville-en-Tardenois by Spads of Spa.77. The escadrille's leading ace, Sous-Lieutenant Maurice Boyau, had burned a German balloon over Bois de Dole earlier that day, and now shared in downing an Albatros, as well as a second that went unconfirmed. Evidently Spa.77's *Jasta* 15 victims survived, but the same cannot be said for Sergent André Gelin, whose Spad XIII became the first—but by no means last—of its type to fall victim to a Fokker D.VII as Berthold turned the tables on his ambushers and shot Gelin down south of

Soissons. Leutnant Josef Veltjens was credited with a second Spad and Leutnant Georg von Hantelmann with a "probable," though Gelin was Spa.77's only casualty. Berthold completed the day by claiming a Salmson 2A2 from Sal.27.

With the fall of Château-Thierry to the 7. *Armee* on May 30, JG.I moved up to occupy the former French aerodrome at Beugneux-Cremaille on June 1. In between, the afternoon of May 31 saw another engagement with the Breguets southwest of Soissons, during which Leutnant Viktor von Pressentin, gennant von Rautter, downed one at 1255 hours for his 15th victory, killing Sous-Lieutenant Maurice Béranger and Sergent Wolf of Br.29. Moments later, however, von Rautter was killed, either by return fire from the Breguets or by a Spad flown by Adjutant Gustave Daladier of Spa.93, who claimed a Fokker Dr.I but may have confused its silhouette with that of the unfamiliar D.VII. Ernst Udet, now commanding *Jasta* 4, downed another Br.29 plane five minutes later for his 24th victory. At 1425 it was *Jasta* 6's turn as Leutnant der Reserve Hans Kirschstein claimed a Breguet of Br.129 over Grand-Rozoy. At 1940 that evening, Leutnant Martin Skowronski of *Jasta* 6 scored his first success over a Breguet near Marizy-St.-Mard and Hauptmann Reinhard scored his 14th over a Spad near Bonneuil five minutes later. Oberleutnant Erich Rüdiger von Wedel of *Jasta* 11 capped the day with a Spad over the Bois de Bourbillon at 2040.

June saw a proliferation of Fokker D.VIIs, accompanied by glowing reports from their pilots and awed reactions from their Allied opponents. There seemed to be only three things wrong with the D.VII. The first was a tendency for its incendiary ammunition to overheat and explode, which was alleviated by cutting ventilating holes in the cowling and ultimately remedied with improved ammunition. Many pilots thought the Fokker would benefit from a better engine and later that summer it got one—the 185-hp BMW, which gave the Fokker D.VIIf that it powered markedly better performance, especially at altitudes of 18,000 feet or higher, and truly made it the terror of the Western Front. The third great fault of the Fokker D.VIIs was that there were not enough of them, and the fighters produced to supplement them almost invariably suffered in comparison.

In mid-May 1918, the Roland D.VI, featuring a fuselage built up of wooden clinkers like a boat, was assigned to *Jastas* 23b, 32b, 33 and 35b. Its performance was not better than that of the Albatros D.Va, and in late May *Jasta* 23b's commander, Leutnant der Reserve Otto Kissenberth, preferred flying a captured Sopwith Camel in preference to his unit's Rolands.

August saw the appearance of the Pfalz D.XII at the front, although its frontal radiator and "N" shaped interplane struts caused Allied pilots to frequently confuse it with the Fokker D.VII. The Pfalz, however, featured the same semimonocoque plywood strip fuselage as the earlier D.III, and wings with a drag-reducing thin aerofoil section inspired by the Spad, conventionally wire-braced with two bays of interplane struts.

In his postwar memoir, *Jagdstaffel Unsere Heimat*, Leutnant Rudolf Stark mentioned that his command, *Jasta* 35b, accepted Pfalz D.XIIs on September 1, "only after much discussion and long telephone conversations," and that every pilot, "climbed into the new machine with preconceived notions and immediately voiced all manner of complaints." His mechanics were already so "spoiled" by the Fokker D.VII's cantilever wings that they complained of the renewed labor required to keep the Pfalz's guy wires adjusted between missions. Later, Stark admitted, the Pfalz D.XII turned out to be a fairly good plane that, "climbed well and could fly along with the Fokker D.VII in all respects, and in a dive it was a bit faster. But in turns and combat it was slow and could not compare with the Fokkers."

Two noteworthy exceptions among the Fokker D.VII's maligned stablemates were the SSW D.III and D.IV, once their engine problems were rectified. In addition, there was another Fokker product— a monoplane which, like the Morane-Saulnier AI, elicited great expectations, only to fall disappointingly short of them.

When *Idflieg* held a Second Fighter Competition at Adlershof between May 27 and June 21, 1918, Anthony Fokker and his staff entered the V28, a parasol monoplane powered by a 110-hp Oberursel Ur.II rotary engine. Fokker's experiments with cantilevered wing structures bore fruit with a lightweight plywood-covered wing that gave the plane outstanding climb and maneuverability, while its

Top: Captain Reed Chambers of the 94th Aero Squadron poses before a Roland D.VIa of Jasta 23b, turned over to the Americans after the armistice. The Roland was one of several supplements to the Fokker D.VII that failed to find favor among German Jagdflieger in 1918. (*U.S. Air Force Museum*) Bottom: A preserved Pfalz D.XII at the Champlin Fighter Museum in Mesa, Arizona, in 2000. Although a good plane, the Pfalz D.XII suffered in comparison to the Fokker D.VII. (*Jon Guttman*)

placement at eye level by means of streamlined steel-tube struts gave the pilot a remarkably good view in all directions. Judged the best rotary-engine fighter of the competition, the V28 was accepted for production as the E.V on July 3, but Fokker had already taken the liberty of starting production two weeks prior to receiving the official order. Fokker's chief engineer, Reinhold Platz, later claimed that the E.V may have cost "less man-hours than any other World War I aircraft." In any case, on August 5, the first E.Vs arrived at JG.I.

Leutnant Richard Wenzl, commander of *Jasta* 6, recalled:

> In terms of aviation technology, the machine was outstand-
> ing, despite the fact that it had been designed for the more
> powerful 140-hp rotary engine. In about a minute and a half
> it climbed to 1,000 metres and in eight minutes to 3,000
> meters, but then, [as a consequence of] a characteristic of
> engine torque, the performance fell off. Nevertheless, in
> terms of climbing ability and technical performance, this
> machine was superior to all previous [fighters], even the
> much-slower [Fokker] Triplane.

By that time, the last German offensive had been stopped and it
was the Allies who were on the advance. JG.I fell back to the aerodrome at Berne on August 11. On the 16th, *Jasta* 6 chalked up its
first success in the new monoplane when Leutnant der Reserve Emil
Rolff shot down a Camel for his third victory, its pilot, Sergeant P.M.
Fletcher of No. 203 Squadron, being taken prisoner. Later that same
day, however, another E.V crashed during a test flight and its pilot,
Vizefeldwebel Lechner, was injured.

On August 18, the RAF intelligence staff began alerting frontline
units, "that Fokker monoplanes have been issued to at least two pursuit flights not working in the Somme area." Then, suddenly, things
went frightfully wrong for the E.V. On the 19th, Rolff was putting one
of the new fighters through its paces over Berne when his wing suddenly broke up at an altitude of 300 meters and he crashed to his
death. Sensing a reprise of the misfortunes that had befallen the Dr.I,
Idflieg immediately grounded all E.Vs. A special crash commission
concluded that condensation moisture that had entered through
wing breathing holes had begun to rot the flying surfaces from within. Improper spar dimensions and faulty construction at Fokker's
Perzina factory were also blamed for the flaws in an intrinsically
sound design. It was the Dr.I all over again.

On August 24, E.V production was suspended until the shoddy
production techniques were rectified. Fokker responded by building
a new wing with strengthened spars, more careful assembly and a var-
nish-coated interior. It was successfully load tested on September 7,

Offizierstellvertreter Friedrich Altemeier of Jasta 24s poses with a Fokker E.V marked with the three-ring personal marking he used on all his aircraft. Although Altemeier was credited with as many as 21 victories—the last on November 10, 1918—there is no evidence that he scored any in Fokker's parasol monoplane. (*U.S. Air Force Museum*)

and *Idflieg* permitted production of the monoplane, now redesignated the D.VIII, to resume on September 24. The first D.VIII was accepted on October 8, and additional wings were built to be retrofitted to the 139 grounded E.Vs. Too much time had been lost, however, and Rolff's fleeting success remains the only positively recorded aerial victory attributed to the much-touted cantilever Fokker monoplane. Likewise, there is no evidence that an even-more-advanced design, the Junkers D.I all-metal low-wing monoplane, even saw combat before the Germans agreed to the armistice.

While the Germans—in a curious prelude to the closing months of a later war—experimented with innovative fighter designs that came too little and too late, Britain was introducing one more new type that could not have been less radical in concept—the Sopwith Snipe. Begun in mid-1917 as a Camel successor, the Sopwith 7F.1 featured wings of equal dihedral, with the upper wing center section lowered to the pilot's eye level in order to improve his forward and upward vision, which had been a longstanding shortcoming of the Camel. The plane's prototypes evolved over the months that followed, adapting the 230-hp Bentley B.R.2 rotary engine, increasing the wingspan with a two-bay rather than the original single-bay interplane strut layout, and altered tail surfaces. After testing at Martlesham in February 1918 and operational front-line evaluation at St. Omer in March, the 7F.1 Snipe was ordered into production, with seven companies being contracted to build 1,700 of the new fighter. Although its structural makeup was little changed from the 1916 Pup, the Snipe achieved the historic distinction by being the first fighter to enter service with the Royal Air Force since its formation on April 1, 1918.

On August 12, No. 43 Squadron received its first Snipe and in mid-September it was at full strength with 24. Alternating between Camel patrols and orientation flights in the new planes, 43's pilots found the B.R.2 engine commendably reliable and the Snipe, with a maximum speed of 121 mph at 10,000 feet, a better overall performer and somewhat more docile than the Camel.

On September 27, No. 43 Squadron's Snipes and S.E.5as of No. 1 Squadron were escorting No. 107 Squadron on a bombing raid against the railroad station at Bohain when the bombers were attacked by Fokker D.VIIs at 0915 hours. No. 1 Squadron intervened first, Lieutenant B.H. Mooney claiming a D.VII in flames over Bertry and Lieutenant C.W. Anning sending one down OOC near Bevillers. Ten minutes later, it was 43 Squadron's turn as Captain Cecil Frederick King and Lieutenant Charles C. Banks drove a Fokker D.VII down OOC near Cambrai. Five minutes later another Snipe pilot, Lieutenant R.S. Johnston, claimed a second D.VII OOC southeast of Cambrai. On the 29th, Captain Augustus Henry Orlebar sent a D.VII down OOC over Renaucourt, raising his wartime total to seven. In all, No. 43 Squadron claimed 10 enemy planes in the last six days of the month, without loss.

Number 4 Squadron, Australian Flying Corps got into action with its Snipes in October and No. 208 Squadron, RAF was just commencing operations when the armistice was signed on November 11. The most famous Snipe of all, however, was E8102, a personal machine assigned to Major William G. Barker while attached to the still Camel-equipped No. 201 Squadron. The Canadian ace fought his epic duel with at least 15 Fokker D.VIIs on October 27, and survived to receive the Victoria Cross.

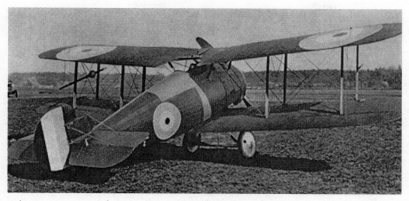

A latecomer in spite of its conventional layout, the Sopwith 7F.1 Snipe carved a niche in aviation history as the Royal Air Force's "first fighter," and by the Victoria Cross earned in one by Major William G. Barker. (*Jon Guttman*)

In January 1918, Sopwith began work on a ground support version of the Snipe, the prototype of which appeared in France for evaluation on May 9 as the T.T. 2 Salamander. Armed with the same twin Vickers machine guns and four Cooper bombs as the Snipe, the Salamander reverted to the angular fuselage that housed an armored box for the pilot, with 11mm-thick steel plate on the bottom, 8mm behind the engine firewall, and 6mm at the sides. Entering production, there were 37 Salamanders in the RAF by October 31, but only two in France, and the war ended before they could see action.

An alternative Snipe variant, completed in April 1918, was powered by the 320-hp A.B.C. Dragonfly radial engine, which gave it a startling maximum speed of 147.8 mph at 10,000 feet. This type, too, was ordered into production, eventually being renamed the Sopwith Dragon. Unfortunately for the British, the Dragonfly engine proved to be as unreliable as it was powerful, handicapping the careers of the Dragon and several other promising fighters that had been designed around it. The Dragon never achieved squadron service, whereas the Snipe would remain a postwar RAF mainstay until 1927.

10

CRESCENDO

The first critical air battle of 1918 occurred far from the Western Front. On the morning of January 20, the battle cruiser *Yavuz Sultan Selim* and light cruiser *Midilli* emerged from the Dardanelles and attacked the British naval base at Imbros Island in the eastern Aegean Sea. *Yavuz*, as it was called for short, was the German battle cruiser *Goeben* and *Midilli* was the former *Breslau,* both of which had slipped past the Royal Navy to be presented to the Turkish navy—an act that had much to do with the Ottoman Empire's fateful decision to ally itself with the Central Powers in 1914. Since then, *Yavuz* and *Midilli*, still operating primarily with German personnel, had affected the balance of power in the Black Sea as well as the Eastern Aegean, occasionally striking at Russian and British bases and having several engagements with the Russian Black Sea Fleet. On this occasion, the raiders sank the British monitors *Raglan* and *M28* in Kusu Bay, but then they ran into a minefield. Striking five mines, *Midilli* blew in two and sank, while *Yavuz* struck three and, as it steamed back to Constantinople, it came under attack by 10 British aircraft, which caused it to run aground on Nagara Bank.

With *Yavuz* thus immobilized, the British had a golden opportunity to bomb and destroy the most powerful warship in the Aegean—and for nearly a week they sent every bomber, floatplane and fighter they could muster against it, joined by airmen from Greece, which had joined the Allies in June 1917. *Yavuz* had no anti-aircraft guns aboard, so the Turkish army and Germans had to deploy them on the surrounding land. The nearest aerodrome, at Chanak-Kale, had a floatplane unit, the reconnaissance detachment *Fl. Abt.* 1, and *Fl. Abt.* 6, a "*Jagdstaffel*" whose available fighter force consisted of two Fokker E.IIIs, two Halberstadt D.Vs, and two Albatros D.IIIs.

The Germans, too, sent up everything they had. Leutnant Emil Meinecke, a prewar flier in *Fl. Abt.* 6 who already had three Allied planes to his credit, recalled of that day: "We had many small air-battles, but we did not dare fly very far out over the sea as our rotary engines were not to be trusted since they already had many hours of service on them and we had too few parts to overhaul them. Still, I succeeded in shooting down one English seaplane." His victim was a Sopwith Baby of 6 Wing, RNAS, which went down off Nagara Point.

Bad weather aided the defenders on the 21st, but the Allied air attacks resumed in earnest on the 22nd. "I was in the air almost constantly that day and had not even time to eat until dark," said Meinecke. "While I was in the air, the ground crew was fueling and oiling one of the other machines and loading it with ammunition. When I landed, I would get out of one machine and into the other and take off. I had one good fight with a Sopwith Camel who was more than a match for me." Meinecke managed to fend it off until its fuel ran low, but jammed guns prevented him from getting any parting shots into it. On the 23rd, Meinecke shot down a Sopwith 1-1/2 Strutter whose pilot, leaping from the burning plane, fell in the Dardanelles off Chanak-Kale. His body was recovered, proving to be Greek naval Flight Sub-Lieutenant Spyros Hambas.

On January 24, Meinecke and his commander, Leutnant Theo Jakob Croneiss, intercepted Sopwiths from Greek naval squadron H2, based at Mudros on the isle of Lemnos. Croneiss sent one down into the Gulf of Saros in flames. "I shot another in the engine and his engine stopped," Meinecke said. "This was confirmed by ground observers, but what happened to him, I do not know since I was attacked by another English pilot and my attention was diverted away." The Greeks confirmed the loss of their two planes, while Meinecke may have been one of three enemy planes credited that day to Captain Aristides Moraitinis. Moraitinis, who had been an observer during the Balkan Wars before becoming a pilot, became Greece's only ace with nine victories, but during a flight from Thessaloniki to Athens in stormy weather on December 22, 1918, he crashed to his death near the summit of Mount Olympus.

Finally, on the night of January 26, the Turkish pre-dreadnought battleship *Torgut Reis* managed to help free *Yavuz* from the shore and towed it to Constantinople, where it would still be under repair when the war ended. On January 29, Meinecke shot a Camel down in flames over Kilia, for his sixth victory. The air battle over Nagara was of some significance as a lost opportunity for air power to destroy a capital ship before Brig. Gen. William Mitchell's peacetime demonstration of airpower on July 21, 1921. Equally significant, however, is the role played by fighter aircraft in the warship's survival.

In January 1918, while the Germans prepared for their spring offensive, France's *Aéronautique Militaire* was expanding its concept of a roving fighter force from *groupes de combat* into *Escadre de Combat No.1*, comprising GC.15 (Spa.37, 81, 93, and 97), GC.18 (Spa.48, 94,153, and 155) and GC.19 (Spa.73, 85, 95, and 96). Led by *Chef de Bataillon* Victor Ménard, the former commander of N.26 and GC.15, the new *escadre* could field 12 squadrons wherever they might be needed to achieve local air superiority. On February 27, the French created a second such unit, *Escadre* No.2 under Commandant Edouard Duseigneur, consisting of GC.13 (Spa.15, 65, 84, and 88), GC.17 (Spa.17, 89, 91, and 100) and GC.20 (Spa.68, 99, 159, and 162).

In March the French enlarged the organization even further, forming two brigades that combined the fighter equipped *escadres* with similar bomber formations, all four comprising a *Division Aérienne* commanded by Colonel Albert-Charles Marie de Vaulgrenant. Thus, Menard's *Escadre* No.1 would operate in Chef de Bataillon Joseph de Göys de Meyzerac's 1e *Brigade* alongside *Escadre* No.12, commanded by seven-victory ace Commandant Joseph Vuillemin and made up of the nine Breguet 14B.2 equipped *Groupes de Bombardement* 5, 6, and 9, and *Escadrilles de Protection* R.239 and R.240 with Caudron

Jasta 12 of Jagdgeschwader II was transitioning from Albatros to triplane when pho-tographed at Toulis on March 15, 1918. The white-nosed, black-tailed Albatros D.Va and Fokker Dr.I at far right both bore the white chevron motif of Unteroffizier Ulrich Neckel. (Greg Van Wyngarden)

R.11s. Duseigneur's *Escadre* No.2 was part of Commandant Philippe Féquant's *2e Brigade*, supporting *Escadre* No.13, comprising GB.3 and 4 and escorting *Escadrille* R.46.

By this duet of combined-arms teams, the French intended to have their fighters seize control of the sky and their bombers make immediate use of it to strike the enemy at and as far behind the battle line as possible. The sheer mass of airpower that the *Division Aérienne* could concentrate in a given area of operations, combined with local units and other reinforcing escadrilles would ultimately overwhelm the German air effort during their offensive and in the Allied counteroffensives to follow.

As it was, the *Kaiserschlacht*, launched on March 21, in what the Germans regarded as a limited window of opportunity, caught the *Luftstreiskräfte* sorely short of the state of preparedness it would have preferred. That especially applied to its fighter force, whose best plane at the time was the Fokker Dr.I, equipping elements of all three *Jagdgeschwader* and *Jasta* 14. This nimble but imperfect dogfighter could only serve as the tip of the *Jagdstaffeln*'s spear, the shaft consisting of the older, less-desired workhorses. At the end of April, for example, the *Luftstreitskräfte*'s Fokker inventory totaled 171 Dr.Is and 19 newly arrived D.VIIs, necessarily supplemented by 928 Albatros D.Vas, 174 D.IIIs, and 131 D.Vs, plus 433 Pfalz D.IIIas.

A lineup of *Jasta* 6 triplanes at Léchelle, which JG.I occupied on March 26. Vizefeldwebel Franz Hemer's Dr.I 595/17, with the wavy line inspired by his curly hair, is at right, with Leutnant Robert Tüxen's white-banded Dr.I 568/17 next to it. (*Greg Van Wyngarden*)

Manfred von Richthofen and Rudolf Berthold, commanding JG.I and JG.II respectively, were already aware of the triplane's limitations—it was slow and its rotary engine, never a German forte, was chronically unreliable. Richthofen hedged his bets by fully equipping *Jasta* 6 and 11 with Dr.Is, but retaining Albatros D.Vas and Pfalz D.IIIas in *Jasta* 4 and 10, the latter of which would receive Fokker D.VIIs once they became available. Likewise, Berthold's *Jasta* 12, 13, and 19 had triplanes, but *Jasta* 15 flew Albatros D.Vas. Oberleutnant Bruno Loerzer intended all four of JG.III's *Staffeln* to use Dr.Is, but in February there were only enough Fokkers to supply *Jastas* Boelcke and 36; *Jastas* 26 and 27 continued flying Albatros D.Vs well into March.

As of early March 1918, the German 2., 17., and 18. *Armees* had 730 planes, 326 of which were fighters, deployed against the British Third and Fifth Armies, which then had 579 operational aircraft, of which 261 were single-seat fighters, in 32 squadrons. In terms of the entire front, however, the RFC, RNAS, and Australian Flying Corps (AFC) had 336 of the Dr.I's most comparable adversary, the Sopwith Camel, equipping 14 squadrons throughout the Western Front, as well as three Camel squadrons in Italy. In addition, the RFC had eight combat ready S.E.5a squadrons whose full complements of 18 each totaled—on paper at least—144 planes.

In the thick of the fighting with the Red Baron's Flying Circus, Camels of No. 73 Squadron at an airstrip near Humières on April 6, 1918, with a Bristol F.2B landing in the background. (*Greg Van Wyngarden*)

While the Allied armies reeled back before the German onslaught, British and French aircraft struggled to regain control of the air while single and two-seat fighters of both sides bombed and strafed ground forces as opportunity allowed. Amid all that, on April 1, the British effected a profound organizational change on their air assets, combining the RFC and the RNAS into an independent air arm, the Royal Air Force. All RNAS squadrons were renumbered in the 200 range, so that, for example, "Naval 8" became No. 208 Squadron, RAF. Under the circumstances, most British airmen were too busy fighting to pay much notice to their change in status at the time.

Operation Michael, a drive toward Amiens that ended on April 5, and Operation Georgette, an offensive in the Lys River area launched four days later, saw a series of classic aerial encounters that made legends of Camel and Fokker triplane alike, culminating in the dogfights of April 20 and 21. In the first, *Jasta* 11 tackled No. 3 Squadron, resulting in three German and at least one confirmed British claim. The actual damage was all inflicted by Richthofen, however, as he shot down Major Richard Raymond-Barker, and 2nd Lt. David G. Lewis in flames. Major Barker, No. 3 Squadron's CO with six victories scored previously in Bristol Fighters, was killed, but Lewis miraculously survived as a POW. The next day's fight pitted *Jasta* 11 against No. 209 Squadron, during which Richthofen latched onto the tail of 2nd Lt. Wilfrid R. May and became so fixated on his inexperienced, desperately jinking quarry that he followed him into Allied territory at low altitude, thus violating his own dicta, until a single bullet—either from May's friend and flight leader Captain Arthur Royal Brown, or more likely from an Australian soldier's weapon fired from the ground—traversed the Red Baron's chest. Richthofen managed to land near Amiens, but died instants later, to be buried with full honors by his foes at Bertangles.

The Red Baron's death was a serious blow to the Germans, not merely because he was the war's ace of aces, but because of his leadership. Neither his personally named successor, Hauptmann Wilhelm Reinhard, nor the man who took over JG.I after Reinhard's death on July 3, Oberleutnant Hermann Göring, quite matched Richthofen's uncanny ability to join his men in the thick of a dogfight while somehow simultaneously managing to keep an eye on all of them. As if that wasn't enough, JG.I lost two more aces on May 2, when *Jasta* 11's CO, Leutnant Hans Weiss, whose score stood at 16, was shot down by Lieutenant Merrill S. "Sammy" Taylor of No. 209 Squadron and Vizefeldwebel Edgar Scholtz, credited with six victories and about to receive his Leutnant's commission, fatally crashed during a takeoff attempt.

After Operation Georgette's cancellation in the face of British counterattacks on April 29, the Germans shifted their power for a strike at the French on May 27, with Operation Blücher-Yorck and its follow-up, Gneisenau, in the Aisne sector between Soissons and Reims. These offensives unleashed the Fokker D.VIIs in force, giving the *Jagdflieger* a sense of confidence they had not known since Bloody April.

Also appearing in German units at about that time were the first parachutes to become standard equipment in airplanes. Unteroffizier Otto Heinecke, a ground crewman in *Flieger Abteilung* 23, had devised a compact parachute pack that gave pilots the same option of abandoning a stricken plane that balloon observers had enjoyed with their bulkier Paulus parachutes since the war began. When the necessity arose, the airman jumped from the plane and a static line attached to a harness around his shoulder and legs would pull the parachute

pack clear of the empennage before a
second static line, secured inside the
cockpit, pulled the canopy from the
pack.

Such parachutes had, in fact,
existed as early as 1916, their
issuance largely being delayed by
high-ranking officers on both sides
who debated whether they would
encourage aircrews to abandon
planes that could be ridden to the
ground, or even undermine their
aggressiveness in the air. The
Luftstreistkräfte, heavily outnumbered even as Germany launched the
Kaiserschlacht, was the first to judge
such nonsense, and the consequent
loss of trained airmen whose lives
might otherwise be saved, to be a
luxury it could ill afford.

At first some pilots, including
Manfred von Richthofen, doubted
the parachutes' reliability as being

Leutnant Gustav Frädrich of Jasta 72s
is helped into his harness, after which
his ground crewman will install his
parachute in the cockpit of his Fokker
D.VII. Appearing at about the same
time as the D.VII, the parachutes were
unreliable, but many German airmen
owed their lives to them. (Jon
Guttman)

worth the 15 kilograms they added to a fighters' weight. Their early
use seemed to justify the skepticism, as an alarming one-third of the
first 70 airmen to bail out were killed, either because their parachutes
caught on the empennage, or because the harnesses gave way under
the stress of a body suddenly jerked out of free fall at 80 mph. The
latter problem was addressed in the late summer of 1918 by reinforced harnesses with wider leg straps that distributed the weight
better and greatly improved reliability. The first demonstration came
during a fight between *Jasta* 46 with S.E.5as and Camels on June 27,
when Leutnant Helmut Steinbrecher successfully bailed out of his
burning plane. Two days later, Leutnant Ernst Udet of *Jasta* 4 was
shot down by a Breguet 14A2 and likewise ended up owing his life to
his Heinecke parachute.

While the new parachutes at least improved a German pilot's odds of survival if shot down, the British balked at issuing them to their single-seat squadrons until September 16, 1918. The French and Americans never did allow their pilots to use them before the armistice.

In spite of the toll the Fokker D.VIIs took on the Allies, they remained outnumbered, and as things turned out several of the Allied fighters, such as the Spad XIII, S.E.5a, and Sopwith Dolphin, were at least able to hold their own against them. Others, such as the Sopwith Camel and Nieuport 28, could outmaneuver them, even though their lower speeds gave their pilots no means to disengage other than fighting their way home.

The *Jagdflieger* would certainly have been happier had the Fokker D.VII reached them earlier, but they were most fortunate that it had not arrived any later. On June 12, JG.II reported, "The Fokker triplanes can no longer be regarded as serviceable for the front." This was primarily because their rotary engines needed to be lubricated with castor oil, a commodity that was not readily available to Germany due to the Allied blockade. German chemists had developed substitutes, such as Voltol and Rizinus oil, but their viscosity broke up much sooner than castor oil's—especially in the summer heat. Consequently, JG.II's last all-triplane unit, *Jasta* 19, was frequently grounded and unable to play a steady roll in *Geschwader* operations until its Dr.Is were replaced by D.VIIs. *Jastas* 14's and 36's triplanes apparently soldiered on into August, no doubt with great difficulty, until they too finally got D.VIIs.

While the Allies absorbed successive blows on the Western Front, on June 15, Austro-Hungarian forces crossed the Piave in a bid to defeat Italy. The Italians were dug in and determined, however, and both their aircraft and the RAF's severely punished the Austro-Hungarian bridgeheads until the 19th, when the offensive stalled, and throughout the Austrian's subsequent withdrawal back across the river. Amid those strafing operations, Italy lost its leading ace and leader of its most elite unit, the 91a *Squadriglia*, when Maggiore Francesco Baracca's Spad XIII crashed near Montello, apparently a victim of ground fire. Baracca, dead with a bullet through the head,

Defending Reims in May 1918, Spa.124's transitionary lineup includes a Spad VII flown by Czech volunteer Adjutant Vaclàv Pilàt (left), and Spad XIIIs flown by Sous-Lieutenants Marcel Robert (No.3, second from left) and Henri Barancy (right). (*Radko Vasicek Collection via Jon Guttman*)

had 34 victories to his credit. The Battle of the Piave ended on June 22 with about 190,000 Austro-Hungarian casualties.

On the morning of July 15, the Germans made their final attempt to drive on Paris and force the French to sue for peace. The French, now joined by American forces, stopped them in their tracks along the Marne River. On the 18th the Germans retreated across the Marne and on the 20th the French went over to the offensive. In the course of a month the Central Powers had irrevocably lost their last chance for victory.

In the air, however, the *Jagdflieger* still seemed to give more than they got. At the end of June the American 1st Pursuit Group transferred from Gengoult to Saints in the Château-Thierry sector to join the French in their operations against the last German offensive. Although the Americans had gained some experience in the Toul sector, their introduction to the "big leagues," in the form of Fokker D.VIIs flown by Germany's most seasoned veterans, was grim. Among the heavy casualties the 1st Pursuit suffered was 1st Lt. Quentin Roosevelt, former President Theodore Roosevelt's son serving in the 95th Aero Squadron, killed on July 14, and six pilots of the 27th Aero Squadron killed or taken prisoner on August 1.

On July 13, the first 14 Spad XIIIs arrived to replace the 1st Pursuit Group's Nieuport 28s. Only one was listed as flyable the next day. On the 25th, the 95th Aero's Spads had a morale-raising debut when 1st Lt. Walter L. Avery landed a lucky hit on a Fokker's carburetor that forced it down in French lines. The captured pilot turned out to be Leutnant Karl Menckhoff, commander of Royal Saxon *Jasta* 72 and a *Pour le Mérite* holder with 39 victories to his credit.

That encouraging start notwithstanding, the Americans found their first batch of Spad XIIIs as troublesome as those first delivered to the French. The 94th Aero Squadron alone reported 124 cases of leaking oil pipes, faulty oil pumps, carburetors, magnetos, gas tanks, gauges, reduction gears, and other problems between July 18 and 31. While the 94th and 95th Aero squadrons were still glad to see the last of their Nieuports at that point, the pilots of the 27th and 147th, whose respective commanders, Majors Harold E. Hartney and Geoffrey Bonnell, had had previous experience with rotary engines in the RFC and had prepared their men accordingly, were disgusted with the Spads. Bonnell objected so outspokenly, in fact, that he was relieved of command and replaced by 1st Lt. James A. Meissner, who after surviving two incidents of fabric tearing from his Nieuport 28's wings while in the 94th, was quite pleased to accept the new Spads.

With no recourse but to make the faulty engines work, Hartney wrote, "Our mechanics dug into their job with fine spirit. Although it meant four days for a complete overhaul of the new water-cooled engine against four hours on the air-cooled Monosoupape, they realized the additional risks being taken by the pilots and accepted the situation with good grace."

While the French and Americans were reversing the German tide on land and in the air, the RAF had kept up its OPs with a growing confidence based not only on numbers but the quality of its aircraft and its squadrons. As with the Germans, British fighter pilots were able to benefit from the experience of squadron and flight leaders whose leadership matched their individual skills in an air war that could not be determined by aces alone.

Although Canadian Major William Avery Bishop had acquired much publicity as the leading RAF ace with 72 victories, postwar examinations of his record call into question the validity of his claims—even in regard to the action on June 2, 1917, that led to his receiving the Victoria Cross. More important at the time was his behavior when he led a new S.E.5a unit, No. 85 Squadron, to France on May 22, 1918. While popular among the men, Bishop continued to display the self-serving lone-wolf tendencies he had shown earlier flying Nieuport 17s in No. 60 Squadron, leading to his recall on June 19, to be replaced by Major Edward Mannock.

Among the war's great flight and squadron leaders was Major Edward Mannock, who would have regarded his 61 accredited victories and Victoria Cross as secondary to assuring the survival and success of his men. (*IWM Q58662*)

"Mick" Mannock's tally of 61 was second only to Bishop's in the RAF, and it was likewise secondary to his value as a leader. Privately harboring an aversion to war and a pathological fear of what he had a premonition would be death in flames, Mannock buried those weaknesses under an outward display of hatred for the Germans and a genuine obsession with the survival of his pilots. As commander of A Flight in No. 74 Squadron earlier in 1918, he had shown outstanding leadership, and likewise as commander of 85 he saw to it that the squadron record reflected the success of his pilots as much as his own. Characteristically, on July 26, he took up a new pilot, 2nd Lt. Donald C. Inglis, and helped him to shoot down his first enemy plane. Moments later, however, the two SEs came under ground fire from German Infantry Regiment No.100, and Mannock's premonition finally came true as his plane was hit and fell burning to the ground. He was posthumously awarded the Victoria Cross.

July had cost the RAF other notables. On the 10th, Major James McCudden, victor over 57 enemies and a VC recipient, was taking off to assume command of No. 60 Squadron when his S.E.5a's engine seized, and as he tried to return to the aerodrome he stalled and crashed, subsequently dying of his injuries. On July 22, 2nd Lt. Indra Lal Roy of No. 40 Squadron was shot down and killed in a fight with *Jasta* 29, after having shot down 10 enemy planes in less than two weeks to become India's only ace. After shooting down a Hannover CL.III on July 31, Limerick-born Captain George Edward Henry McElroy of No. 40 Squadron, a star pupil of Mannock's and the leading Irish ace with at least 46 victories, was killed by an anti-aircraft shell. In spite of such grievous losses, the RAF carried on with an ample supply of other seasoned leaders.

On August 8, 10 divisions of General Sir Henry Rawlinson's Fourth Army, supported in flank by the French 1*e Armée*, opened a devastating offensive at Amiens, involving a skillful coordination of artillery, tanks and troops. In what General Ludendorff called the "Black Day of the German Army," six German divisions collapsed and the British advanced nine miles along a 10-mile front, taking 16,000 prisoners.

The RAF and *Aéronautique Militaire* were much in evidence during the operation, both in close support of the troops and in an effort to destroy the bridges across the Somme and cut off the mauled II. and XVIII. *Armees*. Equally active throughout, however, were the *Jagdgeschwader* and local *Jagdgruppen*, which were credited with at least 42 British aircraft on the first day alone, for the loss of two POWs and two pilots wounded. They continued to exact a heavy toll over the next few critical days, defending the bridges long enough to save the retreating armies from complete annihilation.

That success came at a rising price. On August 9, *Vizefeldwebel* Franz Hemer of *Jasta* 6 was wounded, ending his combat career with 18 victories. On the 10th Oberleutnant Erich Löwenhardt, commander of *Jasta* 10 and Germany's third-ranking ace with 53 victories, collided with Leutnant Alfred Wenz, who had scored five with *Jasta* 11. Both men bailed out of their crippled Fokker D.VIIs, but while Wenz's parachute opened, Löwenhardt's did not and he fell to his death near Chaulnes. During a fight with S.E.5as of No. 32 Squadron that same day, Leutnant Paul Billik, commander of *Jasta* 52 and victor over 31 Allied planes, came down between Vimy and Combles with a dead engine and was taken prisoner. After shooting down two D.H.4s that day to bring his score to 44, Hautpmann Berthold's control column was shot through. In the ensuing crash his already lame arm was injured anew, though even then it took a direct order from Kaiser Wilhelm II for him to relinquish command of JG.II and report to a hospital. On August 13, Leutnant Dieter Collin of *Jasta* 56, with 13 victories, was mortally wounded and the Red Baron's brother, Leutnant Lothar von Richthofen, who at that point had 40, suffered his third wound of the war, serious enough to put him out of it.

A series of British offensives east of the Somme and in Flanders continued throughout September and October 1918, as did French advances on the Aisne and Champagne fronts, all backed by aircraft and all contested by the *Luftstreiskräfte*. To those was added the first major American operation of the war, in which General John Joseph Pershing, commanding 665,000 troops in 19 divisions, backed by 3,220 guns and 267 tanks, aimed to drive the 10 divisions of General Max von Gallwitz's *Armee Gruppe* C from the St. Mihiel salient.

Air support for the push was under the overall command of Colonel William Mitchell, at whose temporary disposal the French had put Vaulgrenant's *Division Aérienne* and the British had volunteered support from the nine bomber squadrons of their Independent Force, based at Nancy. By the time the offensive was launched on September 12, Mitchell's own fighter element consisted of the 1st Pursuit Group, returned from Saints to its new base at Rembercourt, the 2nd Pursuit Group at Toul, made up of the 13th, 22nd, 49th, and 139th Aero Squadrons, and the 3rd Pursuit Group at Vaucouleurs, comprising the 28th, 93rd, 103rd, and 213th Aero Squadrons. As the French had done with their *Division Aérienne*, Mitchell had made the fighter units part of a larger formation: Major Bert M. Atkinson's 1st Pursuit Wing, which also included French GC.16 (Spa.77, 112, 150, and 158), the American 1st Day Bombardment Group (11th, 20th, and 96th Aero Squadrons), Caproni Ca.3 night bombers of French GB.2 (*Escadrilles* CEP.115

and 130) and Italian *Gruppo di Bombardamento* 18 (*3a,* 14*a,* and 15*a Squadriglie*), and a USAS night reconnaissance unit, the Breguet 14A.2-equipped 9th Aero Squadron.

The total Allied commitment to the offensive came to 1,476 airplanes. Among the aerial opposition they would face were local *Jastas* 64w and 65, with the additions of *Jastas* 18, 54s, and 77b, and as of September 3, the formidable JG.II, now commanded by Hauptmann Oskar von Bönigk.

Although most of the American fighter pilots were woefully inexperienced, they had the benefit of group, squadron, and flight leaders with previous experience in a variety of other air arms. Some had transferred from the USAS from previous French service through the Lafayette Flying Corps, or in the RFC, including Canadian-born Harold Hartney, who was given command of the 27th Aero Squadron and later the 1st Pursuit Group. Others were USAS members who had been assigned to French escadrilles or RAF squadrons to gain experience until their own units were fully equipped. Some had trained in Italy before going to France.

On February 18, 1918, the *Escadrille Lafayette* underwent a split metamorphosis, its American personnel joining the USAS as the 103rd Aero Squadron, while Spa.124 resumed operations with French personnel—to which it added three Portuguese, Czech volunteer Sous-Lieutenant Vacláv Pilát, and six-victory Russian ace Capitaine Pavel Argeyev, who would score nine more with the unit. The 103rd Aero Squadron flew Spad VIIs with French *Groupe de Combat* 21 around Reims and on its own in Flanders until July 29, when it was transferred to Vaucouleurs. There it became the nucleus of the 3rd Pursuit Group under Lafayette ace Major William Thaw, who in emulation of GC.12's differently posed storks and GC.21's varicolored bands, adopted variations on the 103rd's Indian head motif for his other squadrons, the 28th, 93rd, and 213th. Another *Escadrille Lafayette* veteran, Captain Ray Bridgman, led the 22nd Aero Squadron. One of the 139th's flight leaders, 1st Lt. David Putnam, had flown with N.94, MS.156, and Spa.38, honing his skills in the latter unit under Lieutenant Georges Félix Madon, who in addition to scoring 41 confirmed victories—and some 60 probables—was one of the war's great mentors of fighter pilots.

Crescendo 259

The 13th Aero Squadron's commander, Captain Charles J. Biddle, had seen previous combat in Spa.73—under Lieutenant Albert Deullin, 20-victory ace, published air tactician and tutor of other aces—and in the 103rd Aero Squadron. Although encouraged by the high level of skill and morale among his pilots, Biddle tried to stress the importance of team effort and, "discouraging the great tendency for one man to try to dash off by himself and be a hero at the expense of the whole," admonishing them that, "Any man who leaves a patrol for such a purpose will be put on the ground for a couple of weeks and confined to camp, and if he repeats the performance I shall send him to the rear."

While not the highest scorer among the balloon specialists, 2nd Lt. Frank Luke of the 27th Aero Squadron, shown posing with a captured German Maxim machine gun, had one of the most meteoric careers, being credited with 14 gasbags and four airplanes between September 12 and 29, 1918, and earning a posthumous Medal of Honor. (Jon Guttman)

Rain and thunderstorms limited air operations when the St. Mihiel offensive commenced on September 12, but the aero squadrons flew whenever they could. Two Fokkers were claimed by 1st Lt. Leslie J. Rummell and 1st Lt. Charles Rudolph D'Olive of the 93rd. That afternoon, Dave Putnam of the 139th engaged eight D.VIIs, downing one for his 13th victory, then saved a Breguet under attack by an enemy formation only to be struck twice in the heart by Leutnant Georg von Hantelmann of *Jasta* 15. Both Putnam and the German who killed him were 19 years old. Ironically, the only success confirmed to a member of the veteran 1st Pursuit Group that day was a balloon burned by 2nd Lt. Frank Luke, an undisciplined young Arizona cowboy who had been nothing but a disciplinary problem since he joined the 27th Aero Squadron on July 25.

The American ground assault caught *Armee Abteilung* C in the act of withdrawing from what it recognized as a vulnerable salient. As a result, by September 16 most objectives were attained, along with the capture of some 15,000 prisoners and 257 guns, liberating 200 square miles of French territory at a cost of 7,000 casualties—one-third of what the U.S. Army Medical Corps had anticipated. In the air it was a different story. While Mitchell's air armada maintained control of the air by its sheer numbers, it paid a heavy price.

A particularly bad day was September 14. That morning, 1st Lt. Sumner Sewell was at the tail end of a 95th Aero Squadron patrol when von Boenigk jumped him and set his fuel tank ablaze. The Spad was credited to JG.II's CO, but its power dive blew out the fire and Sewell crash landed in Allied lines—to be narrowly missed moments later by the wheel of his plane, which had come off during his dive.

The 13th Aero Squadron was jumped by *Jasta* 18 that morning, 1st Lt. George R. Kull being killed and 1st Lts. Alton A. Brody, Harry B. Freeman and Charles W. Drew taken prisoner—Drew having to have his wounded leg amputated. Three of them were credited to Leutnant der Reserve Hans Müller, who would survive the war with 12 victories, and one to Leutnant Günther von Büren. Two Fokkers were jointly credited to 1st Lts. Robert H. Stiles, Gerald D. Stivers, and Murray K. Guthrie, but *Jasta* 18's only casualty was von Büren, wounded. A grieving Biddle lamented that in spite of his relentless warnings, "the new men will get carried away with themselves in a combat and go too strong."

That afternoon, 1st Lt. Arthur Raymond Brooks led C Flight of the 22nd Aero Squadron to escort a Salmson 2A2 on a reconnaissance mission, but all he found at the rendezvous point over Mars-la-Tour were 12 red-nosed Fokkers of *Jasta* 15, which claimed four of the Spads—two by Leutnant der Reserve Johannes Klein, one by von Boenigk and one by Leutnant von Hantelmann. Brooks saw 1st Lt. Philip E. Hassinger shot down in flames, while 1st Lts. Raymond J. Little and Arthur C. Kimber force-landed in Allied lines, the latter with 70 bullet holes in his plane. Over the next 10 minutes, Brooks took on eight of the Fokkers in an effort to cover the retirement of his remaining men until Klein drove him down in Allied lines. Miraculously unhurt, Brooks was subsequently credited with two Fokkers shot down—which he insisted on sharing with Hassinger—

and two damaged, for which he was awarded the Distinguished Service Cross.

September 14 was a good day for Allied balloon busting, however. Sous-Lieutenant Paul Maurice Boyau of Spa.77 teamed up with an LFC escadrille mate, Caporal Edward Corsi, and Sous-Lieutenant Claude Haegelen of Spa.100 to burn a *Drachen* over Etraye. The 27th Aero Squadron added two more to the day's bag when Frank Luke and 1st Lts. Leo H. Dawson and Thomas F. Lennon burned a balloon in the morning and Luke destroyed a second that afternoon. Eight Fokker D.VIIs attacked Luke, but he was saved by the intervention of his only friend in the squadron, 1st Lt. Joseph F. Wehner.

Boyau and three other Spa.77 pilots burned two more *Drachen* on September 15, raising Boyau's total to 14 enemy planes and 20 balloons. Luke also destroyed two and when German fighters descended on him Wehner again thwarted them, sending a Fokker crashing and driving an Albatros down in a steep dive.

On the 16th, Boyau, Corsi, Caporal René Walk, and Aspirant Henri Cessieux went after a *Drachen* at Harville. Boyau and Cessieux destroyed the balloon, but then the French were jumped by seven Fokkers of *Jasta* 15. Cesseiux and Corsi were wounded, but escaped. After evading his first attacker by diving under the burning balloon, Boyau tried to drive a Fokker off Walk's tail, only to be hit by either another German fighter or by ground fire, and Boyau fell in flames, to be credited to Leutnant von Hantelman. Walk, though credited to Vizefeldwebel Gustav Klaudat, force-landed his damaged Spad in Allied lines. That evening Luke and Wehner put on a command performance before their squadron leader, 1st Lt. Alfred A. Grant, their group commander, Lt. Col. Hartney, and Brig. Gen. William Mitchell, jointly destroying one balloon, then Luke burning a second and Wehner a third.

Having made themselves the most talked-about phenomenon in the USAS in five days, Luke and Wehner burned two German balloons near Labeuville, on September 18, but were then attacked by *Jasta* 15. Luke sent two Fokkers down to crash and after failing to spot Wehner, he joined Sous-Lieutenant Pierre Gaudermen and Adjutant Reginald Sinclaire of Spa.68 in destroying an LVG C.V in

French lines. Although he had scored five victories within half an hour, Luke could not have gone unaffected by the loss of his best friend, who had been mortally wounded by Leutnant von Hantelmann—the third ace killed within a week by the young former hussar, who would survive the war with 25 victories.

With St. Mihiel successfully concluded, the AEF turned to its next target, the Meuse-Argonne region. Shortly before that campaign began, on September 24, the newly promoted Captain Edward Rickenbacker relieved Major Kenneth Marr as commander of the 94th Aero Squadron. Applying the ambition that drove him as a race car driver and as a fighter pilot to his squadron, "Rick" started off by insisting to his pilots that, "No other American squadron at the front would ever again be permitted to approach our margin of supremacy." He likewise insisted that the mechanics see to it that the 94th's Spads and their engines would be in perfect running order at all times.

The next morning, Rickenbacker flew a lone patrol over Verdun and Douaumont. Soon after turning east toward Étain, he spotted two German two-seaters (identified as LVGs by him, but as Halberstadts in his citation), escorted from above by five Fokkers. "Climbing for the sun for all I was worth," he wrote, "I soon had the satisfaction of realizing that I had escaped their notice and was now well in their rear. I shut down my engine, put down my nose and made a bee line for the nearest Fokker." Catching the D.VII by surprise, Rickenbacker reported that it crashed near Billy at 0840 hours. He then plunged through the Fokker formation to attack the two-seaters, shooting one down in flames and, as the regrouped Fokkers dived on him, "I put on the gas and headed for my own lines."

No German loss has been found to match Rickenbacker's Fokker claim for September 25, but the deaths of Sergeant Heinrich Lender, and Leutnant der Reserve Fritz Knipp of *Flieger Abteilung* 36 over "Maas-Ost" fit his two-seater in flames. Twelve years later, on November 6, 1930, he received the Medal of Honor from President Herbert Hoover for his actions that day.

The Meuse-Argonne offensive saw the AEF encountering much more difficult terrain than it had around St. Mihiel, against a determined enemy who had had plenty of time to prepare defenses in depth. The intensity of the six-week land campaign was matched in the air. The USAS was stronger and its pilots more experienced, but the Germans, aware that JG.II and the local *Jastas* would not be enough to stem the growing American preponderance, transferred JG.I from fighting the RAF to tackling the USAS. On September 25, the Circus came to town—in this case Metz-Frescaty aerodrome.

That night the Americans unleashed a barrage from 3,928 guns and at 0530 hours on September 26 troops from nine divisions advanced through the dawn mist. Only five German divisions opposed them, but they were well entrenched in three defense lines or *Stellungen*, bearing the Wagnerian names of Giselher, Kreimhilde, and Freya, and unlike their comrades at St. Mihiel they had no plans to withdraw—not with a four-track railroad at their backs that was vital to sustain the German war effort to the north. As the American drive slowed, both sides committed more soldiers to the contest— some 400,000 Americans of the First and Second armies, plus the adjacent French XVII Corps, against 40 German divisions, primarily from General Georg von der Marwitz's V. *Armee*.

Again, the air battles were often epic and the Allied losses high. The *Jagdflieger* claimed 64 victories on September 26, for the loss of one pilot brought down a prisoner and five wounded. Among the latter was Oberleutnant Ernst Udet of *Jasta* 4, struck in the thigh after downing two D.H.9s of No. 99 Squadron, Independent Force, to bring his total to 62. On the same day Lieutenant René Fonck of Spa.103 was credited with six victories—his second sextet in a day, having accomplished the same feat back on May 19. Fonck, whose self-absorbed personality kept him from gaining the admiration reserved for the late Georges Guynemer, nevertheless finished the war as the Allied ace of aces, with 75 victories.

While Fonck's career barreled on to its climax, one of France's pioneer fighters was making a belated bid for acedom. Since his capture on April 18, 1915, Roland Garros had made several attempts to escape the Germans before finally succeeding on February 14, 1918. Aggressive as ever, after training on the Spad XIII, he rejoined

Spa.26 and on October 2, he claimed two Fokker D.VIIs, one of which was confirmed for his fourth victory. On the 5th, however, Sous-Lieutenant Garros went missing, having last been seen battling seven Fokkers southwest of Vouziers. He was probably killed by Leutnant der Reserve Hermann Habich of *Jasta* 49, who claimed a Spad near Somme-Py.

On September 29, Frank Luke pulled an evening raid that destroyed three balloons, but was brought down mortally wounded by ground fire near Murvaux. In 18 days he had been credited with 14 balloons and four airplanes, a meteoric career capped by a posthumously awarded Medal of Honor.

Luke's balloon forays, usually alone save for a wingman to ward off enemy fighters, seemed consistent with his wild cowboy temperament and his apparent lack of fear. Such tactics may, in fact, have been the best for eliminating the gasbags, however, as the 1st Pursuit Group discovered on October 10, when General Mitchell sent the 94th and 147th Aero Squadrons out in a large-scale operation to eliminate two balloons at Dun-sur-Meuse and Aincreville. Rickenbacker selected 1st Lts. Reed Chambers and Hamilton Coolidge of the 94th to attack the gasbags at 1550 hours, while the rest of the group covered them. The Germans were equally determined to defend their *Drachen*, however, and elements of JG.I gave the Americans what Rickenbacker called "a regular dogfight," in which he claimed two Fokkers, Chambers claimed another, and a fourth was shared by Coolidge and 1st Lt. William W. Palmer. The 147th Aero Squadron was also heavily engaged, with 1st Lt. Kenneth L. Porter claiming one Fokker and sharing a second with 1st Lt. Oscar B. Myers and 2nd Lt. Wilbert W. White; another was credited to Captain Meissner and 2nd Lts. George A. Waters and Ralph A. O'Neill; and a fourth fell to 2nd Lt. William E. Brotherton before he was shot down in flames. When a Fokker got on another 147th member's tail, 2nd Lt. White turned and rammed it head-on.

Rickenbacker was belatedly going to Brotherton's aid when he saw another Spad under attack and recognized his former squadron mate, Jimmy Meissner, "smiling and good-natured as ever, with two

Escaped from the Germans and back in action, Lieutenant Roland Garros boards his Blériot-built SPAD XIII S15409 of Spa.26. He scored his fourth victory on October 2, 1918, but was killed three days later, probably downed by Leutenant der Reserve Hermann Habich of Jasta 49. (*Musée de l'Air et l'Espace, BA26287*)

ugly brutes on his tail trying their best to execute him." Rickenbacker fired a long burst and wrote, "The Hun fell off and dropped out of control, the other Fokker immediately pulling away and diving steeply for home and safety."

For all the claims made over them, the Germans recorded only one Fokker destroyed—that of Leutnant der Reserve Wilhelm Kohlbach of *Jasta* 10, who parachuted from his plane after colliding with White's Spad. (Rickenbacker claimed to have seen one of the Fokker pilots he downed take to his parachute, evidently confusing him with Kohlbach.) *Jasta* 10 also credited Spads to Leutnant Justus Grassmann and Leutnant der Reserve Aloys Heldmann, their victims presumably being Brotherton and Meissner, although the latter made it home. Even fighting over their home turf, the Germans could sometimes be as capable of overoptimistic confirmation as the Allies.

As for the whole operation's primary objective, Chambers and Coolidge never did get at the balloons. In retrospect, Rickenbacker wrote:

> I was never in favor of attacking observation balloons in full daylight and this day's experience—the aroused suspicions of the observers, the pulling down of the balloon as strong

airplane assistance at the same time arrived, and the fate of Lieutenant Brotherton, who tried unsuccessfully to dive through the defensive barrage—is a fair illustration of the difficulties attending such daylight strafings. Just at dawn or just at dusk is the ideal time for surprising the Drachen.

October 10 also saw the "Don Cossack of the Air" grounded. Since returning to action with Spa.89 on June 5, 1918, Sous-Lieutenant Viktor Federov had shared in downing a Halberstadt two-seater over Belrupt on September 18, and claimed a fighter in flames over Damvillers for his sixth victory on October 9, although Brigadier Raymond Tertain was killed in the action, probably by Leutnant Oliver von Beaulieu-Marconnay of *Jasta* 19. Newly promoted Lieutenant Federov was wounded the next day, probably by Leutnant der Reserve Friedrich Noltenius of *Jasta* 6. Federov survived the war, only to die at St. Cloud of tuberculosis on March 4, 1922, at age 36.

On October 25, Major Charles Biddle was given command of the newly formed the 4th Pursuit Group at Toul, combining the just-operational 25th and 141st Aero squadrons with the 17th and 148th, which had been transferred from 65 wing, RAF. Both the 17th and 148th Aero squadrons had been equipped with Sopwith Camels and had seen considerable combat in the British sector. Only the 141st saw aerial combat before the armistice, claiming two victories. The 25th, equipped with S.E.5as and filled with RAF veterans, flew its first patrol on November 10, just a day before the war ended. The 17th and 148th were being re-equipped with Spads when the war ended.

For the Central Powers' air arms, the last three months of the war could best be called a fighting retreat. On September 2, the British advanced at Drocourt and Quéant, moving on to Havrincourt and Epéhy on the 18th. On September 27, General Sir Henry Horne's First Army advanced between Epéhy and St. Quentin, while General Sir Julian Byng's Third Army stormed the Canal du Nord, east of Cambrai, again forcing the Germans to retreat to avoid being cut off.

Supporting the push were 1,000 aircraft of the 1st, 3rd, 5th and 9th RAF brigades. German fighters claimed 33 British planes that day, 15 of which, including four of the new Sopwith Snipes, were credited to elements of JG.III for the loss of Leutnant Fritz Heinz of *Jasta* Boelcke. *Jasta* 5 claimed others, including Leutnant Fritz Rumey's 45th victory over a Camel of No. 54 Squadron. *Jasta* 5 participated in a wild melee over Cambrai with S.E.5as of No. 32 Squadron, in which Lieutenant Frank Lucien Hale, an American from Arkansas, claimed three Fokkers to bring his total to seven, and South African Lieutenant George Edgar Bruce Lawson claimed his fifth and sixth victories. Lawson crashed into his second Fokker, which probably accounted for the only actual German loss of the action: Fritz Rumey, his upper wing damaged and shedding fabric, bailed out at 1,000 feet, but his wildy spinning Fokker prevented his parachute from deploying properly and another leading German ace fell to his death.

On September 28, British and Belgian forces began advancing through Flanders and on the 29th the Allies were breaking through the Hindenburg Line. October 8 saw the Second Battle of Le Cateau. As the German army reeled back, the *Jagdflieger* fought on in defiant fury between frustrating but necessary moves with their steadily withdrawing armies, from one aerodrome to another.

Elsewhere, Germany was losing allies one by one. On September 15, French and Serbian forces ended years of stalemate in Salonika with a decisive victory over the Bulgarians at Dobro Pole. As mutinies broke out in its retreating army, Bulgaria sued for peace, signing an armistice on September 29. On October 30, the Ottoman Empire, likewise facing Arab revolts and imminent collapse in the face of British offensives in Syria and Mesopotamia, signed an armistice at Mudros.

Austria-Hungary's battered army in Italy had also been crumbling since the failure of its last attempt to storm the Piave in June. In contrast to the swift French and British counteroffensives launched on the Western Front, however, Italy's supreme commander, General Armando Diaz, carefully husbanded his land and air forces for what he expected to be a truly decisive breakthrough. By little or no coincidence, the Italians chose October 24, the anniversary of the first day of the Battle of Caporetto, to launch a diversionary attack in the Monte Grappa sector to attract Austro-Hungarian reserves, followed by a general assault across the Piave. Soon the Italians, with French and British support and all aided by overwhelming numbers of aircraft, were over the river and advancing while the Hapsburg Empire itself began to disintegrate. On October 28, Czechoslovakia declared itself an independent republic, followed by the southern Slavs the next day. Vienna called for an armistice on the 29th, but the Italians ignored it. The Austro-Hungarian army in Italy was split in two on the 30th, and the empire followed suit on the 31st, when Hungary declared its independence. The Austrians signed an armistice and their troops began laying down their arms at 1520 hours on November 3, but the Italians, eager to grab the territory that had been their goal since they entered the war, pressed on through the southern Tyrol right up to the effective deadline of 1500 the next day. The Battle of Vittorio Veneto, as the Italians called it in 1923, had cost them 38,000 casualties against 30,000 Austro-Hungarian casualties and 428,000 prisoners.

That left Germany alone to face the Allies' wrath, yet on the same day the Austrian armistice went into effect, its *Jagdstaffeln*—including *Marine Feld Jasta* 4, fighting on in spite of a mutiny that had broken out in the navy on October 30—claimed 38 Allied planes shot down, including four Sopwith Snipes of No. 43 Squadron by Leutnant Karl Bolle, commander of *Jasta* Boelcke. The next day's 11 claims included a Spad XIII by "Alo" Heldmann of *Jasta* 10 and another by Oberleutnant Erich Rüdiger von Wedel, the 350th and last for *Jasta* 11; their victims, Sergent Jean André of Spa.88 and 1st Lt. Louis L. Carruthers of the 93rd Aero Squadron, were both taken prisoner.

On November 6 the Americans finally achieved their breakthrough in the Argonne, occupying the east bank of the Meuse opposite Sedan on the 7th. The *Jagdflieger* were credited with three British bombers and four Spads on the 6th, the latter including the last victories for both JG.I and JG.II. In one case, Leutnant Ulrich Neckel, commander of *Jasta* 6, shot down 1st Lt. Ben E. Brown of the 28th Aero Squadron, who had just teamed up with 1st Lts.

Martinus Stenseth and Hugh C. McClung in driving down a German two-seater, which he saw flip over on its back. Brown later described what occurred after he scored his first and only victory:

> I was about 200 meters high and as I began to turn toward our side I was suddenly attacked from the rear. I turned square around quickly to get out of the enemy fire and flew back underneath a Fokker. Almost immediately another Fokker got on my tail and I began turning to get away from him. There were four Fokkers after me. One came down to about my level and I straightened up and opened fire on him but was forced to quit the attack by other Fokkers on my tail. I was now so close to the ground that maneuvering was difficult and I could no longer get away from the stream of tracers. Bullets were coming through the cockpit and I was hit in one finger. I fell into a flat spin, throttled the motor and straightened out as much as possible. The machine crashed and I was unconscious for awhile from the jar, but was quite all right a few minutes later. The German soldiers had pulled me out from the wreckage and bound up my finger. Nothing whatever was taken from me....All the German officers I met were very polite. The four Fokker pilots who chased me down came to Loupy le Château to shake hands with me. Lieut. Neckel was their flight commander. He told me who he was and then complimented me for getting the bi-place. They seemed to be a very sporty lot of pilots.

The *Jagdflieger* claimed a balloon and four airplanes—three of them confirmed—on November 10, while in the American sector Major Maxwell Kirby claimed a Fokker for the 94th Aero Squadron's 70th and final victory. Game though the *Luftstreitskräfte* was to fight on, however, Germany itself had had enough. It too signed an armistice with the Allies, which went into effect at 1100 hours on November 11. The guns fell silent and once the combatants had convinced themselves it was really over, the celebrating began.

AFTERWORD

Legend and Legacy

Whatever actual material contribution to victory fighter aircraft had made on the Western Front, they had established traditions to which many squadrons—though they could not have realized it at the time—would add in the conflicts destined to follow the then-so-called "War to End All Wars." For now, the adjutants tallied up the statistics and completed the records for posterity.

One flying officer who felt a personal satisfaction at armistice time was Captain Rickenbacker, who had made good on his vow to make the 94th the top squadron in the AEF—with 70 victories, 26 of which were his. The 94th also boasted the highest score and the American ace of aces, as well as the distinction of producing the first USAS victory and first USAS ace, both courtesy of 1st Lt. Doug Campbell. A close second to the 94th, with 66 victories, was the 148th Aero Squadron, whose exploits with the RAF could probably have been forgotten, had it not been for a book co-authored by one of its aces, Elliott White Springs, whose title became a byword for all the Americans who flew in British service: *Warbirds*.

The top-scoring French unit, Spa.3, had 175 Germans to its credit, followed by its sister "Stork" escadrille in GC.12, Spa.103 with 111—73 of which were scored by one man, René Fonck. If leadership may be measured by comparing victories to losses, then two other escadrilles and their commanders stood out. Since its reorganization on February 18, 1918, Spa.124 had lost two pilots in a training accident, but since its return to combat under the commands of Capitaine André d'Humières and Lieutenant Henri Bergé, it had only lost one man wounded, while being credited with 26 enemy planes—nine by its Russian member, Capitaine Pavel Argeyev.

Formed on August 22 under the command of Spa.37 veteran Lieutenant Bernard Barny de Romanet and assigned to GC.12, Spa.167 flew its first sortie on September 26 and in the course of October shot down 10 German aircraft—eight by Romanet, raising his total to 18—without suffering a single casualty.

Britain's highest-scoring single-seat fighter squadron by the end of the war was "Fighting Fifty-six," whose veritable galaxy of star S.E.5 pilots, such as Albert Ball, Jimmy McCudden, Geoffrey H. Bowman, Arthur P.F. Rhys Davids, Richard A. Maybery and Hank Burden, had accounted for 401 enemy planes, albeit at a heartbreaking cost (Ball, McCudden, Rhys Davids, and Maybery were among its many dead). Its record was far exceeded by the two-seater teams of No. 20 Squadron, whose F.E.2d crewmen had been credited with 203 enemy planes, including those of noted Richthofen disciple Leutnant Karl-Emil Schäfer and the Red Baron himself, and whose Bristol F.2B crews raised its overall tally to 619. In appraising those and other British squadron records, however, it is unavoidable to note that only a fraction of those fantastic scores can be matched by postwar documentation of enemy losses.

Because they usually fought on their side of the lines, a much greater percentage of claims by the German *Jagdstaffeln* could be confirmed by wreckage or victims who force landed intact. Leading the pack, appropriately, was Manfred von Richthofen's red-nosed *Jasta* 11, with 350. It had paid for that record with 17 pilots killed in action plus two in flying accidents, two taken prisoner, and 19 wounded. An equally a propos second was *Jasta* Boelcke, with 336 for the loss of 31 men killed in action, two in accidents, two POWs, and nine wounded.

There was an interesting dichotomy of response to the war's end to be seen in the *Jagdgeschwader* to which the two leading *Jastas* belonged. Ordered to surrender its aircraft to the French, JG.I's commander, Oberleutnant Hermann Göring, noted with some satisfaction that his crack pilots consistently made the worst landings of their careers, leaving behind a field strewn with pranged Fokkers. Oberleutnant Bruno Loerzer's JG.III, on the other hand, did not sabotage the fighters it turned in to the British, but their new owners found detailed victory lists of their respective pilots scrawled in chalk on the fuselage sides, courtesy of their proud mechanics.

Whichever way they expressed their defiance, the German fighter pilots had for the most part fought to the very end. In consequence, a good many of them took in the news of the Kaiser's abdication and their country's capitulation with a combination of incredulity and disgust. In many cases that bitterness and the belief that they had done their part and others had let them down, lent itself to widespread acceptance of the myth, encouraged by the rising National Socialist Worker's Party throughout the 1920s, of a German army stabbed in the back by war profiteers, communists, and traitors... predominantly Jewish. It is no coincidence that some of the most devout Nazis included fighter pilots such as Robert Ritter von Greim, Josef Veltjens, Rudolf Hess and Hermann Göring.

In all fairness, though, a good many *Jagdflieger* regarded the Nazi ideology as running counter to their sense of honor, to say nothing of human decency. Josef Jacobs, with 48 victories, was among them, as was Carl Degelow, 30-victory ace, commander of *Jasta* 40s and the last pilot to receive the *Orden Pour le Mérite*. Degelow's last deputy commander and trusted comrade-in-arms, the prewar flier and nine-victory ace Willy Rosenstein, was also ill-disposed to accept the Nazis' idea of what constituted a patriotic German—he was Jewish.

Of the conclusions one can draw from the first struggle for control of the air, perhaps the most surprising is how inconclusive in itself it had been. On the Western Front, the greater overall industrial capacity that France and Britain enjoyed over Germany allowed them to maintain the initiative in spite of the heavy losses they suffered against adversaries who made the most of their defensive stance. For all the élan with which the *Jagdflieger* fought at the time of the armistice, the statistics foretold the inevitability of what lay ahead. As of November 11, there were 1,069 Fokker D.VIIs at the front, with 78 *Jagdstaffeln* having anywhere from six to 12 of them on strength. A grand total of 2,768 had been built. In contrast, nine French contractors had built

8,472 SPAD XIIIs, of which 893 were delivered to the USAS. While 320 of the famous Dr.I triplane is known to have been built by Fokker, Sopwith and five other firms built 5,695 Camels. In addition, 2,765 S.E.5s and S.E.5as had been built, and Bristol Fighter production would total 4,747 by the time production ceased in September 1919. Austria-Hungary had fared even worse—compared to some 12,000 Italian warplanes produced in the course of the war, its factories had built a total of 5,180 to support its army and naval operations from Russia to northern Italy.

The Allies' advantage lay in more than just numbers of aircraft. They also had access to undiminished supplies of fuel, lubricant, and rubber, while the Germans resorted to wooden or steel-sprung wheels and chemical compounds such as rizinus lubricant, a castor oil substitute that broke down far quicker in the rotary engines for which it was meant. Also, in contrast to Germany's finite manpower, the RAF's ranks were being amply filled with replacements from Canada, Australia, New Zealand, and South Africa; France's multinational volunteers constituted a veritable Foreign Legion of the air, and Americans had turned up in all Allied air arms as well as the USAS.

Paradoxically, then, while the German *Jastas* were inflicting heavy casualties on the Allies in the air in the war's last months, they remained consistently outnumbered three to one and were consequently unable to protect their reconnaissance and bombing airplanes or their balloons, let alone their weary, broken ground troops. For all that, they put up an astounding fight, but it was a losing fight just the same.

When World War I began, the fighter plane did not exist. By the end of 1915, the single-seat "scout" had completed its transition from a front-line surveyor to a deadly weapon. In 1916, the first tactical fighter doctrine was written, with refinements to follow. Over the next two years the fighter successfully went to sea, also taking on such adjunct roles as bomber interceptor and escort, balloon destroyer, night fighter, night intruder, ground strafer, and close support plane.

The war's last year showed how far aviation in general had come, with sleek, swift fighting machines that showcased the culmination of its most noteworthy structural refinements. It also showed how accepted a weapon the airplane had become, as the once-knightly dogfights gave way to sprawling air battles involving scores of fighters locked in earnestly mortal combat.

Many of the war's innovations proved to be too far ahead of their time. Radial engines, cannon armament, monoplane wings, cantilever wing structures, and all-metal construction found limited acceptance at best, and the wood-and-wire biplane would continue to predominate in the immediate postwar years. As engines became more reliable and powerful, and construction methods more refined, however, those passing glimpses of things to come in 1918 would become the norm by 1938.

Aside from electronic warfare, jet power, and guided missiles, there was little that occurred in the air during succeeding aerial conflicts that had not at least been tried out in World War I. Human nature being what it is, however, that factual legacy of the first air war has been accompanied by a legacy of myth.

Even while they welcomed the publicity that might help prod the United States to enter the war on the Allied side, the American volunteers of *Escadrille* N.124 privately winced at the exaggerated, sometimes laughably fantastic stories that an adoring French press spread of exploits that they justly thought could easily have stood on their own merits. Save for a handful of glory seeking individuals such as Billy Bishop and René Fonck, the same could be said of most of the first fighter pilots. Fortunately for posterity, they represented a literate generation and, unlike the heroes of the Trojan War, a great many of them wrote their own stories during, and in the decades after, the Great War. Those products vary in accuracy and quality, but even the most self-serving, such as Fonck's autobiography, contain much useful information and insights into the time, if approached with a knowledge of the author. Jimmy McCudden, a mechanic before he

Top: Sous-Lieutenant Louis Risacher (five victories) with his Spad XIII of Spa.3 in 1918. (*Louis Risacher album via Jon Guttman*) Bottom: Louis Risacher visits an old friend at the Musée de l'Air at Meudon in November 1981. (*Jon Guttman*)

became a pilot, and a professional as well as a patriot, left behind a remarkably detailed and reasonably precise account of events in his long and varied fighting career, told in an almost paradoxically lively manner.

For all that wealth of literature, every generation needs its Hector and Achilles, and the first air war certainly provided them for all countries involved. Since the conclusions of their actual exploits, the very real stories of men such as Manfred von Richthofen, Werner Voss, Georges Guynemer, Charles Nungesser, Albert Ball, Mick Mannock, Francesco Baracca, Raoul Lufbery, Eddie Rickenbacker (a first name, catchy though it may be, that he personally disliked) and Frank Luke have had to run a gauntlet of embellishment at the hands of the succession of people who have retold them in each succeeding decade. While they were alive, many were more than pleased to "keep the record straight," as was the self-sworn purpose of Charles H. Dolan, the last living pilot of the *Escadrille Lafayette*, right up to his death on December 31, 1981.

Sometimes though, veterans learned something new themselves, as did 13-victory American ace George A. Vaughn Jr., who once described his generation as "an endangered species," when he got to compare his memories of a dogfight on September 22, 1918, with *Jagdgeschwader* III's records of the same fight and remarked with considerable interest that the two accounts "dovetail remarkably." Others left behind valuable perspectives of the times they knew. Asked by a youngster how he could go up in "rickety crates" like the Spad XIII, former 103rd Aero Squadron member Martin F. McQuilken pointed out that it was not a rickety crate to him at the time, "What did I have to compare it to—the Wright Flyer? When I flew it, the Spad XIII was among the latest, best planes you could fly."

Others left reminders of how widely attitudes of the time could differ. Max Holtzem, a Pfalz test pilot before he scored two uncredited victories with *Jasta* 16b, emphasized the importance of chivalry toward his opponents in the air. On the other hand, seven-victory French ace Jean Fraissinet flatly stated: "You speak of 'chivalry.' Should it shame me to write that I was one of the first to fire at a parachute that drifted into enemy lines, from which was suspended an observer no doubt armed with photos taken of our defensive installations?" If Fraissinet's sentiment seems uncharacteristically more coldly pragmatic than the popular "knight of the air"stereotype, it must be added that he was a cavalrymen serving alongside the infantry in the trenches before he became an aviator.

For serious scholars of the first air war, especially that generation—now itself dying off—who knew many of those warriors before they faded away, it can be galling to see books or films take artistic liberties that present a distorted image of people and their exploits, which were more than dramatic enough as they actually were. One can only hope the next generation of chroniclers will be equally or more conscientious.

Left: The last great World War I aces reunion in November 1981 included a personal reunion between two former Sopwith Pup pilots in No. 3 Squadron, RNAS: English ace Leonard H. Rochford (29 victories) and Canadian Alfred W. "Nick" Carter (17 victories) Right: Old enemies also met in Paris, in this case Aloys Heldmann of Jasta 10, Jagdgeschwader I (15 victories) and Kenneth L. Porter of the 147th Aero Squadron, 1st Pursuit Group (six victories). (*Jon Guttman*)

Just the same, the legends are no less valid a part of the first fighter pilots' legacy than the technical realities. Those first recountings in books and pulp magazines enthralled countless readers and inspired a new generation of flyboys to follow "Captain Eddie" and the Red Baron into the sky. There, many champions of that new generation, and of a third, a fourth, and a fifth, emerged to leave their own mark in the clouds above Spain, Poland, Finland, Britain, Malta, Russia, the Solomons, North Africa, Normandy, Burma, the Marianas, the Philippines, Okinawa, the Yalu River, Kashmir, North Vietnam, Sinai, the Golan Heights, the Falklands, the Bekaa Valley, and Iraq.

As mankind stubbornly refuses to leave war behind as it enters the 21st century, the nature of warfare continues to change. Among other things, the aerial warfare that those first fliers developed has taken a new turn, with computerized warplanes that practically fly themselves and even unmanned reconnaissance and missile-armed attack drones that can be operated by proxy from afar. In another twist, the end of the Cold War and its replacement with asymmetrical warfare threatens to render the fighter plane as we used to know it obsolete.

Terrorists don't seek air superiority, but operate stealthily under, and in spite of, that air umbrella they've conceded to their enemy. Pending a confrontation between conventional military powers, the latest generation of stealth fighter pilots may well be denied their chance to emulate the aces of old simply because there is nothing comparable to fight.

If that is true, then the first fighter aces, likened unto knights jousting in the air with machine guns instead of lances in 1915, may have come around full circle. As the state of the art of aerial warfare they pioneered advances apace, the time may already be coming nigh when they will again be regarded in the same manner as the medieval knight—supreme warriors in their day, but likewise warriors of the past.

Regardless, one way or the other, by fact or by legend, as long as mankind remembers its heroes, they too will be remembered.

SOURCES

Gregory Alegi, *Hanriot HD.1/HD.2*, Albatros Productions Ltd, Berkhamsted, Herts, 2002.

Rinaldo d'Ami, "The Italian Front Revisited: Expanded notes," *Cross & Cockade (USA) Journal*, Vol. 17, No.1, Spring 1976, pp.48-47.

Chaz Boyer, *For Valour: The Air VCs*, Grub Street, London, 1992.

J.M. Bruce, *War Planes of the First World War: Fighters, Volume Two and Five*, Doubleday and Company, Inc., Garden City, NY, 1968.

J.M. Bruce, *Vickers FB5*, Albatros Productions Ltd, Berkhamsted, Herts, 1996.

Baron Willy Coppens, "Belgian Aviation...1914-1918," *Cross & Cockade Journal* (USA), Vol.5, No.2, Spring 1964, pp.105-108.

Richard Duiven, "Das Königliches Jagdgeschwader Nr.II," *Over the Front*, Vol.9, No.3, Fall 1994, pp.196-229.

Brian P. Flanagan, "Emil Meinecke, Fighter Ace on the Dardanelles," *Cross & Cockade Journal* (USA), Vol.12, No.3, pp.244-248.

Norman Franks, *Sharks Among the Minnows*, Grub Street, London, 2001.

Norman Franks, Frank Bailey and Rick Duiven, *The Jasta War Chronology*, Grub Street, London, 1998.

Norman Franks, Hal Gilpin and Nigel McCrery, *Under the Guns of the Red Baron*, Grub Street, London, 1995.

Norman Franks, *Bloody April...Black September*, Grub Street, London, 1995.

Norman Franks, *Sopwith Triplane Aces of World War 1*, Osprey Publications, Botley, Oxford, England, 2004.

Norman L.R. Franks, Frank W. Bailey and Russell Guest, *Above the Lines*, Grub Street, London, 1993.

Tomasz Goworek, "The U.S. Army Air Service's first air-to-air victim may have arranged his own capture," *Military History*, October 1994, pp.10-16.

Peter L. Gray, *The Fokker D.VII*, Profile Publications, Ltd. No.25, Leatherhead, Surrey.

P.M. Grosz, *Fokker D.VIII*, Windsock Datafile 25, Albatross Productions, Ltd., Berkhamsted, Herts, 1991.

P.M. Grosz, *SSW D.III-D.IV*, Windsock Datafile 29, Albatross Productions, Ltd., Berkhamsted, Herts, 1991.

P.M. Grosz, *Fokker E.I/II*, Albatros Productions Ltd, Berkhamsted, Herts, 2002.

P.M. Grosz, George Haddow and Peter Schiemer, *Austro-Hungarian Army Aircraft of World War I*, Flying Machines Press, Mountain View, CA, 1993.

Jon Guttman, *Nieuport 28*, Windsock Datafile 36, Albatross Productions, Ltd., Berkhamsted, Herts, 1992.

Jon Guttman, "Plumage: Spa.156: L'Escadrille des Deux Martinets," *Over the Front*, Vol. 9, No.1, Spring 1994, pp.71-74.

Harold E Hartney, *Up & At 'Em*, Ace Books, New York, NY, 1971.

Peter Kilduff, *The Red Baron Combat Wing: Jagdgeschwader Richthofen in Battle*, Arms & Armour Press, London, 1997.

Peter Kilduff, *Richthofen: Beyond the Legend of the Red Baron*, Arms & Armour Press, London, 1993.

Viktor Kulikov, "Morane-Saulnier Type G," *Windsock International*, Vol.10, No.4, July/August 1994, pp.31-36.

Wing Commander Gwilym H. Lewis, DFC, *Wings over the Somme, 1916-1918*, William Kimber & Co., Ltd., London, 1976.

Frederick Libby, *Horses Don't Fly, A Memoir of World War I*, Arcade Publishing, New York, NY, 2000.

Major James T B McCudden, *Flying Fury: Five Years in the Royal Flying Corps*, Ace Publishing Corp, New York, NY, 1968.

Vadim Mikheyev, *Sikorsky S-16*, Flying Machines Press, Stratford, CT, 1997.

James F. Miller, "Eight Minutes Near Bapaume," *Over the Front*, Vol.21, No.2, Summer 2006, pp.120-138.

Alex Revell, *British Single-Seater Fighter Squadrons on the Western Front in World War I*, Schiffer Publishing Ltd., Atglen, Pa., 2006.

Christopher Shores, Norman Franks, and Russell Guest, *Above the Trenches*, Grub Street, London, 1990.

Robert A. Whittaker, "Dragon Master of Tsingtao, *Aviation History*, January 1995, pp.34-80.

Robert L. Willett, "The Tsar's Ace," *Aviation History*, March 2008, pp.41-45.

INDEX

Aircraft Groups

ACKNOWLEDGMENTS

History is a synthesis of constantly growing and accumulating knowledge. So it is here, in what is probably not so much of an earthshaking revelation as it is the latest product of that ongoing process. Toward this current end—or merely juncture—I wish to acknowledge the invaluable help provided by the following colleagues in the scavenger hunt for both information and photographs: Frank W. Bailey, Jack Eder, Colin Huston, Alex Imrie, Norman Franks, William Nungesser, Colin A. Owers, Walter Pieters, Les Rogers and Greg van Wyngarden, as well as the late August Blume, J.M. Bruce, Rick Duiven and Peter M. Grosz. An added word or more of thanks must go to Laura Pfost, the patiently supportive lady in my life who put up with my absence and occasional unintelligible utterings in the months leading up to manuscript deadline, and then helped in the proofreading.

Posthumous thanks are also extended to some of those veteran airmen I have known, whose collective recollections gave me a somewhat better understanding of the first air war as they experienced it: John O. Andrews, Sir Harold Balfour of Inchrye, Gottfried *Freiherr* von Banfield, Antal Boksay, Arthur Raymond Brooks, Douglas Campbell, Pierre Cardon, Louis L. Carruthers, Pierre de Cazenove de Pradines, Willy Coppens, Baron d'Houthulst, Charles H. Dolan, Victor Groom, Jean Fraissinet, Aloys Heldmann, Livingston G. Irving, G. DeFreest Larner, Gwilym H. Lewis, Francis Carlo Lombardi, Donald R. MacLaren, Martin F. McQuilken, André Martenot de Cordoux, Hans-Georg von der Osten, Kenneth L. Porter, Louis Risacher, Sir Hugh W.H. Saunders, Carl-August von Schönebeck, Henri Hay de Slade, William McKenzie Thompson, Armand de Turenne, George A. Vaughn Jr. and Robert Paul Waddington. This book is dedicated to their memory—and to their comrades-in-flight.

CPSIA information can be obtained
at www.ICGtesting.com
Printed in the USA
FFOW03n0159281017
41624FF